THIS IS CHARLIE BIRD

THIS IS
CHARLIE BIRD

CHARLIE BIRD
WITH KEVIN RAFTER ~

Gill & Macmillan

Gill & Macmillan Ltd
Hume Avenue, Park West, Dublin 12
with associated companies throughout the world
www.gillmacmillan.ie

© Charlie Bird 2006
ISBN-13: 978 07171 4075 6
ISBN-10: 0 7171 4075 X

Index compiled by Helen Litton
Typography design by Make Communication
Print origination by Carole Lynch
Printed and bound by MPG Books, Cornwall

This book is typeset in Linotype Minion and
Neue Helvetica.

The paper used in this book comes from the wood pulp
of managed forests. For every tree felled, at least one
tree is planted, thereby renewing natural resources.

A CIP catalogue record for this book is available
from the British Library.

5 4 3 2

All photographs have been supplied by courtesy of
Charlie Bird, unless otherwise noted.

To Orlu and Neasa

CONTENTS

ACKNOWLEDGMENTS

My career in journalism would not have been possible without the support and understanding of Mary O'Connor and our two daughters, Orla and Neasa. They are owed the biggest 'thank you' of all. This book would probably never have been written without the cajoling of Kevin Rafter and his efforts since the summer of 2005. Oorla Rafter put up with Kevin and me over the months when the book was being written. She also kindly read the manuscript and offered to buy the hat! Ben, Brian and Adam Rafter offered some noisy distraction. Right from the beginning, Faith O'Grady provided considerable encouragement for the project.

In truth, this book would not have been possible without the thousands of people, who, over a quarter of a century of news reporting, have been central characters in the stories I have reported on. I also owe a great deal to many people in RTÉ. It would be impossible to name everyone—so instead, thank you to all my colleagues in Montrose, past and present, for putting up with me. I would also like to say thanks to my colleagues in the world of journalism in Dublin. I know there have been times when I have tried their patience.

A few people deserve specific mention. George Lee and I began work on our investigation into National Irish Bank in 1998. It was the start of a rewarding relationship and a close friendship which saw us live through some difficult times together. Thank you, George.

It is difficult to measure the influence my boss, Ed Mulhall, has had on my career, especially over the past decade. Ed's guiding hand, his courage and his conviction at the height of the NIB investigation contributed enormously to the success I have had in recent years. I cannot thank him enough.

In life, we are fortunate to meet exceptional people. Joe O'Brien is one of those people, and I have been lucky in having him as my close friend. Both as a work colleague and as a friend, Joe has supported me through good and bad days. Ray Burke, my news editor in RTÉ, is one of the best journalists in the business. Thanks are owed for his ongoing support and also for his suggestions for this book. Billy Hanrahan in the RTÉ News Library was ever helpful with requests for material as the book was being written.

I would like to single out one group of people for special mention. During my foreign assignments, I have met so many courageous and dedicated volunteers working with Irish and international relief agencies. We all owe an enormous debt of gratitude to the people who work for organisations like Concern, GOAL, the Red Cross and Trócaire.

Finally, I would like to thank the man whom I still describe only as the 'duffel-bag man' and the other whistle-blowers who have had the courage to come forward with their stories. It is because of them that Irish banking, among many other areas of life in Ireland today, has been changed for the better.

Déanfaidh mé iarracht níos fearr an chéad uair eile.

Charlie Bird
June 2006

LIST OF ILLUSTRATIONS

Between pages 76 and 77
—Togged out for Sandymount High rugby team.
—Speaking from the back of a lorry at a Young Socialist rally outside the GPO in 1969/70.
—Contentment in the early 1970s came from my pipe and a pint of Guinness.
—At the podium at a Labour Party conference, most likely in 1970.
—With Mary O'Connor in County Kerry in the early 1970s.
—With documents discovered in a dump in Ringsend in Dublin in the mid-1970s.
—Interviewing Neil Blaney, as a radio reporter.
—At a Fine Gael press conference during the February 1982 general election.
—Chasing after Jim Gibbons during a leadership heave in Fianna Fáil in October 1982.
—Journalists sweltered in the heat at the airport in Algiers during the 1985 hijack drama.
—With Fr Niall O'Brien in Bacolod Prison in the Philippines in 1984.
—The humanitarian crisis for the Kurds who fled Saddam Hussein's regime after the first Gulf War left a huge impression on me.
—Reporting on the plight of the Kurds meant travelling considerable distances on foot.
—Inside Nelson Mandela's prison cell on Robben Island.
—Talking to Des O'Malley on the plinth outside Leinster House in 1985.
—I interviewed Charlie Haughey on his final day as a member of Dáil Éireann in 1992.
—As we waited for the results of the final heave against Charlie Haughey's leadership, in November 1991, the crowd started to sing 'There's only one Charlie Bird'.
—In September 1990, while on holidays on Inis Oírr, I met Brian Lenihan.

—Fianna Fail's negative advert for Mary Robinson's 1990 presidential bid.
—Dick Spring and Mary Robinson at a press conference, two days after she had won the presidential election.
—Filming material for an RTÉ documentary on Mary Robinson.
—With President Mary Robinson and her husband, Nick, in the private quarters of Áras an Uachtaráin, in 1997.
—At a trade union protest outside Leinster House in 1986, against the controversial Section 31 ban.
—Interviewing Gerry Adams in 1994.
—The IRA statement, declaring its August 1994 ceasefire.

Between pages 172 and 173
—My notebook with the wording of the IRA statement announcing its restored ceasefire in July 1997.
—Albert Reynolds was always available to answer questions from the media during his term as Taoiseach.
—John Bruton became Taoiseach unexpectedly in late 1994.
—Interviewing Brian Cowen in November 1994.
—Trying to get a little quiet ahead of an interview with Bertie Ahern.
—A few moments of relaxation with Bertie Ahern and Celia Larkin during their official visit to China in 1998.
—Recording a piece-to-camera for a television news report, with the Great Wall stretching out behind me.
—The red carpet was rolled out in Tiananmen Square in Beijing.
—One of the confidential documents that sparked RTÉ's investigation into wrong-doing by National Irish Bank.
—Neither George Lee nor I had any idea that our NIB investigation would cause us to be involved in the longest-running libel case in the history of the state.
—My boss in RTÉ, Ed Mulhall, was a tremendous support during the libel action.
—A brief handshake with Beverley Cooper Flynn at the conclusion of the case in April 2004.
—As Finance Minister, Charlie McCreevy was initially sceptical of RTÉ's investigation into NIB.
—Liam Lawlor leaving the Flood/Mahon Tribunal in his typically robust style.

PROLOGUE

I had a single folded sheet of paper in the inside pocket of my jacket. It was a statement from RTÉ, dated 28 April 2004. I had read it only a few minutes earlier but the consequences sent a cold shudder throughout my entire body. The words written on the page made for depressing reading.

> Following the decision in the Supreme Court this morning on the appeal taken by Beverley Cooper Flynn TD, RTÉ stressed that the judgment did not in any way affect the integrity of the stories that led to the case. The organisation expressed disappointment that the Jury's verdict in this case could not stand because of the trial judge's failure to address the Jury on the issue of majority voting in accordance with law.

Only one statement had been prepared. Everybody in RTÉ believed Beverley Cooper Flynn was going to win her Supreme Court appeal. The accepted view was that we were going to lose on a legal technicality. As I walked into the entrance hall of the Four Courts in Dublin, I felt as low as I had ever felt in almost a quarter of a century as a news reporter.

It seemed a lifetime ago since a source from the trade union world had given me explosive information showing that one of the country's leading financial institutions had been actively encouraging its customers to evade their taxes. The name of the Fianna Fáil TD from Mayo was never mentioned nor was she referred to when the initial television reports were broadcast in early 1998. But it did not take long to find out about Cooper Flynn's promotion of the tax scam during her previous career as a financial advisor with National Irish Bank. She denied the substance of our reports and ultimately took a libel action to the High Court.

The case had been a traumatic time for everybody involved. I hated every day of the trial. I heard terrible things said about me which were totally untrue, things that if said outside the court would in themselves have led to a defamation action. It turned out to be the longest libel case in the history of the state. I lived through the strain of every minute.

I had worked on the NIB investigation with George Lee, RTÉ's Economics Editor. We were a good team and we had smiled broadly when the jury in the High Court case found in our favour although the celebrations were modest enough. On the evening of the judgment, George and I went for a Chinese meal and talked through the twists and turns of the news investigation and the subsequent trial. The state was millions richer thanks to our having exposed the NIB tax evasion scheme, while customers of the bank had been reimbursed the monies illegally taken from their accounts in false charges and fees. It was all down to good journalism which, I like to think, was what swayed the jury in our direction.

The High Court case was not, however, the end. Despite the jury's having found against her, Cooper Flynn appealed to the Supreme Court. It had taken six years to get to April 2004 but now a final decision was about to be made by five of the leading judges in the land. Senior management at RTÉ had taken a view on the proceedings in the appeal case. A mistake had been made by the judge in the High Court case; it had nothing to do with the substance of the libel trial but a chink had been opened for Cooper Flynn's lawyers to exploit. We were going to lose. The station's statement had been prepared, and the only copy was in my pocket.

> RTÉ reiterated its commitment to stand firmly behind the stories and the journalists involved and to defend, in a new trial, its position that none of the broadcasts in the summer of 1998 damaged the reputation of Beverley Cooper Flynn TD.

The prospect of a new trial and the stresses that would bring was just unthinkable. We were back to the beginning of my nightmare. I was going to read part of the statement out on the steps of the Four Courts as Cooper Flynn enjoyed her victory. 'My colleague George Lee and I stand over the stories on the NIB off-shore scheme which we broke…'

The fact that the Revenue Commissioners had already received €50 million from their investigations into the NIB scheme would matter little. The fact that a jury in the High Court had supported RTÉ's view that tax evasion was promoted by Beverley Cooper Flynn would also matter little. Despite talk of a technicality deciding the Supreme Court appeal, I knew that a loss was a loss. The political pressure was going to be enormous. There were people in Fianna Fáil, and I suspected in the other parties, who were only waiting to give RTÉ a good kicking. Beverley Cooper Flynn was going to be able to talk about the Supreme Court finding in her favour. And, despite fighting talk, I was unconvinced about the appetite in RTÉ for a re-run of the libel case.

The fallout inside the station had the potential to bring down the shutters on investigative journalism. I feared that I would find myself being pushed sideways. I suspected that the positions of those who fought for the NIB investigation to be broadcast, and who were closely associated with the court battles, could have become very difficult. The investigation was not about only those reporters who were seen in front of the camera. Many other people in RTÉ—especially the station's Director-General, Director of News and Director of Legal Affairs—had been highly supportive of the investigation. A negative outcome could also have had serious consequences for the careers of these individuals.

It was all too depressing to think about. When the doors opened to the Supreme Court, the time for thinking was over. As I walked into the courtroom, I felt the tiredness in my bones. I was weary of my NIB reports and everything that had emerged from what had been an award-winning news investigation. Most news stories are over and done with when they are broadcast. Television news is very much defined by deadlines. Meet the deadline and then move on to the next story. However, the NIB story was different. It had become a central part of my life for six years. I had lived with the cloud of these legal proceedings hanging over me.

Not only was I tired of NIB, but on that particular morning in the Supreme Court I was also exhausted from travelling. Two days previously, I had been in Bogotá in Colombia. Half a day earlier, I had been in New York. The blue shirt and blue and white tie I was wearing had been purchased in Bloomingdale's, in a quick run through the New York department store. My transatlantic flight had touched down in Dublin only at breakfast time. There had not been even enough time to drive home to my house in Ashford in County Wicklow. So I had showered and changed in my daughter Neasa's apartment in central Dublin. I was a bundle of nerves.

I was glad to have both of my daughters alongside me as I walked into the Supreme Court in April 2004. Neasa, a barrister, and Orla, a public relations executive, had grown up with my career in journalism. They were born in the 1970s as I was making my way as a researcher in the current affairs department in RTÉ. During their school years, I was a television news reporter, working long hours and often away for weeks at a time. But they always understood the nature of my job and they have always been interested in what I do for a living. I am lucky as a father in having a good relationship with my two daughters, and I have been fortunate in seeing them both succeed through university and into their respective careers.

I have been lucky in my job. Sometimes I have even stopped and wondered how I got so far. I have reported from all corners of the world, on famines, on earthquakes and on wars. I have interviewed presidents and prime ministers. I have worked on so many big stories and have had my fair share of exclusive reports. But now, five judges in the Supreme Court were about to make a decision that would cast a shadow over everything I had ever done as a news reporter. In a sense, what people thought and said about my career in journalism was going to be defined by the outcome in the Supreme Court in April 2004.

The small courtroom was packed with reporters and lawyers. I knew many of the faces. There were nods of encouragement from several colleagues. My boss, Ed Mulhall, was seated upstairs in the same place he had positioned himself during the entire court case. I hoped it was a lucky seat but the RTÉ statement in my pocket said otherwise.

One of the court officials came over and smiled at me. 'I've reserved seats for you,' he said. George Lee was at my shoulder. The seats were at the top of the courtroom just across from the legal teams. George walked ahead as I nervously turned to another person in the courtroom whom I knew. 'How's this going to go?' I asked. His response hit me like a bolt of lightning. 'You'll be all right,' he whispered.

I stopped walking and looked straight at this man. 'What are you saying?' I asked, now speaking in a hushed voice also.

'You'll be all right,' he again said quietly.

'With everything?' I wanted to know.

'Yes,' came the reply.

I had taken the RTÉ statement from my inside pocket as I came into the courtroom. I was holding it tightly in my right hand. 'I won't need this,' I thought to myself as I sat in beside a very serious-looking George Lee.

One of the court officials was now putting out various documents on the benches where five judges of the Supreme Court would presently sit. I had a sneak preview of what the judgments were going to conclude. I was finding it difficult to contain my excitement. I had a scoop, and, like a good reporter, I wanted to broadcast the news. I reached over to my colleague and whispered quickly, 'George, I've just been told we're going to win.'

He looked at me as if I had just arrived from an alien planet. 'What?' he asked.

I tipped RTÉ's solicitor Eamon Kennedy on the shoulder. 'We're going to win,' I said, the smile on my face getting ever wider.

Before another word could be exchanged, the five judges trooped in—Keane, Denham, McGuinness, Geoghegan and Fennelly. Everyone in the courtroom stood up. It's a cliché, but it was true—there was a hushed silence as Ronan Keane, the Chief Justice, started to talk. The outcome was not clear from his opening words. For those listening in the courtroom, the judgment could still have gone either way— Beverley Cooper Flynn or Charlie Bird? But I was ahead of the crowd on this one. RTÉ was going to have to prepare a new statement.

'I would dismiss the appeal and affirm the order of the High Court,' were the final words spoken by the Chief Justice. The other four judges backed this conclusion. We had won and, for the second time in my life—the previous occasion was at the end of the High Court case—I found myself with my arms wrapped around George Lee. We had won. It was over.

Chapter 1

BERMUDA AND MACROOM

I have two birth certificates. One records the date of my birth as 4 September 1949, while the other says I was born five days later, on 9 September 1949. I have no idea why I have two birth certificates, or how it's possible for a person to have two birth certificates. Nevertheless, that's how it is with me and so I have a choice of birthdays. For what it's worth, I always celebrate on the ninth.

Bird is an English name. My father's family was originally from the south of England and settled in Bermuda. As a child, I was told that we were related to a Bird who had been a royal governor somewhere in the Caribbean. Although the story was untrue, it furnished the Birds with a fictitious but distinguished family history. In fairness, it was probably more a case of exaggeration than outright lies. I have in my possession, for example, a small silver dress sword which my grandfather brought with him from Bermuda. His father, my great grandfather, and two brothers left Portsmouth sometime in the 1850s and took up residence in the north west of Bermuda at a place coincidentally called Ireland Island. The name came not from this country, but from an individual whose surname was Ireland. At any rate, the Royal Navy connection with Portsmouth almost certainly accounted for my family's presence in Bermuda, where there had been an important Royal Navy base since the eighteenth century. One of my great uncles is listed as an Inspector of Machinery in census data from 1881.

My grandfather, Timothy Bird, was born in Bermuda in 1870 and lived there until sometime in the 1880s, after which, for reasons unknown to me, he decided to move to England where he worked as an electrical engineer in Portsmouth, thus completing for the moment the circle which his father and uncles had begun in the previous generation. With the introduction of electric street lighting at the turn of the twentieth century, his services were in considerable demand. It was this that brought him across the Irish Sea to work on a project in Macroom, County Cork. At that time, Macroom was a small country town but it was one of the first places in Ireland to have electric street lighting. My grandfather oversaw the installation of the lights and he never left Macroom. He married a woman from a well-to-do local Catholic family in the mineral-water business. My grandfather 'took the soup', in reverse, in order to marry, converting to Catholicism and breaking with the family's traditional Protestant heritage.

My grandparents ran a hotel in the town, near the railway station at the location known locally as 'Bird's corner'. They weren't wealthy, but by the standards of the early twentieth century they were comfortable and were firmly part of Macroom social life. There's a stained-glass window in the local church dedicated to my grandfather's memory. The Birds of Macroom were not an overtly political family. I think they would have been Michael Collins people in terms of their attitude to the Anglo-Irish Treaty in 1921. The historian, John A. Murphy, who hails from Macroom, told me that he remembers my grandmother selling poppies to commemorate the dead of the First World War. He even recalls my grandmother calling to his own family home, and his mother telling my grandmother, 'I won't be buying those poppies but you've great courage selling them around here.'

My mother's family—the Murrays—were cattle dealers in County Cork. One of her brothers, Tommie Murray, was a member of the British Army. He was travelling home from Rosslare to Fishguard on the *St Patrick* in June 1941 when his ship was attacked by German aircraft. She broke in two and sank. My uncle, along with nine other passengers and ten crew members, was killed. He's buried in Macroom in a grave that is exactly the same as thousands of Second World War graves in the north of France and elsewhere. His headstone recalls that he was a private in the Essex Regiment and that he was 40 years old when he died.

My grandparents had four sons and a daughter. The girl, my aunt, went to live in the United States. The sons, including my father, were boarders at Clongowes Wood College near Dublin. One of them qualified as a doctor and practised in England; another was an engineer with the ESB; the third worked as a bank manager. My father did least well of that generation, spending much of his working life either at sea or in jobs in Dublin which didn't allow him to fulfil his potential.

There were few jobs and even fewer prospects in Ireland in the late 1930s. Like many of their generation, my parents—Jack Bird and Delia Murray—went to England after they married. They lived in Romford outside London during the Second World War. My mother sometimes told stories about when the aircraft sirens sounded. They used to gather a few precious possessions and run for the local bomb shelter. It must have been very frightening. Their house was bombed twice by the Germans but my parents were unhurt and returned to Ireland before the war was over.

My father had worked as a ship's engineer before getting a job with the ESB in Dublin. He held that job for many years, but a mixture of economic necessity and his love of life at sea prompted him to take a job as a third engineer with Irish Shipping. The wanderlust kept drawing him back to life at sea, and his absence was just taken for granted in our house when I was growing up. The ships in the fleet were called after different species of Irish trees and at various times my father sailed on the *Irish Oak*, the *Irish Ash* and the *Irish Pine*. There was always great excitement when he came home, bringing with him exotic gifts from far-flung places. I still have a handmade wicker hat which he brought back from China. I also remember getting postcards from all sorts of strange-sounding places, like Port Said and Cape Town.

My parents rented a house in Sandymount where they started to bring up their children. I was the youngest of four boys. There was an eight-year gap between myself and my eldest brother, so I was very much the baby of the family. I was golden brown at birth as my mother had a thyroid problem during the pregnancy which had been treated with iodine. My father thought it appropriate that I be christened Charles Brown Bird although I have always been known as Charlie. For many years, I suspected that my parents' decision to go with Charles may have had something to do with the fact that the name was fashionable at that time due to the birth of Prince Charles in Britain. However, I have since discovered that the name Charles actually goes back several generations in the Bird family.

We lived in Sandymount until I was around six or seven years old. Ronnie Delany had been a neighbour. For years, I was reminded by my mother that a young Charlie Bird had been pushed around Lee Crescent in Sandymount in his pram by the man who went on to win

Olympic gold in the 1,500 metres in Melbourne in 1956. My lasting childhood memories, however, are more associated with Goatstown where my family moved to in the mid-1950s. Goatstown in south County Dublin was still a country village. The housing boom was only just starting. Eden Park, where we lived, was surrounded by country-side. It was a wonderful environment for a growing boy to explore. The old railway line from Bray to Harcourt Street in Dublin city centre ran through nearby Dundrum. This area became my world. I worked my way through the area, field after field. I remember playing soccer on the local streets.

As with all childhoods, there were some intriguing adults to be discovered. Jack O'Donnell, a cobbler, left a lasting impression on me. He worked from a small shop in Drummartin. He spoke Irish, loved children and played the tin whistle and the uileann pipes. I suppose with my father away so much, I looked to Jack as a father figure. He was originally from Bray in County Wicklow and was mad into the GAA. He brought many local children, myself included, to Croke Park to see the famous Kilkenny hurling teams of the time in action. I delivered shoes for Jack all over the Goatstown area. I know I was on an errand for him on the day John F. Kennedy was shot dead in Dallas in November 1963. I also delivered prescriptions for a local chemist shop. I had a variety of part-time jobs from about the age of seven. I think I started out delivering daily newspapers for a Mrs Ryan, an elderly woman who ran a small shop opposite The Goat public house. Right through my teens, I worked after school during the week and also on Saturdays.

The money I earned was always handed over to my mother. She then used to give me something back. It was the same even after I left school and started to earn regular wages. Each week, I gave over my pay packet to my mother. My parents, and in particular my mother, were very strict. That was not unusual in that era as for most people corporal punishment in school and at home was just part of everyday life. I never caused huge problems. I was never in trouble with the gardaí. I never came home drunk or anything like that.

When my father finished at sea, he worked as a welder in Bridgefoot Street. He was a proud man and I'm sure the job hurt his pride and self-esteem. He had come from a family of some means. His brothers had all developed good professional careers. But now, in his sixties, he was coming home in the evenings with blackened hands. Then, total disaster in the form of cancer. He fought a losing battle against the disease in his final years and was only 65 when he died in February 1971. He passed away on decimal day when the country switched to the currency which survived until the introduction of the euro. I wasn't close to my father—he was away at sea for much of my childhood. To me he was a man who sent postcards from faraway places and, when he did arrive home, brought with him what seemed at the time like quite exotic gifts. I do recall fondly the days when he came back from his travels as I was allowed to miss school but, to be truthful, I didn't know him very well. I was a child in a different era. My relationship with my own children is totally different and it is only now as they have reached adulthood that I realise what my father and I missed out on.

With my father away so much, my mother was the dominant parental presence in my life. Even as I grew into my teens, my mother remained the traditional strong disciplinarian. I used to go dancing in the Stella House dance hall in Mount Merrion. A very young Van Morrison and his band, Them, were regulars at the Stella House. I was 16 or 17 at the time. If I arrived home late, my mother would lock me out. I was left in the garage to sleep on an old curtain. The severity of this response contributed, along with other things, to the very mixed views I held for many years about my mother, with whom I suppose I did not have a particularly close relationship.

I moved out of home only when I got married in early 1974. After that, my mother lived alone in the house in Goatstown. She never acknowledged the progress I was making in my career, something I grew to resent. There was never any word of praise or encouragement. We never got to confront these issues as she was killed in a road accident in 1983. She was struck while crossing the road outside the Cornelscourt shopping centre. She was in her mid-seventies. The accident happened on a Thursday and she died the following Sunday in Loughlinstown hospital. I remember visiting her in intensive care over that weekend. The hospital was sealed off with armed gardaí on the main entrances. The IRA had attempted to kidnap millionaire businessman Galen Weston. But gardaí were alert to the plan and a gun battle ensued. Several of the kidnappers were injured. Some of them were being treated in the same emergency ward as my mother, who was dying from the injuries she had sustained in the car accident. The hospital was off-limits to all but the relations of critically ill patients. I can still see the look on the faces of the gardaí as I walked along the corridor leading to the emergency room—their expressions said, 'What's he doing here?'

My mother was buried in the cemetery in Deansgrange. It brought the family together for probably the last time. My brothers and I were brought up in different times. I know my parents meant well by us and they did their best to give us a start in life. As with my father, I would like to have had a different relationship with my mother. There were things I would like to have discussed with her but sadly we never had the opportunity to have those conversations. I am grateful that I have succeeded in avoiding a similar situation with my own children.

———

If my school years were anything to go by, I was destined to achieve very little in life. I went to a number of national and secondary schools. I struggled in them all. My parents decided to enrol me in Sandymount High School. It was located near Lansdowne Road and was fee paying. My three brothers were by that stage all working, and, while the fees were just about manageable, it was a big sacrifice for my parents. For that I will always be grateful to them: they struggled to give me the gift of a good education.

The school was multi-denominational and co-educational, which was very unusual in Ireland at that time. This experience left a big impression as many years later I would help with the establishment of the Bray School Project—the country's second multi-denominational national school. Both my daughters went there, and my wife, Mary, was chairperson of the school's board of management for many years.

I had never been in a class with girls before and, having no sisters, I was somewhat intimidated at the outset. But I quickly settled in. We often went on 'mass-mitches'—a whole gang of us used to take off to nearby Herbert Park for an afternoon. The boys used to support the girls at their hockey matches and they used to cheer us on at rugby matches. I played rugby for the school team but not very well. We trained on the back pitches of Lansdowne Road. I only ever scored one try and that was during a match played on pitches where the RTÉ Radio Centre was later built. Actually I think I slipped on the ball as it went over the try line but the score was given!

The school also had an active debating society. I was elected Auditor in my final year and was one of the organisers of the first inter-schools debating society in Dublin. But for all my extra-curricular exploits I was not what might be described as academically skilled. I liked English and history but had a real problem with maths. I was also easily distracted and a bit lazy when it came to school work. I had my part-time jobs and was delivering papers or working in The Goat Bar when I should have been doing my homework. By the time the Leaving Cert had come around for me, I had as good as opted out of school. I remember one teacher saying, 'Charlie, I think you should give up maths altogether. Is there any chance you could help me get the path outside my house fixed with the contacts you have?'

My lack of academic success was a huge personal disappointment. However, I was not a complete failure in school. I loved the debates in class and I was never shy about contributing to discussions. But I was not cut out for studying and I never performed well in formal examinations, particularly in maths.

I never really considered going to university. I failed my Leaving Cert because I didn't pass my maths exam. I was hugely disappointed when the results came out. It was an awful day. It wasn't as if I was the only person in my class not going to university, but most of the people I knew were. It was hard not to look at them and then at myself, and wonder if I had messed up completely. It was not the last time in my life that having missed college affected me like that.

For years, I resented my own poor academic record. I have always regretted not having had the opportunity to go to university. Yet, somehow, this apparent failure has been a great personal motivator. Despite failing my Leaving Cert, I have got to the top of my profession. It has been a long climb and I have worked hard but I have not let missing diplomas or degrees get in my way. If anything, my achievements have probably been built on the back of my earlier failures. I was going to prove that teacher wrong—I may have given up maths but I was never going to give up on making something of myself.

I would love to have studied history or politics if I had gone to university. These were the subjects that I was passionately interested in. Actually my first political act occurred while still a schoolboy in 1966. Ireland was caught up in the celebrations marking the fiftieth anniversary of the 1916 Easter Rising. There was a lot of talk about the men of 1916 and how they had taken the fight to the British in the name of Irish freedom. The leader of the rebellion, Pádraig Pearse, was presented as an Irish hero. I was nearing the end of my second-level education, and I remember being captivated by a classroom discussion about Irish history and what had happened at Easter time, half a century previously. There was great excitement about a military parade planned for O'Connell Street in central Dublin. Flags and bunting were on prominent display across the capital, including Goatstown.

We were not what might be called a political family. Nevertheless, I was obviously attracted by the pomp of the Rising anniversary and found a way to make my own small contribution to the national celebrations. There was a big palm tree in the field behind the garden of our semi-detached house. The tree was probably 60 feet high. I climbed it as far as my 16-year-old legs would safely take me, and I tied a flag on a branch before making my way back down to the garden below. The green, white and orange flag fluttered in the wind. I was chuffed at my achievement. I'm not sure why I did it. I was only a teenager and knew nothing of the world.

Something about the atmosphere generated by the fiftieth anniversary of the Easter Rising definitely rubbed off on me because, in early March 1966, I found myself responding to the destruction of Nelson's Pillar in O'Connell Street. The 134ft monument—the foundation stone of which was laid in 1808—had been erected in Dublin city centre to commemorate the Battle of Trafalgar. The pillar offered great views over the city skyline and I was one of the tens of thousands who had walked the steps to its viewing gallery. An explosion in the early hours of 8 March 1966 destroyed the upper half of the granite pillar, throwing the statue of Admiral Nelson onto the street. I don't think the noise was heard out in Goatstown but word quickly spread. When I heard the news, I suggested to one of my schoolfriends, Cathal O'Shea, that we go into town. We gave school a miss that morning and took the bus into the centre of Dublin. It wasn't clear who was responsible for toppling the pillar although a group of IRA men later admitted to planting the explosives. They saw the pillar as a symbol of Britishness and, in an odd sort of way, believed that destroying it was an appropriate way to celebrate the Easter Rising. I didn't give too much thought to the reasons why Nelson's Pillar had been destroyed. Like any young boy of my age I was attracted by the excitement of a massive explosion in central Dublin.

A big crowd had gathered at the top of O'Connell Street. The gardaí were trying to keep order. The stump of the pillar was still in place. There was rubble all over the street and the head of Nelson was lying forlornly on the ground. My initial thought was to take the Admiral's head. It was a crazy idea. The head was too big and we would have needed a truck to get away with it, not to mind the attention we'd have attracted. So instead I wrapped my arms around Nelson's head. There was a great deal of humour among the crowd. We filled up our school bags with lumps of rubble. Souvenirs! With little more to do, we decided to return to school. Showing up late was better than not showing up at all. I suspect the class teacher had never been given such an excuse from a pair of mitching pupils. Having surveyed our bags of rubble, however, he decided to excuse the absence.

With my school days coming to an end, I thought about joining the British Navy and got the application forms. I suppose the Bird sea-faring tradition had an influence especially with my father's career, but my parents ultimately talked me out of it. I also thought about a career in television where my brother Colin was an actor in the first soap series, *Tolka Row*. Jim Bartley, who in later years became well known as Bella in *Fair City*, played opposite Colin in *Tolka Row*. Colin, who was the eldest in the family, later worked as a scriptwriter for RTÉ before becoming press officer for the Industrial Development Authority. He subsequently became a press officer for Justin Keating when he was a government minister in the 1973–77 Fine Gael/Labour coalition.

My brother Frank was the nearest to me in age. Of the four boys in the family, we were also the most alike in appearance. Some of his friends knew him as Cheeko. Another of my brothers was christened Richard Bird although he has always been known as Dickie Bird. A famous family story relates that when Dickie was a teenager, a garda stopped him cycling through Clonskeagh for not having a light on his bike. 'What's your name?' the garda enquired.

'Dickie Bird,' my brother responded.

'Don't be so cheeky,' the garda replied as he marched Dickie off to the station in Dundrum where the soon-to-be embarrassed garda eventually realised his error.

Dickie later went to work in the oil business in the Middle East where he stayed for many years.

I was never that close to any of my three brothers. There was a big age difference. They were out working while I was still a kid in school. I do regret that we were not on better terms, but we were never a close-knit family. There was some connection with our relations in Macroom, though, and I remember visiting some cousins in County Cork. Interestingly, the Macroom connection was useful to me later in my career in journalism. In the early 1990s, there was considerable controversy over the sale of state-owned land in Ballsbridge in Dublin. A government-appointed inspector examined the deal. The so-called Telecom affair implicated some of the biggest names in Irish business including the stockbroker, Dermot Desmond.

Desmond was providing a media briefing on the Glackin report on the background to the land deal. The RTÉ news desk asked would I help out Vincent Wall, who was then RTÉ's business correspondent. I had never met Desmond not to mind talking with him before 1992, but it was obvious that he was intrigued by my presence. By then, I was beginning to get a reputation as someone who turned up when there was trouble. He was more used to dealing with the business and finance reporters who dominated the audience at the briefing. At one stage, Desmond turned and directed a question at me: 'What the fuck are you doing here? You're not a business journalist.' It was said half in jest and half as a question. When the briefing was concluded, Desmond came over to me.

I knew he had a family connected with Macroom so I mentioned my own link. He smiled at me. 'You've got trusting eyes,' he said. 'And now I know why—it's because you're from Macroom.' As he left, he gave me his phone number, a precious commodity for a journalist. I rarely covered business stories so I had few enough reasons to call him, but on the few occasions that I have dialled the number over the years, it's been mainly to discuss Charlie Haughey, who had a close relationship with Desmond from whom he received several sizeable donations. In the late 1980s, Haughey, as leader of Fianna Fáil, championed the International Financial Services Centre in Dublin, an idea pushed by the stockbroker from Macroom.

Several years after my encounter with Desmond over the Glackin Report, I passed him on the street in central Dublin. 'You must come and have coffee,' he said, although in fact lunch was eventually arranged. I turned up at Desmond's offices in the IFSC. His private chef cooked lunch for the two of us. Two very good bottles of wine were consumed. Despite his reputation for coyness, I found Desmond very affable. The conversation was relaxed. The topic of Charles Haughey dominated our conversation. Desmond strongly defended the former Taoiseach. 'I have never regretted anything I did for him,' he said. It was late afternoon by the time I bade him farewell. As I left, he said to me, 'I wouldn't like this to get into the paper.' And it never did, until now!

Ben Dunne also had a family connection with Macroom. I approached the former supermarket businessman one time when he was leaving the McCracken Tribunal at Dublin Castle where he had been answering questions about his financial relationship with Charlie Haughey. Making small talk, I mentioned that we both had family connections with the County Cork town. 'We could be related,' Dunne ventured, before turning to me with a mischievous smile and adding, 'I suppose I'll have to leave you some money in my will.'

———

Money was not very high up my list when I left school in 1968. Few things were. I had no real sense of what I was going to do to earn a living, not to mind what I was going to do with my life. I laugh now when I say my first job was making perfume. It's not totally true. Just after I left school, I got a job in the Pond's factory in Rathgar. I worked alongside one of the qualified chemists.

My job was to load up the chemical mixers. It was a Monday-to-Friday, nine-to-five existence. I wasn't very happy there but I got paid at the end of every week so I had some money in my pocket. I stayed at the job for well over a year. In early 1970, I left Pond's and went to work as a clerical assistant in a company called Stewart Industrial in Dublin city centre. It was a Northern Ireland company which sold drill bits all over the country. I was processing shipping documents.

These jobs left me with some money to spend. I enjoyed my pints of Guinness; I bought a tweed jacket and started to smoke a pipe. For a time, I even changed my name to its Irish-language version. My spare time was increasingly taken up with political involvement. There was an upsurge in left-wing activism in Dublin. It was the same all over Western Europe. I got involved in the Labour Party and with the Young Socialists. These were exciting times. I had just turned 20 years of age and was without a concern in the world. I joined protest marches against the apartheid regime in South Africa and against the Vietnam War. I went to meetings organised by the Dublin Housing Action Committee and marched on protests for better public housing and an end to homelessness.

In January 1970, the all-white South African rugby team arrived in Dublin. The Springboks were touring Britain and Ireland and the opening match of the tour was scheduled for Lansdowne Road. I was one of those on the picket outside the Royal Starlight Hotel in Bray where the Springboks were staying. There was a huge crowd outside the stadium on the afternoon of the match: 10,000 protesters marched from the city centre to Lansdowne Road. I helped to carry a Labour Party banner. Despite the size of the crowd, the demonstration passed off without any serious incidents.

All this activity was for me the equivalent of student politics. I loved every minute of it. Dublin was alive. O'Dwyer's Pub on Merrion Row was a regular meeting place. On Saturday afternoons, I could be found outside the GPO on O'Connell Street. In a good week, over a hundred people used to gather to listen to various individuals speaking from the back of a milk lorry. I climbed up onto the platform a few times, taking the microphone in my hand and talking for a few minutes.

It was all exciting stuff but I was restless and wanted more from my life. So, early in 1970, I decided it was time to 'find myself'. I left my job, packed a few belongings into a bag and bought a bus ticket to County Galway. My ultimate destination was Inis Oírr, the smallest of the three Aran Islands, and home at that time to 345 people. I had visited the Aran Islands the previous summer and had fallen in love with Inis Oírr, and, to be honest, I had also found my first love on the island.

Áine O'Connor was a researcher in RTÉ. She would later marry an RTÉ colleague, Larry Masterson, before making her name as a talented television producer. She enjoyed great success with the movie, *In the Name of the Father*, and was a partner of Gabriel Byrne and later David Duffy of *Fair City* fame. Tragically, Áine died at 50 years of age, in 1998. She was simply stunning, beautiful and full of life. We knew each other slightly in Dublin from mixing in the same wider circle of friends. But we hit it off on Inis Oírr. And over the next six months or so, we went out together. I was the true romantic—I remember taking her on a date to a Young Socialist meeting! Áine wasn't overly impressed. It was lovely, but I was way out of my depth!

Some months later, I returned to Inis Oírr. Bizarre, as it may now seem, I had an idea that I would settle down there. The sense of isolation on the island was attractive. The steamer out of Galway, the *Naomh Éanna*, could not land at Inis Oírr as the harbour was too small, so locals used to come out in currachs to collect goods and people. I had arranged to stay with Orla Knudsen, or Orla the Dane as he was known to all on the island.

A Danish national who had arrived on the island in 1954, Orla was a self-taught weaver who worked from a loom built from driftwood. He was a quiet man who supported his bachelor lifestyle by the sale of ties and colourful cloth. Poetry and painting filled his leisure hours.

Orla lived in a small cottage with two downstairs rooms. I brought a blue tent and pitched it in the attic. What I was at, I am not really sure. I suppose I loved the romantic image of this rural world and had aspirations to follow in the footsteps of Orla the Dane. I wore an Aran sweater, smoked my pipe and talked with Orla about the ways of the world. These were the actions of a young man without any responsibilities.

It was a flight of fantasy—an adventure which lasted for a few months. I eventually bade farewell to Orla and returned home to Dublin. He actually passed away at the end of 1970. I got a job on a construction site in Ringsend. The Glass Bottle factory was being built and I was told, 'There's good money on the buildings.' I spent a couple of months there, and at one stage was responsible for the fact that the gardaí were almost called.

I usually worked with a pneumatic drill, breaking rocks up into smaller pieces. It was a bit like a prison sentence. I was always looking for an excuse to do other work on the site. One morning, I saw my opportunity when the foreman was looking for someone to drive the dumper around the site. 'I'll do it,' I volunteered. What I didn't tell him was that I had never sat behind the wheel of any vehicle in my entire life. He gave me the keys and I got into the dumper. But as soon as I switched on the ignition, I knew I was in trouble. I couldn't control the damned thing: it just took off on me. I didn't know how to stop it. So I jumped off the dumper as it sped forward, and watched it turn upside down as it landed in the newly laid foundations of the factory. It was now an ex-dumper, and it was time for Charlie to get another job!

I then spent a few months back working with a subsidiary of Stewart International. But it was a stopgap position as I looked for a job in the media. It seemed a logical step given my huge interest in current affairs and the impression being made on me by the number of people I was meeting from the world of journalism. In fact, through my involvement in politics and various protest groups, I got to meet and mix with a huge number of interesting people. In particular, I remember the Earleys from Clonskeagh. They helped me get the ill-fated building-site job. Mrs Earley was a member of the Labour Party but her husband had aligned himself with the Communist Party. They were friendly with Peadar O'Donnell, the Donegal writer who had fought in the Civil War and was involved in various left-wing struggles in Europe. I joined the Earleys when they went to visit O'Donnell at his house in Drumcondra. He was an old man but I felt I was meeting an iconic figure from Irish history.

———

I was a member of the Labour Party by the time the 1969 general election was called. My brother Colin had actually been an unsuccessful Labour candidate at the local elections in 1967. It was his only electoral involvement as he then went on to concentrate on his acting career. In what was still largely one-channel land, his presence on TV at the time was a big deal. By 1969, Labour had adopted a radical policy agenda and campaigned under the slogan, 'The Seventies will be Socialist'. A number of high-profile candidates like Conor Cruise O'Brien, Justin Keating and David Thornley were selected for Labour. I was an active member of the Clonskeagh branch of the party and was given responsibility for the canvass in the area where I lived.

The party did well in Dublin in the 1969 general election but failed to make a significant electoral breakthrough. The following couple of years were dominated by internal debates about the question of a future pre-election coalition with Fine Gael. The issue dominated the party's national conference in Galway in 1970. I spoke from the podium, introducing myself as 'Bird, Clonskeagh branch'. The coalition debate was filmed by RTÉ. It was one of the station's first live colour transmissions. The footage of that very party member with his long hair and youthful enthusiasm is still in the RTÉ archives library.

I was very much aligned with the anti-coalition wing of the party. After the debate in Galway, many delegates adjourned for a drink to a local hotel. A very drunk Frank Cluskey—who at that stage was a Dáil deputy—was involved in the debate about coalition which had continued in the bar area. To a senior party figure like Cluskey, I was simply a nuisance—one of the Young Turks who were causing the Labour leadership such trouble. Cluskey took exception to some remark I made and he took a swing at me.

Noël Browne took a different view. Browne had near iconic status with many on the left because of his time as Health Minister in the 1948–51 inter-party government. Now a member of the Labour Party, Browne was opposed to the idea of a coalition arrangement with Fine Gael. He had spearheaded opposition to the leadership position. Some time later, Browne invited me to lunch with him in Leinster House. I wasn't particularly close to him but I suppose it was his way of saying thanks for the support I had given him. It was my first time ever in the parliament building. We ate in the members' restaurant. It's all changed now but back in the early 1970s, the service in the restaurant was very formal. The waiters were dressed in black and wore white gloves. There were special plates with silver knives and forks.

I suppose I was somewhat in awe of the environment but Browne was not long knocking me back into reality. 'This place is useful for only one thing, Charlie,' he said. 'And that's swinging out of the chandeliers.' What exactly he had in mind I don't know, and I didn't ask!

I backed Browne at the 1971 Labour Party conference in Cork where the coalition debate was resolved. I again spoke from the platform at a fringe meeting. My photograph was in the newspapers the next day, a fresh-faced Young Turk. Bernadette Devlin, the Westminster MP for Mid-Ulster, was another speaker that day. Eventually the opponents of the leadership strategy led a walk-out from the main conference, and I joined them. The Young Socialists were among the groups leading the opposition within Labour to the idea of coalition with Fine Gael. Peter Graham was the driving force behind the Young Socialists which he had helped establish in 1968 and which was loosely aligned to Labour. With the zeal of an enthusiastic recruit, I made it my business to attend Young Socialist meetings every Wednesday and Saturday. I used to take the bus into town and head for the group's basement offices off

Mountjoy Square to discuss political ideology and plan demonstrations and protests. We were going to change the world.

There were all sorts of groups which joined together at various protests and marches. I remember John Feeney who was involved in a left-wing Catholic organisation. John went on to become a journalist with the *Evening Herald* newspaper. His brother Kevin was later a senior counsel involved in RTÉ's legal cases concerning National Irish Bank, and, in early 2006, he became a High Court judge. Another brother, Peter, has held a number of senior positions in RTÉ including the post of editor of the current affairs programme *Frontline* which I worked on for a time in the late 1970s.

To be honest, this left-wing world had an air of unreality about it. There were all sorts of labels—Marxists, Leninists, Trotskyites and Maoists were among those I can now recall. I remember one distinct difference was that we drank in different pubs. The Young Socialists were regarded as Trotskyites. They congregated in O'Dwyer's pub on Merrion Row, while the so-called Stalinists from the Connolly Youth Movement made themselves at home across the street in O'Donoghue's. Looking back, I know I could barely have spelt the word Trotsky at that time, not to mind appreciating what the term Trotskyism actually meant.

Peter Graham was affable and a good public speaker. I got to know him reasonably well. He was a few years older than me—in his mid-twenties. He was from the Coombe area in Dublin and, I think, an electrician by trade. He was very well connected. He had spent some time in London in 1969 and got to know Tariq Ali, one of the leading Trotskyites in Europe. Tariq was from a wealthy family in Pakistan who in the mid-1960s had been President of the Oxford Union. He was very involved in left-wing politics in London as well as leading the campaign against the Vietnam War. Through this opposition, he earned a reputation in debates with figures like Henry Kissinger. After one of these debates had been televised in the United States, the actor Marlon Brando invited Tariq to dinner. Given this pedigree, the association made Peter all the more impressive in Dublin. In early November 1971, Peter left the Hume Street offices and went for a drink with some friends. He then left for his flat near St Stephen's Green. What happened after he arrived home has never been resolved. Sometime before 1 a.m., two men rang the doorbell of the elderly caretaker of the flat complex, asking where Graham lived. Some minutes later, there was a commotion and what locals said sounded like a gunshot. A man was reported as having been seen running from Peter's flat with blood on his hands. Peter had been shot in the head with a .45 bullet.

All sorts of rumours spread. There was talk that Peter was linked to plans to smuggle weapons into the Republic for the IRA's use in Northern Ireland. I was unaware of his having had any links to left-wing republican groups. He had never advocated the use of violence. He had no involvement in the IRA and nobody really knew why he had been killed. It was frightening. Gardaí came to my home in Goatstown. They wanted to know what I knew. The answer was very little. My fingerprints were taken. There was a big row about what would happen to the fingerprints but the gardaí assured all of us who had known Peter that the material would be destroyed when their investigations were concluded. I was actually given my set of prints which I still have to this day.

Bernadette Devlin came from the North for Peter's funeral. Tariq Ali travelled from London. I walked near the front of the long funeral procession. Wearing a dark sheepskin coat and a polo-neck sweater, I looked every inch the radical left-wing activist. As we walked through the cemetery, in front of me a man held the Starry Plough flag. At the graveside, we all lifted our left arms high with clenched fists in solidarity with Peter. I was pictured alongside Tariq Ali right in front of the burial plot which was covered with floral wreaths. It's an amazing photograph. Tariq Ali gave the graveside oration. 'Peter was the ideal example of the worker militant,' he said, before adding, 'We have our own ways of dealing with such people.' I was not really sure what I was doing there.

I went around the country to address meetings of the Young Socialist Movement. In late January 1972, I was speaking in Limerick when news started to come through about what had happened during a civil rights march in Derry. It seemed some marchers had been shot dead. I travelled back to Dublin by train. At Limerick Junction, I found myself in the same carriage as Breandán Ó hEithir and Fred Cogley who were on their way back from a rugby match. There was little news about the events in Derry. When we got into Heuston Station, there was a snow storm and all buses and cars were off the roads. I remember walking home to Goatstown with Breandán.

The news from Derry was bleak. Thirteen people had been shot dead by British soldiers. The images on the television were truly awful. There was huge outrage and anger across the island as the atrocity was quickly dubbed 'Bloody Sunday'. I joined a protest demonstration the following weekend in Newry. I was also part of the large protest in Dublin which marched to the British Embassy. I had no idea that it would end with the embassy being burned to the ground. It was a dramatic act in a very tense period. I remember walking home from the march and meeting Micky Mullen, one of the top trade unionists in the country. 'What happened?' he asked me.

'The embassy is on fire,' I responded.

He simply nodded which I took as a form of approval. They were dangerous times when even mild-mannered individuals with no compulsion towards violence were not sure themselves what direction they wanted events to turn.

I had travelled north of the border on several occasions over the previous few years. The re-emergence of conflict in Northern Ireland and allegations of mistreatment of nationalists had generated considerable debate at many of the meetings I attended. I joined several civil rights marches in Derry where I was interviewed on Radio Free Derry about attitudes south of the border. There were always buses leaving Dublin on a Saturday morning for some location in Northern Ireland where a protest march was being held. And you were nobody on those trips if you were not arrested by the police or army. I had that badge of honour! One Saturday afternoon, I was picked up by the British Army and taken to the local army barracks. After about an hour in a cell, we were released.

By the end of 1972, I was drifting out of the Young Socialists and the Labour Party. I was, however, to have one final fling with political activity. Tony Heffernan, a close childhood friend, asked me to get involved in the 1973 general election campaign. We had grown up together in Goatstown and were friends for many years. He was involved with Official Sinn Féin and I agreed to act as director of elections for Peigean Doyle, the OSF candidate in Rathmines. We all did our best but she was well beaten. It was my final involvement in party politics, although for Tony Heffernan it was only the latest in what became lifelong political activity. In later years, he worked as press officer for the Workers' Party, Democratic Left and more recently as a senior advisor to Pat Rabbitte in the Labour Party.

———

I had drifted through a number of different jobs, but because of the circles I was in, I had started to think about a career in the media world. Seeing my brother Colin on the black and white television screen in a way prompted my desire to get involved in journalism. I knew several *Irish Times* people from my time working behind the bar in The Goat, including Donal Foley who was a regular. From the Ring Gaeltacht in County Waterford, Donal was full of enthusiasm when he spoke about his job as news editor with *The Irish Times*. He was responsible for recruiting a number of new young reporters—people like Conor O'Clery, Maeve Binchy and Nell McCafferty—and some years later, he helped to direct me on my first steps into a career in journalism.

It was probably through Donal, and Breandán Ó hEithir from RTÉ, that I first met Eoghan Harris. They all used to drink in The Goat. Eoghan was a producer in RTÉ although he wouldn't have known me very well. But when I was going out with Áine O'Connor, we were introduced properly. He would have known about my Labour Party involvement, and my interest in a media career. I remember Eoghan helped with an article I wrote about the building industry; he made some suggestions and offered some advice. I wasn't really sure how I was going to break into journalism or a related job, and started doing some freelance research for *Hibernia*, a fortnightly current affairs magazine, which was published by John Mulcahy. The government information bureau was established in the early 1970s and I applied for a job there. But without a university qualification I was never going to be considered: that old bogey again.

I made one ultimately abortive attempt to get a job in provincial newspaper journalism. A new newspaper was being set up in Carrick-on-Shannon in late 1970 in competition with the *Leitrim Observer*. I saw an advert for reporters and immediately applied, not that I had any journalistic experience. The man behind the venture, John Keaney, ran a photo shop in Carrick-on-Shannon, and when I arrived in the town, dummy versions of the new newspaper were being produced. I lasted six weeks. I had no experience and it showed. We both agreed that it was for the best that I return home to Dublin.

However, my desire for a career in the media was undimmed. In early 1971, I heard that *The Irish Times* was looking for a library researcher. Donal Foley organised the interview for me, and I did enough at it to be offered the job. I was ecstatic and probably insufferably smug telling people that I worked in the Reference Library of *The Irish Times*! But it was such an exciting place to work. The printing presses were downstairs and there was always a hum of activity. The newspaper was home to some brilliant reporters and writers—people like Eugene McEldowney, Dick Walsh, Elgy Gillespie and Mary Maher. When I carried reference files down to the newsroom, I sensed the excitement. I was seeing real journalism at first hand, in the middle of what was a golden age for the newspaper. 'I want to do this,' I decided. Being exposed to this environment was important in confirming to me that this was very much the career I wanted to follow.

The library offices were on the same floor as the newspaper's photographic department where I became friends with Pat Langan and Jack McManus, two of the staff photographers. I still have very clear memories of the day in May 1974 when bombs went off in central Dublin. Twenty-five people were killed when three car bombs exploded at 5.30 p.m. I was sitting at my desk in the reference library when I heard the explosions. A short time afterwards, there was huge activity in the office next door to the reference library as photographers came rushing in with their images to be developed. The scenes their cameras had captured on the streets nearby were truly awful. Loyalists were blamed for the attacks.

Douglas Gageby was editor of *The Irish Times* when I worked in D'Olier Street. From a Northern Ireland background, he had set the newspaper on a modernisation course from his appointment in the mid-1960s. Gageby would often come up to the library in the evening to look for files to check facts in stories written for the following day's edition. He also had a habit of going into the photographic department where I often saw him request crowd-scene photographs that were to be carried on particular pages waiting to go to print. The photograph would be blown up for him and he would divide it into sections. He would then take out a magnifying glass and count each head in one section to get an estimate of the number of people on the march. The exercise was to check the accuracy of the estimations reporters had put on crowd scenes. I was amazed at this attention to detail.

My life was moving at a fast pace. I met Mary O'Connor in the middle of 1972 while she worked with Aer Lingus. Although she turned down my first request for a date, I persisted, spending every penny I had at the local florist. The flowers worked and we were married early in 1974. I was dabbling in journalism while I worked with *The Irish Times*, writing a monthly review of left-wing publications. I would gather up the latest magazines and newspapers, and write up a commentary on who was saying what. This was really my first foray into journalism. I think I got six or seven articles published. But despite this energy and enthusiasm, I was never going to progress in D'Olier Street. I had a permanent pensionable position but I was outside the newsroom, and that was where the real action was taking place.

I got my big break early in 1974 when Eoghan Harris arrived into the reference library. He was working on a television project but had been given permission to do some research in D'Olier Street. Eoghan was a dynamic producer with the *Seven Days* current affairs programme on RTÉ television. We got talking. 'Would you be interested in working in RTÉ?' he asked me. I hardly had to reply as the positive response was written all over my face. 'There's a researcher job going with *Seven Days*,' Harris told me, adding the all important words: 'You should think about applying.'

Chapter 2 ～

| STARTING OUT

I t was two o'clock in the morning as I drove down Tara Street in Dublin, crossing from the south of the city to the north side via Butt Bridge. Despite the late hour, plenty of activity was visible as I approached Liberty Hall. Blue emergency lights were flashing, and I could see several ambulances lined up outside the Dublin city morgue. Less than an hour earlier, I had been awoken in my bed at my home in Bray by the sound of a ringing telephone.

The voice at the other end of the line was that of Mike Burns, the man who had given me a break into news reporting a little over a year previously. Burns was 'Mr Radio' in RTÉ and was responsible for all the radio output in the newsroom. He would walk though the office smoking a cigar, and had so many contacts in the diplomatic services that it was often joked that he was a CIA spy. 'Charlie, there's been a big fire in north Dublin. Can you get there as quickly as possible?' Burns asked, although it was a question which hardly needed a response. It was the early hours of Saturday, 14 February 1981.

The Stardust fire was the biggest story I had worked on in my short time as a journalist. It happened at a time when I was still learning my trade as a general reporter on television and radio in the RTÉ newsroom. I am not sure why it is—the numbers who died, their young age, maybe the fact that it was an Irish story, or possibly a combination of all these things—but years later, the Stardust remains a story that retains a deep and lasting personal impression for me.

I was not sure exactly where the Stardust was located on Dublin's north side as I responded to Burns's telephone call. But there was no need to stop to ask for directions on that awful night. I simply followed the ambulances, fire engines and garda cars as they made their way out towards Artane. Hours earlier, over 800 young people had gathered at the Stardust nightclub in Artane to celebrate St Valentine's Day. The disco was under way when a fire started sometime before midnight. The blaze spread quickly amid panic. Later, at a public tribunal of inquiry, it emerged that a number of the fire exits at the venue had been either locked or chained.

Rescue efforts had been hampered by steel plates which had been welded over toilet windows. By the time I came on the scene, firefighters were winning their battle with the blaze. But lives had been lost. In all, 48 young people were dead. Local hospitals were under huge pressure, coping with the hundreds of survivors who were injured in the inferno. The emergency services did all they could. There was huge activity, with fire engines and ambulances coming and going. It was a bitterly cold night. There was ice everywhere and I recall that as water would leak from the fire hydrants, it would immediately start to freeze. By dawn, the scale of the tragedy was evident. It was Ireland's worst fire disaster. Reporters on the scene, including myself, were collecting what information there was from the gardaí. The fact that so many who had lost their lives had been so young made the tragedy much worse. There was a terrible silence at the scene, broken only by the occasional fall of rubble in the charred interior of the Stardust complex.

The bodies of the dead had been taken to the city morgue which I had passed hours earlier. The injured—many suffering disfiguring burns—filled several hospitals. There was a real sense of shock among those who came to witness the destruction. People were silent as they looked on. A local shopkeeper allowed me to use his phone so I could file a report for the early-morning radio bulletin. This was a world before mobile phones and 24-hour rolling news. The country woke up to the news that 48 young people on a night-out were dead.

Taoiseach Charles Haughey arrived early in the morning. The Stardust building was in his Dáil constituency. He had some words of comfort for the families who had lost loved ones. He announced that the Fianna Fáil Ard Fheis which should have been the main news story that weekend would be cancelled. The reporters, who included myself and Eamon Mallie, with whom I later worked in Northern Ireland, followed Haughey through part of what remained of the burnt-out building. The scale of the disaster was overwhelming. What had been the inside of the complex had been gutted by the blaze.

Later in the morning, I was sent to the Mater Hospital where many of the survivors were being treated for their burns. Initially the media were not allowed in but the hospital authorities eventually relented. It was an important decision because the television pictures brought home to the public just how awful the fire had been and showed the terrible injuries suffered by those who were fortunate to be alive. I have a vivid memory of speaking with one young man, Martin Dowling, who was sitting up in his bed. His eye lids had been burnt and his hands were wrapped in white bandages. He was the son of the head waiter at Leinster House. He raised his hands up for the camera and an image was captured which became synonymous with the Stardust. I also interviewed two women who had been working in the Stardust when the fire broke out. The heavy smell of smoke was the first indication that something was wrong, they told me.

Later in the afternoon, I was asked to compile the lead report for the main evening television news. It had been a huge collective effort by many RTÉ staff who had worked at the Stardust site. The normal television schedule had been cleared. A decision had been taken to cancel that evening's edition of the *Late Late Show*. As I wrote my script for a radio report, Mike Burns sat down beside my desk and together we found the right words to tell the tragic story. He might have been a senior manager in the newsroom but when there was a big story to be covered, Burns just rolled up his sleeves and helped out in whatever way was needed.

Burns and I, together with dozens of others in RTÉ, worked through until after ten o'clock that evening. I had never been so close to a major news story before. But it did not end with reporting the devastation brought by the fire. It was the middle of winter and, over the following days, the people of Artane buried their dead. It seemed that there was a never-ending series of funerals. So many young lives had ended prematurely.

The tribunal of inquiry found the Butterlys, the family who owned the Stardust, guilty of negligence for keeping emergency exits locked. From the evidence presented, it was concluded that the fire had been started by a cigarette which ignited the foam beneath a slashed seat cover. The decorations for the Valentine's night celebrations ignited, and, within minutes, the entire building was ablaze. The tribunal concluded that the fire had probably been started deliberately. It was a contentious conclusion. Many of the families of the victims continue to believe that the truth has never emerged and that the tribunal failed to uncover the full facts about who was responsible for the Stardust tragedy.

Occasionally after the fire, I bumped into one particular man in central Dublin. Peter Hobbs, a stockbroker in Dublin, had lost his brother in the Stardust. Along with others, he campaigned for many years to discover the truth about what had happened at the dance hall. Whenever we met on the street, we would make eye contact and give each other a 'hello' by way of acknowledgement. What do you say to a man like that and the other families who lost their loved ones? It's a question to which I have returned again and again during my career in journalism in relation to a whole array of stories. For most people, the Stardust disaster faded away, but for the survivors and the victims' families, the campaign for justice continued. In February 2006, on the twenty-fifth anniversary of the fire, I interviewed Billy Fitzpatrick, who had spent more time in hospital than any of the other survivors, as he recovered from his terrible burns. Despite the passage of time, his story still had a powerful impact. RTÉ's powerful drama-documentary on the tragedy pushed the injustice done to these people up the news agenda once more.

The Stardust disaster in February 1981 was my first big news story although I had actually arrived in RTÉ in the summer of 1974. It had been an amazing journey which I could hardly have envisaged when I left my permanent staff job at *The Irish Times* for a short-term contact as a researcher in the current affairs division of the national broadcaster. I was newly married. My wife, Mary O'Connor, and I were renting a house in Blackrock as we saved to buy our first home. The 1970s were bleak economic times with high interest rates and high unemployment. Like many other young couples at the time, we weren't what might be called 'well-off'. There's no doubt that my decision was a risk. However, to be perfectly honest, that consideration was totally outweighed by the opportunity that was now going to become available to me.

I couldn't believe that I had made it into RTÉ. The current affairs division was located in prefab cabins at the back of the television building. I remember the big desks which were home to large metal typewriters. Television was still a novelty to Irish people in the 1970s. RTÉ was the only station available in most houses. So, when the RTÉ cameras and microphones arrived in any town in the country, it was a huge deal for the local community. It was all very exciting. I spent most of the following six years as a researcher, mainly in current affairs although for a short time with the *Late Late Show*. But as I quickly discovered—not long after my arrival in 1974—there was a curious kind of respect for anyone associated with the magical and mysterious world that brought television pictures into people's homes every day.

The presenters and reporters on RTÉ programmes were well-known faces. Some of the biggest television names were working in the current affairs division: household names like Ted Nealon, Brian Farrell, Paddy Gallagher and John O'Donoghue. They were an ambitious group. Very early on, I became conscious of the competitive tension between the presenters. When one particular presenter was going on his annual holidays, he lobbied—unsuccessfully—to be on air full time before he departed so as to compensate for his absence from the television screen while on leave. 'You can fuck off. There'll be no prima donnas in this office,' was the public rebuke that met the request. But in truth there were plenty of big egos in RTÉ television. When one presenter from another programme was ill, his wife actually rang up to request that that night's programme be cancelled!

My job as a researcher was to explore stories to see if there was enough material to warrant including the item on the flagship *Seven Days* current affairs programme. I would talk to potential guests, take notes on their stories and write up briefs for reporters and presenters. I was one of a number of researchers, including Eugene Murray, who in later years served as a senior executive in RTÉ. As I quickly discovered, television was a labour-intensive operation, involving a huge cast of people. Technology would transform broadcast journalism over the following years but in the 1970s, every filmed report needed a researcher, reporter, producer, production assistant, cameraman, soundman, and electrician. Travelling to film anywhere outside RTÉ's base in Donnybrook in Dublin was a big operation.

My first assignment brought me over the border into Northern Ireland. I was given a few contact numbers and asked to investigate the possibility of *Seven Days* producing a programme on the so-called 'Murder Triangle' along the border where the IRA was killing Protestant farmers. I drove to Monaghan town and got a taxi from there into the North. I visited families in Fermanagh who had lost loved ones to the IRA, and spent two days making contacts and taking notes. I had been north of the border before but never like this, on my own, and I was terrified for every second.

I spent quite of bit of time in Northern Ireland during my first couple of years in RTÉ. I met leading loyalists who were involved in the 1974 strike which broke the power-sharing Sunningdale government. I arranged for loyalist leader Andy Tyrie to be a guest on *Seven Days*. Each time I went across the border, I was very conscious of my southern accent. I was involved in researching two programmes based in Belfast, one of which dealt with sectarianism between Protestants and Catholics. When I was in Belfast, I stayed at the Europa Hotel in the centre of the city which was fast gaining a reputation as the most bombed hotel in Europe. It was common to hear explosions at night time. There were tensions with republicans because the Section 31 broadcasting ban precluded RTÉ from transmitting sound interviews with members of the IRA and Sinn Féin.

I quickly found my feet in the current affairs division. I was working on quick turnaround programmes which were a scramble to get on air, as well as longer documentaries. I recall being asked to research price comparisons between a similar basket of goods in Dublin and in London. I headed into Dublin city centre and bought an agreed list of goods, and then I set off for London, in search of the same products. As I settled into my seat on the Aer Lingus flight to London, I remarked to myself how fortunate I was—it was the first time I was ever in an aeroplane.

A short time later, I joined Brian Farrell on a trip to the Hague to interview a leading Dutch politician about the Europe Economic Community, as the European Union was then known. I think I was brought along because I had made some phone calls in relation to the item, but that didn't matter to me—it was just great to be involved. Brian Farrell was a big name who combined his television job with a position as an academic in University College Dublin. He wrote his scripts in longhand with a fountain pen. They were then passed over to a typist. As a young researcher, I was charmed by his generosity. 'Will you come for tea?' he would say, including me in a group which occasionally went to the nearby Montrose Hotel for something to eat on evenings when we were going to be late in the office.

I was working with some great people and I was gaining in confidence. I was being given more things to do. When there was a row about contraception legislation, I was sent off to order condoms from a shop in England. I had a nose for a story. When *Seven Days* decided to do a programme on Clann na Poblachta, I tracked down some rare film footage compiled by the party in 1948. It was the first time this footage of Seán MacBride's party was seen on television. I remember meeting a young teacher from County Meath by the name of Noel Dempsey, when researching material for a film on the fiftieth anniversary of the foundation of Fianna Fáil. He was impressive and we decided to include him in the studio discussion about the party. It was one of the future minister's first television appearances.

Gerry Murray was the head of the current affairs division when I arrived in 1974. Eoghan Harris had tipped me off about the job vacancy but it was Gerry Murray who actually offered me a contract. He was nothing like what I had expected of someone in charge of *Seven Days*. He was a charming, quiet-spoken man who would smoke his pipe as he chaired editorial meetings. Gerry Murray was unassuming but he had a fiery group of ambitious producers in his division. Current affairs in RTÉ in the 1970s was driven by people like Eoghan Harris, Joe Mulholland, John Kelleher, Pat O'Connor, Seán Ó Mordha, Michael O'Connell and Peter Feeney.

I worked with Joe Mulholland on the successful 'Dublin by Night' documentary; few programmes in the history of RTÉ television used as much film in their making. Mulholland was a big personality who would many years later become Director of News when I was RTÉ's chief news correspondent.

Eoghan Harris was another forceful character. Everything he did, even the shortest of reports, was controversial. His concept of balance was very different from that of most people in RTÉ. While undoubtedly a complicated individual, on form, he was a broadcasting genius. He was also encouraging and would include researchers in everything that was happening. I did the research for a number of documentaries which Harris produced for *Seven Days*, including a controversial one about the development of an oil refinery in Dublin Bay, which later won a major television award. Everyone knew that he was political and was involved with Sinn Féin, The Workers' Party. There were allegations that that party's agenda was setting the agenda for RTÉ's current affairs output. The subject of a Workers' Party clique in current affairs was never an issue for me. I had left my political involvement behind. I never saw any evidence of bias. It would have been impossible for Harris and those sympathetic to his views to influence every report on every programme.

In the late 1970s, Mary McAleese joined the current affairs team. She came from an academic background in Northern Ireland. Years later, there were stories of clashes between McAleese and people like Harris and Mulholland over the coverage of Northern Ireland. From what all sides subsequently said, there were clearly differences but I have to say that I never witnessed any tension. However, I left current affairs in the middle of 1979 so I may have missed some of the famous fireworks. I was the researcher on one programme on which McAleese was the reporter. A significant number of Irish women were travelling to Britain to terminate their pregnancies, as abortion was illegal in Ireland. My research put me in contact with a young woman who was prepared to allow her journey from Dublin to an abortion clinic in England to be recorded on film. The production team, including McAleese and myself, set off together with the woman, on the ferry from Dublin to Liverpool. The woman didn't want to be identified so all the shots of her were in silhouette. She had expressed concern about friends or relatives noticing her clothes so I brought one of my wife's coats for her to wear when the camera was on. She went through with the abortion. McAleese was good to work with. But if at the time somebody had said that she was a future President of Ireland I wouldn't have believed them. Nor would I have believed that, a quarter of a century later, I would be one of the main RTÉ reporters covering an election contest that put McAleese into Áras an Uachtaráin. Her presidency has been very different from that of Mary Robinson but I admire their shared commitment to Northern Ireland.

Politics and elections were very important to the output of the current affairs department. I worked as a researcher on the election results programme for the 1977 general election. John Kelly, a Fine Gael TD for Dublin South, had been Attorney General in the outgoing Fine Gael–Labour coalition. Kelly was a guest on the radio results programme, and I was sent to the Radio Centre to collect him when he came off-air to escort him to the television studios. The results were going badly for the outgoing government. Jack Lynch and Fianna Fáil were on their way to a famous overall majority victory. On our short walk between radio and television, Kelly stopped, let out a loud sigh and reached into his inside coat pocket. He produced a silver hip flask, took a swig out of it and turned to me, saying, 'God, things are really bad.'

I recall travelling by train with Ted Nealon and Eoghan Harris to cover a story in Cork. We stayed in the Imperial Hotel. On occasions like those, you learned to drink. The sessions would continue well into the early hours. It was part of that era in journalism. RTÉ crews ate well and drank hard. But as we sat in the bar of the Imperial Hotel on that occasion, we noticed another group of revellers engaged in a very strange activity. They were burning money. A whole stash of twenty-pound notes was alight in ash trays on their table. As it turned out, they could well afford to burn the notes; we were told that they had won a huge amount of money on a horse called Gay Future. It was an amazing betting coup which led to the conviction of the horse's trainer.

It was a major scandal. The horse had been entered in a race meeting at Cartmel while two other horses from the same stable were entered in races at other tracks. A huge number of medium-sized bets were laid, backing Gay Future for a double with either of the other two horses. Those two horses were withdrawn from their races, meaning the doubles were turned into singles—all on Gay Future. Another twist was added to the tale when soapy water was rubbed into the legs of Gay Future to give the impression the horse was sweating. Punters were put off backing the horse, leaving its odds at 10-1. There were suspicions when the horse romped home. But that night in Cork, there were several big winners. I think they stood us a drink from their winnings.

Production dinners were frequent and legendary in RTÉ in the 1970s. Expensive meals in good restaurants, with equally good wine, were common events. I remember being part of a production team that travelled to Edinburgh. I don't recall the story but I have a vivid recollection of a dinner on our first night which was followed by a big drinking session. Scotch was ordered. There was huge laughter as the toast was proposed. 'To Thackaberry,' we all said as we raised our glasses. 'To Thackaberry.' At that time, Liam Thackaberry was the man in charge of travel and subsistence expenses in RTÉ. He would be getting the receipt for the whisky we were consuming in vast quantities!

The expenses system in RTÉ was generous at that time and was nothing like what operates today. The relaxed attitude to expenses was not confined only to staff at the station. Staff and guests would usually congregate after the evening programme in the hospitality suite. Vincent Scally looked after the guests. He would pour the drink, usually spirits, and ensure that taxis were ordered to take the guests home. It was a familiar routine. Vincent would confirm the fare with the taxi company, and then put the exact amount into an envelope. The envelope would be discreetly given to the guest. It was said that there was one particular individual who even after his elevation to government minister—and with his state car parked outside the television buildings—would still expect an envelope containing the taxi fare.

I did, however, experience a very different approach when I worked on the *Late Late Show* for several months in 1979. It was a short interlude between my role as a researcher in current affairs and my arrival in the RTÉ newsroom as a reporter. Gay Byrne was the biggest star in Irish broadcasting at the time. Some people were almost reverential and every morning they would rush to say 'Good morning, Gay' when Byrne arrived in the office. I liked Byrne and over the years always found him to be a kind and encouraging man. He would always stop and ask, 'How are you?' before adding, 'You're working too hard. Take some time off.' It was an amusing remark from a man who himself put in so many hours in RTÉ between his radio and television commitments.

During my short time working with him in 1979, I was sent to London to prepare the ground for a special edition of the *Late Late Show*, based around the theme of showcasing Irish talent in the United Kingdom. I spent about six weeks in London, lining up the guests for the programme. I would meet with potential guests, talk through their stories and then write notes for Byrne to use when he did the actual television interview. I had tea with the romantic novelist Barbara Cartland and went clubbing with Arsenal soccer star Liam Brady. He drove a nifty sports car which my taxi followed on our way to a fashionable night club in Pall Mall. Ferdia MacAnna—who had had a musical career as Rocky De Valera, was also in London working on the *Late Late Show*. We shared an apartment and lived every minute of our time there.

As the date for the special programme drew nearer, Byrne and Colette Farmer—of 'Roll it there, Colette' fame—arrived to record some promotional material. I collected them at Heathrow Airport, and we spent the day going to various locations in central London which had been selected to record Byrne's 'pieces-to-camera'. That evening, the entire *Late Late* team in London adjourned for a meal at an Aberdeen Angus steakhouse. When coffee was served, Byrne called for the bill. 'What did you have?' he asked me. I had seen a relaxed attitude to expenses in my short few years in RTÉ but now I was witnessing a more measured approach. The *Late Late Show* presenter ensured that each of us paid our own way.

Gay Byrne was a vital cog in the RTÉ machine, and discussions with my colleagues in the canteen would often turn to the subject of how RTÉ would cope if he ever left and how we would cover the story. The *Late Late* presenter had spoken a few times about leaving but the one really serious offer came with the emergence of Century Radio, the country's first national commercial station. There was big money at stake when Century was awarded its broadcasting licence at the start of 1989. I covered the story, and Oliver Barry, the music promoter who was backing the venture, hinted in an interview with me that some big RTÉ names were about to jump ship. Other sources confirmed that they had used Byrne's name in their pitch for the licence, and that he had been offered a million-pound deal.

Back in the RTÉ newsroom, it was decided that I should approach Byrne. I walked the short distance to the back of the Television Building where Byrne was working in the *Late Late Show* offices. When I got there, Eugene Murray from *Today Tonight* was coming out the door empty-handed. Byrne was staying tightlipped.

'I'm here with my news reporter's hat on, Gay,' I said.

'I'm not talking, Charlie. I've already told Eugene Murray that,' he replied.

I tried again. 'Gay—come on.'

I was about to leave without a comment when he smiled at me. 'Look, I've been made an offer. I'm thinking about it and I'll make up my mind by Thursday. Now fuck off—you've got what you want. Goodbye.'

I had my story confirmed. RTÉ's biggest name was in negotiations with the soon-to-be-launched national radio rival. It was the lead story for the nine o'clock news. But first we decided that RTÉ had better be approached for a response. I rang the RTÉ press office and was told that someone would get back to me. However, within minutes, I had the Director-General of RTÉ on the phone. It was bizarre. Vincent Finn was my ultimate boss. 'I'll talk to you off the record,' he said.

'I'm amazed at your story, Charlie, because we're in discussions with Gay and my belief is that his new contract will be sorted out to everyone's satisfaction in the morning,' the RTÉ DG added. I had no idea what was going on. We did our story for the nine o'clock news and, sure enough, by teatime the following day, RTÉ issued a statement announcing that Gay Byrne had signed a new contract. I told this story some years later on the final *Late Late Show* that Byrne presented. Afterwards, one of his colleagues reproached me. 'Gay would never use bad language,' this person stated. But Byrne had. He had told me to 'fuck off', not that over the years he was the only one to do so.

––––––

The opportunity to travel the world has been one of the benefits of my career in RTÉ. In more recent times, I have reported on the Asian tsunami, the earthquake in Pakistan, the emergence of the post-apartheid South Africa and the genocide in Rwanda. I have witnessed at very close quarters terrible suffering but I have also got to meet many memorable people. In truth, my foreign travels started long before I entered the RTÉ newsroom as a reporter in 1980. Over the previous six years, I had more than made up for the fact that my first aeroplane journey happened only on that trip to London in 1974.

I remember, in particular, the excitement of travelling to the United States for the first time in the summer of 1976. John Kelleher, one of the young, ambitious producers in the current affairs division, was assigned to produce a special programme about the two hundredth anniversary of American independence. It was a big documentary for RTÉ who had signed a partnership deal with public service television in the US to fund the film. The programme focused on different generations among the Irish community who lived in the working-class neighbourhood known as 'Southie' in Boston. Two years previously, the area had been home to riots driven by a cocktail of race and class prejudices when the city's authorities attempted to introduce integrated schools.

I was the researcher on the documentary, 'Southie—My Home Town'. We spent six weeks in Boston filming material for the programme which was broadcast on RTÉ and also throughout North America. We stayed in a number of different locations in Boston but one house in Swallow Street in Southie sticks in my memory. The area was rough, rundown and seedy. There were drug-dealers and prostitutes on every corner. I was terrified every moment we stayed in Swallow Street although it was only the appearance of cockroaches in the house that convinced John Kelleher that it was time to move elsewhere.

The Southie area runs down to the sea, with Logan Airport across the water. We spent a day waiting for an Aer Lingus plane to land. John Kelleher wanted the image of the shamrock on the plane landing in Boston. It was a single shot in a big-production documentary but that was, as I was discovering, what television was sometimes about. One of those interviewed was a politician brother of crime boss James 'Whitey' Bulger who was later charged with 19 murders and has been on the FBI's 10 most wanted list for over a decade.

A year after the Southie film, I travelled to the Soviet Union as the researcher on a current affairs documentary on the sixtieth anniversary of the Russian Revolution, directed by Pat O'Connor. The soft-spoken Waterford man was one of the most affable people I have ever worked with. He went on to become a successful Hollywood director. Our trip to the Soviet Union was an incredible experience. It was a different world. I remember sitting in a bar somewhere in Armenia when news was first broadcast that Elvis Presley had died, although, in fact, he had been dead for almost a week before the Russian authorities approved the release of the information on state-controlled television.

We had several official minders for the duration of the trip. They kept a very watchful eye on what we filmed and who we interviewed. We filmed the workers of a collective farm in Armenia. The locals killed a sheep in our honour, and the dead animal was cooked in a hole in the ground. The fields were filled with huge water melons. We sat with these peasants, drinking vodka and champagne and eating caviar, against the backdrop of a snow-capped Mount Ararat. Some of the locals started to sing a Russian folk song. I took up the challenge and burst into a rendition of 'The Auld Triangle'. There was no way of knowing just how many of these activities had been pre-arranged by the Soviet authorities but what was clear from the weeks I spent in the region was that ordinary people had very little freedom.

Thirteen years later, as a news reporter, I returned to a very different Soviet Union. Mikhail Gorbachev was ushering in economic and social changes as communist rule was collapsing all around central and Eastern Europe. The new era was very clearly evident when I arrived in Moscow in February 1990. Having changed travellers' cheques for roubles, the lady at the cash desk in the airport told me I should not pay more than ten roubles for a taxi to take me to my hotel. But all the taxi drivers just threw up their hands and walked away from me. They wanted dollars. The revolution had really arrived. So, ten roubles became ten dollars and we were on our way. Given that the exchange rate was six roubles to one dollar, I paid six times the correct rate for the trip; I also broke the law as it was still technically an offence in the crumbling USSR to give dollars as payment. But few people in the *glasnost* Soviet society were following the rules any more.

Unfortunately the sight of a dollar didn't make it any easier to make a telephone call in Moscow in 1990. On my first night in my hotel, I asked to make a call to Dublin. It was about 11 p.m. I was politely informed I could 'request' a call at nine o'clock the following morning after which I could expect to be connected within a couple of hours. Trying to communicate with Moscow was equally problematic as I discovered some days later when I arrived in Baku, the capital of Azerbaijan. When I asked about calling Moscow, the woman in my hotel smiled. 'Telephone Moscow, maybe hours, maybe not,' she responded. During my three-day stay in Baku—a city in a state of emergency in those dramatic days in Russian history—I was able to get through to Moscow only twice. Attempting to ring Dublin wasn't even a possibility.

I had a memorable flight from Moscow to Baku. Foreigners were the last to board internal flights, for some reason. There was a relaxed attitude to bringing baggage on board—bags of all shapes and sizes were welcome. I didn't understand the announcement from the air hostess but from the sound of wheels emerging from the undercarriage of the aircraft, I reasoned that the two-hour flight to Baku was nearing an end. However, minutes passed without the plane making a descent. After a second announcement, there were loud gasps from several passengers. I started a conversation with the man sitting next to me. He had very broken English but enough for me to comprehend that the weather was too bad in Baku for the plane to land. 'Another Republic,' the man kept saying. We landed at a grey and miserable airport terminal. I had no idea where I was. Nobody spoke English. There were no telephones and the toilet and coffee machine were broken. Fourteen hours later, we took off again and to this day I can recount that I went to the Soviet Union and visited a place I knew only as 'another Republic'.

On 19 January 1990, Soviet troops shot dead over 200 demonstrators in Baku. Gorbachev had loosened the communist stranglehold on East Germany and other Soviet-controlled countries, but the birth of democracy in parts of the USSR came at a bloody cost. A huge carpet of carnations covered the graves of the martyred dead. The graves were in a car park overlooking the Caspian Sea. The car park had been converted into a cemetery after the Red Army's brutal crackdown. Since the shooting, Baku had become a city of protest, with the majority of the population refusing to return to work. A midnight curfew was in place and, on two occasions, soldiers threatened to shoot us when we filmed them. I attended a demonstration against state corruption. Throughout the meeting, I was handed scraps of paper to pass to the person in front of me. Everyone had their own idea about how the meeting was progressing and they were sending their suggestions to the speakers at the top platform. Democracy was at work.

———

I have been privileged during my career in journalism to have experienced such events at close quarters. I could never have imagined such a fortunate scenario as I made my way in RTÉ's current affairs department in the 1970s. It was a roller-coaster environment which was not without its hiccups. When Conor Cruise O'Brien was a government minister, he rang RTÉ to complain about a researcher who had contacted the Department of Justice about some matter. I was that researcher. What was unusual was that O'Brien was actually Minister for Posts and Telegraphs and had responsibility for RTÉ. It was the first time I had come across this type of communication, although it was mild compared to what happened with a programme on the operation of the Irish sweepstakes.

The sweepstakes was a national institution. A little like the modern-day National Lottery, it raised money for good causes—most particularly, Irish hospitals. The sweepstakes also generated huge profits for its promoters. A number of countries, including Britain, the United

States and Canada, banned the sale of Irish Sweep tickets in their jurisdictions. But that did not prevent the Irish Hospitals Trust Ltd—the privately owned company behind the enterprise—from smuggling tickets into these countries.

There was a lot of talk about the operation of the sweepstakes in the 1970s. The *Sunday Independent* journalist, Joe MacAnthony, had revealed that less than 10 per cent of the value of tickets actually went to Irish hospitals. The story showed the power of those backing the sweepstakes. Lucrative advertising from the Irish Hospitals Trust was withdrawn from the Independent Group for several months. MacAnthony eventually left his job and had little choice but to emigrate to Canada in search of employment.

RTÉ's current affairs division decided to have another look. Michael Heney was the reporter assigned to the programme which was directed by Michael O'Connell who was later involved in the independent production sector. I was asked to do the research. I had worked with Michael Heney on Pat O'Connor's documentary about the sixtieth anniversary of the Russian revolution. He was diligent and incredibly thorough in how he did his job. I regard him as one of the most incisive reporters produced by RTÉ in all my years in journalism. An award-winning reporter, he wrote an important book on two Tallaght men who were wrongly convicted of joyriding.

We identified a consignment of sweeps tickets being placed in a container at Dublin Port to be transported by ship out of Ireland. The container was destined in the first instance for the Netherlands. I was sent there and somehow talked my way into the area in the port where the containers were located. We had proof of the illegal activity being undertaken by the Irish Hospitals Trust. There was some sensitivity in RTÉ over the programme. The Hospitals Trust became aware that we were snooping around its operation. A letter was dispatched to the Director-General of RTÉ, and it was decided that all material, including the proposed script, had to be cleared by the Director-General before broadcast.

One of the people I contacted about the programme provided me with a dynamite piece of information—this person gave me a government memorandum which was openly critical of the operation of the sweepstakes. The person in question was Dónal Ó Morain, who, ironically, had previously served as chairman of the RTÉ Authority. But rather than applauding our investigative work, one senior programme executive argued that it would be unpatriotic to use the memorandum. I couldn't believe it but, as a junior member of the production team, I was not involved in the many arguments that followed. There was huge tension in the office. It was the first time I saw a side of RTÉ that I did not like. Ultimately the sweepstakes programme was not broadcast. A great deal of work and a huge amount of resources were wasted.

I was always trying to progress from my researcher position. Several times, I applied for positions that were advertised in RTÉ. Moving on to the producer grade was the obvious career advancement. Producers were the key figures in television output at that time. The audience saw the reporter on screen but most of the important editorial decisions were taken by the producer who also controlled budgets. These people were what I called the elite officer corps in RTÉ.

Each time there was a competition for new producers in the current affairs division, I prepared a curriculum vitae and an accompanying paper with my views on why I deserved promotion. I still have one of these typed submissions. It's from sometime in early 1979 and was obviously my final throw at progressing from my researcher job in current affairs. The submission includes an impressive list of programmes to which I had contributed over the previous five years. I made a good case for my being given the vacant producer job. But the powers that be decided otherwise. Many of the jobs I wanted were allocated to an elite within RTÉ. Whatever about aptitude, drive and energy, many of these people differed from me in one important respect—they had been to college.

This situation really upset me. I had outgrown my researcher role and was itching for a new challenge. But it seemed I was not going to make the grade. In late 1979, I applied for a job as a reporter in the RTÉ newsroom. Mike Burns, the head of radio news, was on the interview panel. He called me a little while later. 'You've got the job,' he said. I couldn't believe it. This was my big break. I was going to be a journalist.

I had been around RTÉ long enough to know that if my stint in the newsroom did not work out, I could always return to current affairs as a researcher. On my first day in my new job in early 1980, I had a small dictionary in my trousers pocket. I couldn't spell and those were the days before computers and software spellcheckers. As a researcher, I had generally had time when typing up my notes. Now I was in a more pressurised environment and was afraid that I would be found out. I was so nervous that I would blow the big opportunity that had come my way. Frequently over those first few months in the newsroom, I would sneak out onto the corridor to look up a particular word to ensure that I was spelling it correctly.

I did not have to travel far from RTÉ for my first news report. The annual general meeting of the Irish Countrywomen's Association was being held in the RDS in Ballsbridge. There was no piece-to-camera (ptc) in my report. It was a straight voice piece to the pictures. I had 40 seconds, which was basically 120 words. Nothing had ever seemed so difficult. I laboured at my typewriter for most of the afternoon. Barry Linnane, a news editor who I discovered was a truly brilliant news man, saw that I was making heavy weather of my script. He sat at my desk and made a few suggestions about getting the right amount of information into the limited time available. With a script written, I edited the pictures and recorded my voice. The report was broadcast midway through the main evening television. When I saw the credit super go up on screen— Report: Charlie Bird—I felt as if I'd just won the sweepstakes.

My first big story came in early July 1980. Two gardaí had been shot dead at a bank robbery in the midlands. I was one of the reporters sent to cover the story. I filed reports for the main television news programmes and did my first piece-to-camera. I had recently purchased a light-brown corduroy suit which must have been fashionable at the time but, in truth, I looked awful. But there I was—on the television news as a reporter for the first time. As mentioned previously, before the more recent advances in technology, television reporting was a huge labour-intensive operation. Nothing could be done quickly. Everything was shot on film, which had to be processed before it could be edited and broadcast. The raw film of stories, such as that of the shooting of the gardaí in County Roscommon, had to be sent back to Dublin by either train or car. To make the six o'clock news, all filming had to be finished by 3 p.m. Sometimes, to overcome these deadlines, reporters would simply sit in the studio when the news was broadcast and read their scripts live as the pictures were transmitted.

The transformation in how broadcast reporters do their jobs has been huge. For example, I have only to think of the bombings in London in July 2005. The bombs went off just after 9 a.m. I arrived in London just after lunchtime and worked with a cameraman throughout the afternoon, filming the bombed areas and talking with people who had witnessed the attacks. At about 5.30 p.m., we were sitting on a traffic island in the middle of a busy road with a small digital editing machine putting together my report for the top of the *Six One News*. As traffic passed slowly alongside us, Magnus Kelly, the cameraman and editor, worked under tremendous pressure. London was that day in a state of panic, the city's transport network at a standstill, with hundreds of thousands of people facing considerable uncertainty about how they would get home, but thanks to the huge advances in television technology in recent years, we were still able to get our work done. All the editing and voice recording was done there on location and then, with the help of a mobile satellite van, the report was sent back to RTÉ in Dublin where, because of the advent of mobile phones, everyone knew exactly what to expect in the report and when to expect it. Unfortunately in 1980, as I embarked on my career in broadcast journalism, on-site editing and satellite vans were all in the future.

As I was a general news reporter, I could be assigned to any story on the news list. In those early months in the newsroom, I reported on petrol shortages, supermarket price wars and preparations for the 1981 Eurovision song contest. I didn't know a lot about Ben Dunne in those days. The supermarket boss was publicity shy despite overseeing one of the most public and profitable businesses in the country. He never gave interviews. Once during the story about the price charged for milk and bread, I rang the main telephone number at Dunnes. It was a routine call which I expected to end with the standard 'no comment' response. The voice at the other end of the line never identified himself but he agreed to speak to me off the record. It was Ben Dunne. We would talk again many times in later years but in very different circumstances in Dublin Castle.

Reporters in the RTÉ newsroom were regularly moved between television and radio. During the 1982 Falklands War, I was presenting the *News at 1.30* on Radio One when reports came through that the British had sunk the Argentine ship, the *Belgrano* with the loss of over 300 lives. Those were dramatic days but I knew I wasn't ready for a presenting role. I would break out in beads of sweat at having to present the daily radio news programmes. One evening when I was presenting the *News at 6.30*, my voice actually went completely. It was a terrifying experience to sit in a radio studio with a live microphone and have no words coming out of my mouth, especially with the knowledge that hundreds of thousands of people were listening. I think the programme ended early on that particular evening. It was the worst period in my career in RTÉ, and I was delighted when the time came for me to return to news reporting.

Derek Davis was a well-known reporter in RTÉ at that time. A likeable character, he later reinvented himself as a hugely successful presenter on light-entertainment programmes. I wasn't long in the newsroom when Davis called me aside and put a fatherly arm around my shoulder. 'I want to give you some advice, young man,' he said. I was listening attentively to what this seasoned reporter had to say. 'I think you should change your name,' he ventured. I was stunned. 'It's like this. People will never take an RTÉ reporter by the name of Charlie Bird seriously. Charles Bird has a better ring about it.' I had been christened Charles Brown Bird but I had always been known as Charlie Bird, and I was not going to change my name now. So I said, 'Thank you very much for the advice,' and kept going with Charlie Bird.

Chapter 3 ～

A NEWS REPORTER

Rory O'Connor called me into his office. From Knocknagoshel in County Kerry, Rory was a colourful character who was head of television news in RTÉ. He always called me 'Charl-es Bird' in his broad Kerry accent. 'Charl-es Bird, how are you? That was a good report you did the other night,' he said, before adding, 'Or was that you, or was it some other reporter?' You could never be sure whether or not Rory was being serious but he was good at giving reporters a break and I certainly benefited from the encouragement and trust that he showed in my abilities. 'You're going to the Philippines,' Rory said to me. I didn't like to argue, not that I had any objections even if the first thing I did when I left Rory's office was to look up the Philippines on a map.

Since I had joined the RTÉ newsroom a few years earlier, I had established myself as one of the main general reporters. I was always hoping that the big stories would happen on my shift. Sometimes they did. Sometimes they didn't. But now, in early 1984, I was being given my big break. It was my first foreign assignment as a newsroom reporter. The story was hugely important to my development as a journalist in RTÉ. It also made my name and face far more recognisable with the general public. The Fr Niall O'Brien story connected with people in Ireland— people paid even more attention than normal to what was being reported from the Philippines. I travelled to cover the Philippines on three separate occasions, staying for three weeks at a time.

It was a huge adventure. I had never been to that part of the world, and I was nervous. This was very different from when I was in current affairs as a researcher and went abroad on stories with colleagues. I was now travelling alone, without any backup support. I was the on-air person, expected to deliver the story. It was a huge challenge but one I was determined to meet.

Niall O'Brien had been brought up in Blackrock in south Dublin. He was ordained in 1963 and almost immediately afterwards set off for the Philippines where his order, the Columban Fathers, was involved in missionary work. For two decades, he was based on the island of Negros where he worked closely with the workers on the local sugar plantations. The Blackrock man was heavily influenced by Pope Paul VI's encyclical, *Populorum Progressio*, which was published in 1967 with an appeal to church members to take positive actions to help the poor and downtrodden. I later heard O'Brien describe his life and work as the 'social gospel'.

The local priests in Negros questioned the socio-economic system which failed to improve people's living standards. They backed labour unions and workers' rights. The authorities were not very impressed with the priests. Many vested interests were being challenged. What was being propagated, the authorities claimed, was communism. A clash was probably inevitable, but few could have forecast that it would have led to three priests— O'Brien, an Australian and a Filipino—and six lay church leaders being arrested and charged with murder. If the men were found guilty, the death penalty was a possible sentence.

With all the connecting flights involved, it took me almost two days to get from Dublin to Manila, the capital of the Philippines. A member of the Columban Order met me at the airport. The first thing I noticed was the heavy military presence; the airport was surrounded by armed soldiers. This was a country under martial law, and the Marcos dictatorship held a tight grip on power. The atmosphere in Manila was tense, almost intimidating, and I was glad to leave the city. There are almost 7,000 islands in the Philippines, including Negros in the west of the country. My destination was Bacolod City on the island of Negros, where I was hoping to seek out Niall O'Brien. The Irishman was one of nine people accused of organising the killing of Pablo Sola, a sugar farmer and rancher.

The Irish priest had been attempting to build a small Christian community with his colleagues, Fr Brian Gore from Australia and Fr Vicente Dangan, a local priest. Only 1.5 per cent of the local population were landowners. The divide between rich and poor was huge. There were 332,000 families in Negros but 330 families controlled 45 per cent of the sugar land, 20 families owned 60 per cent of the fishing catches and 14 families had the rights to timber concessions covering almost

350,000 acres. O'Brien and his colleagues wanted to fight extreme poverty. They were convinced that the murder charges were being brought in an attempt to silence the church.

After their arrest in February 1983, the three priests were placed under house arrest, where they remained for eight months before deciding to join their co-accused in prison. The group—three priests and six lay church workers—became known internationally as the 'Negros Nine'. O'Brien was in his prison cell when I arrived in Bacolod. The prison was not what I had expected, and was more like a compound. Most of the prisoners were rural peasants, and their wives and children were allowed to live with them. When I arrived, the people were cooking meals, and clothes were hanging from makeshift washing lines—all of this inside the prison walls.

Niall O'Brien was prisoner number 30856. I arrived with a bottle of whiskey under my arm. It was a welcome gift. He later recounted our first introduction—'I thought it was strange that an Irish reporter was called Bird, but then when I woke up in prison in the morning and saw him perched at the end of the bed looking at me as if he were a bird, I though it even more strange.'

I visited O'Brien every day. It took a while to get to know him. I think he felt he had a duty of care to me as the Irish journalist who had come to visit. 'Are you all right?' he would enquire, especially when my throat sounded croaky. I often shared a meal with him in the cell. A charcoal fire was kept lighting to cook food, and rice, vegetables and sardines were always on offer.

The Irish priest was living in appalling conditions although he never complained. His cell was small with no covering on the concrete floor. There was a small table in the centre of the room. A cloth screen covered the toilet area, which was really just a hole in the ground which led to the local sewer. There was a truly awful smell—totally overpowering. I was never sure where the smell came from—maybe rotting vegetables, or a dead animal—and I never got used to it. The heat didn't help; the weather was desperately hot.

The local bishop had appointed the three priests as chaplains to the jail in Bacolod where they spent six months. Mass was said every day in the prison compound. But inside the walls it was often hard to judge the atmosphere with the authorities. While the Negros Nine were relatively safe because of the international spotlight on their case, other prisoners were not so lucky. Poor treatment was commonplace. Shots were fired one afternoon, and I never knew if they were intended for one of the prisoners.

I spent nine weeks in all in the Philippines and I filed dozens of reports from Bacolod. Most of my reports were sent by phone to radio and television programmes. I even used the phone in the warden's office. RTÉ's coverage certainly raised O'Brien's profile in Ireland and helped to get greater attention for the Negros Nine. It was a big story in Australia, too, where Brian Gore also became a national figure. I think the case generated huge public attention because of the very real fear that the men would be hanged.

As the months dragged on, the story just got bigger. I was on air every evening. Sometimes I would just ring in a voice piece for television news and they would add the necessary pictures. Occasionally, I would use the facilities of one of the Australian networks. Either way, I gained a huge profile. Niall O'Brien also helped. No matter what radio interview he did, the priest jokingly made reference to my continued presence in the jail.

Arriving in Bacolod City was like stepping back in time. The place was filthy and the poverty was extreme. Not long after I booked into the Sea Breeze Hotel, I caught sight of a rat running through my bedroom. The hotel was infested with rats; to see a mouse was a treat. In addition to the rats, the place was full of cockroaches, which were hard to miss especially as many were the size of a fist. I had never been so close to such destitution. When I wasn't reporting on the Negros Nine, I managed to get a camera crew and spent some time filming in the local slums. The people had nothing. It was obvious what had inspired Niall O'Brien and his colleagues. I remember doing one story on the death of an infant girl. Her family was so poor that the little one was buried in a shoe box.

If the poverty in Bacolod opened my eyes, the total normality of prostitution was another shock. Women and girls were everywhere around the hotel. I had never seen prostitution on this scale. There was one unpleasant incident involving an Australian reporter who was covering the Negros Nine story. This man had a different girl sent to his hotel room each evening. Everyone knew what was going on, and he made little attempt to hide his nocturnal activities. One morning at breakfast, there was a heated discussion about the teenager who had visited him the previous night. The Australian sat at his breakfast table, smoking a cigarette as he complained to the local madam. The girl had left him 'disappointed' and the madam was getting an earful. This man's words had serious consequences for the girl whose family was dependent upon her earnings as the main income in the house. Whatever prospects she had of getting a job in Manila would disappear in the absence of a regular income. The Australian knew all this but he still persisted with his complaint. The madam sacked the girl.

Plenty of visitors came to see Niall O'Brien. In February 1984, Bishop Eamon Casey arrived. The Bishop of Galway was also patron of Trócaire, the Irish Catholic Church's aid agency for the developing world. He stayed at the local Archbishop's palace. I went up to the house to meet Casey. I can still clearly recall him in the main reception room with all its wooden furniture. He was sitting in a white vest with his braces on. The perspiration was pouring out of him but he was full of life and personality. He produced a bottle of whiskey and we shared a few glasses. We talked about the situation facing O'Brien and his colleagues. A date for the trial was due to be set in a matter of weeks.

The evidence against the Negros Nine was flimsy but that had not prevented the Marcos regime from allowing the case to proceed. There were huge crowds outside the courthouse on the day the trial began. Many people held posters supporting the Negros Nine. I was shocked at how Americanised the courtroom appeared. A sign over the judge's seat read: 'Silence in court. Sponsored by Pepsi Cola'.

A great deal of circumstantial evidence was presented, linking the accused to the murder scene. One man, who signed a statement implicating O'Brien, eventually, admitted that he had never met the Irish priest or any of his colleagues. I examined the man's wrists and discovered burn marks left by tight ropes. He had been tortured and presented with a statement which he had signed under duress. It was clear that the authorities in Negros were determined to get a verdict.

The pressure of the trial took its toll on O'Brien and Gore, in particular. Brian Gore was hospitalised in March 1984 with heart trouble. When I visited the prison around St Patrick's Day, I found O'Brien tired and drained. I remember mentioning this during a radio interview and, later that afternoon, Niall was on the phone to his mother in Dublin to tell her not to be worried by what I was saying. The prisoners' spirits were raised by the number of St Patrick's Day cards which arrived by post from Ireland. Almost 350 cards arrived in Bacolod, all of which were stuck up on the walls of the men's cells. I know I recorded some of the mass the priests said on St Patrick's Day, and it was later broadcast on radio at home. But these were small distractions from the main concern facing the accused. Contacts between the Irish government and the regime in the Philippines were ongoing. Garret FitzGerald's government in Dublin was using contacts in Washington to put pressure on Ferdinand Marcos to resolve the case. The international media attention was causing unease in the upper sections of the regime. Whatever about the attitude of the local authorities in Negros, the case had become a huge PR disaster for Marcos.

Irish government officials arrived in Manila in late June. A deal was on the table. The Irish officials, representatives of the Columban Order and senior figures in the Marcos regime were involved in negotiations. I got word that an agreement had been signed which would see the case dismissed. I rang the Bacolod prison and O'Brien was brought to the phone. I told him the news: all the charges had been dropped with no further legal action to be taken. The priests were to leave the Philippines while the lay leaders were guaranteed protection when they returned home.

On 3 July 1984, Niall O'Brien walked out of Bacolod prison. There were crowds of supporters and a large contingent of journalists at the prison gates. Despite his term in prison, the Irishman had lost none of the original fight which had caused such conflict with the local authorities. 'I am filled with deep joy to be out of this terrible prison, but it is no worse than the conditions under which many people must live. We have been in prison because we worked to change these conditions— we will continue to work to change them because we believe that as long as half the world is hungry, no one is free.'

Some of the Australian reporters decided to mark the end of their reporting duties in Bacolod. 'The Brotherhood of Bacolod' was established, and I was given honorary membership. Each reporter received a specially framed plaque which had a script containing humorous references to the Sea Breeze Hotel and the rats. 'Where there's a will, there's a way,' was the motto.

Back in Dublin I returned to RTÉ and covered whatever story came my way. My standing was increasing all the time. I had the title Special Reporter and I was being assigned to bigger news stories. Sometime in early 1987, I got a call at work from a man named Paul Mercier. A friend of his, Roddy Doyle, had written a play called *Brownbread* in which I was a character. I had never heard of Paul Mercier or Roddy Doyle. 'Would you voice your part?' Mercier asked, while offering me reassurance that the project was a serious one. 'Pat Kenny also has a part,' he added.

I rang Pat Kenny. 'Roddy Doyle is an up-and-coming writer,' he said. 'There's no harm helping them out.' So I arranged to meet Mercier and Doyle at the SFX Theatre on Dublin's north side. Doyle, I discovered, had published a novel the previous summer. It was called *The Commitments*. I could later say I knew the Booker Prize-winning novelist long before he was famous, and, in a way, he helped to make me a little more well-known.

Brownbread was Doyle's first play and it was hilarious. It was about three young fellows from the fictional Dublin suburb of Barrytown who kidnap a Catholic bishop. The twist in the story arrives when it emerges that the bishop was born in New York, so US marines invade Barrytown. I played the part of a news reporter called Charlie Bird, which involved recording my lines for a tape machine in the SFX.

My voice is first heard at the start of Act Two when the US Marine Corps arrives on Bull Island in Dublin Bay. The three kidnappers—Donkey, John and Ao—are holed up with their bishop, listening to me on the radio.

CB: From my position here I can see the five Sikorsky Night Hawk helicopters stationary on the fairway. And there are three, no, four more in the air. I can clearly see a large gun, possibly a Gattling or a Howitzer—

Donkey: A Howitzer! Jaysis.

CB: —protruding from the side door of one of the helicopters.

Donkey
not joking: Fuckin' hell. The business wha'.

CB: The helicopters are a chilling sight. So graceful yet so menacing.—A jeep has come over the dunes to my right! And another one! They're going towards the club-house.

John: So wha'!

CB: The dunes are blocking my view of a large part of the combat base but there must be at least a thousand men here.

Ao: There'll be no ridin' there tonigh', wha'.

The lads laugh half-heartedly

CB: The base is like a small busy town.
John
scornful: Jesus! With soldiers an' fuckin' helicopters in it!
CB: I'm now being approached by two Marines. One of them
        appears to be a sergeant. Yes, he's a sergeant.
Donkey: Shoot the fuckin' eejit.
CB: Both men are armed.
Donkey: Good.
CB: They want me to turn off my—
The tape recorder is turned off
Donkey: Good.
*The tape recorder is turned back on. The background noise of helicopters
has been replaced by tweeting birds. Ao chuckles.*
CB: I am now walking down the Causeway Road, away from the
        Marine combat base. I am not going to look around because I
        have been told that if I do, I will, quote, get a bullet in my ass.

It was great fun. I recorded my lines and then turned up to watch the
play on the opening night in September 1987. Brendan Gleeson, who
later went on to considerable international acting success, had a part,
along with the voices of Pat Kenny, Dave Fanning and myself. I also got
a mention in one of Roddy Doyle's novels and I had a part—again play
ing myself—in *When Brendan Met Trudy*, the movie for which he wrote
the screenplay. My break into the movies was, however, mixed, as my
role as a news reporter in a film about the late Veronica Guerin never
made it into the final cut of that movie.

These artistic endeavours were all very well but I still had to earn my
living as an RTÉ reporter, although there was another distraction as I
was also heavily involved with the National Union of Journalists and
chaired the union branch in the newsroom. My involvement was largely
during the 1980s when there were many rows and battles with management. On one occasion, I went to see Rory O'Connor about some
union matter. I was not long back from covering a story about the sink-
ing of the *Kowloon Bridge* oil tanker. 'This place is like the *Kowloon
Bridge*,' I said in exasperation. Suddenly Rory was on his feet and up
from behind his desk with his fists waving in the air. 'How dare you?'
the Kerry man kept shouting and, for a moment, I thought he was
going to hit me. But Rory O'Connor was like that. He never held a

grudge and, five minutes later, he had forgotten about our row.

As head of television news, Rory O'Connor was one of a number of solid news men who were the foundation of the RTÉ newsroom. Many individuals like Rory, who was ex-*Irish Press*, had received their training in the world of print journalism. During the 1970s and until the late 1980s, RTÉ was the sole Irish broadcast outlet for news. After I came into the newsroom in 1980, I learnt so much from Rory O'Connor, Mike Burns, Barry Linnane, Barney Cavanagh, Eddie Liston, Dano Halloran and Jim Flanagan. They were an important group especially in helping RTÉ to cover the conflict in Northern Ireland. It was a crucial period which was not made any easier for RTÉ staff by the restrictions imposed by the Section 31 broadcasting ban.

Wesley Boyd was Director of News during most of that period. From County Fermanagh, he had come to RTÉ after a successful career in print journalism, in which he had had the notable distinction of being the first Diplomatic Correspondent for *The Irish Times*. Interestingly, this Northern Presbyterian succeeded two former IRA chiefs of staff as Director of News at the national broadcaster. With an unassuming style, Wesley ensured that the station reported news in a fair and consistent way. He wasn't really a man for walking the floor in the newsroom, but I could see that he oversaw operations from his office, with Mike Burns in radio and Rory O'Connor in television.

Despite the quality of the staff, there were, however, some downsides to how RTÉ operated. At that time, there were no systems or structures in the organisation—not to mind access to facilities—for how to deal with foreign stories. My trips to the Philippines to cover the Niall O'Brien story confirmed for me—if confirmation were needed—that RTÉ was a small station with limited budgets which looked for the local interest in all international events. In those years, it was rare enough for news reporters to be sent to cover big foreign stories. And when they were sent, journalists operated in very difficult circumstances, as RTÉ literally begged and borrowed facilities. We operated on a shoestring. I cannot count the number of times when I was abroad that the goodwill of the BBC and ITN was the only reason I had access to camera crews, editing equipment and transmission facilities. RTÉ reporters operated on a 'bottle of whiskey' policy, with gifts to other broadcasters smoothing our way.

The station's position was helped by the conflict in Northern Ireland as broadcast stations all over the world were often indebted to RTÉ for access to pictures from the North. This was especially so in the case of the BBC and ITN, which only enhanced an already good relationship with the two neighbouring British stations. Throughout the 1980s and into the early 1990s, newsroom reporters working on foreign stories were in many cases reliant on the goodwill of their colleagues. The BBC would often shoot material at press conferences for RTÉ and then send it back to London on the back of its own reports. Once the pictures were in London, newsroom staff in Dublin could arrange to get them sent over. This happened many times and I would then record a voiceover down a phone line, and someone in Dublin would put the report together, editing the pictures to my voice recording. It was all very ramshackle but that was how we did our business.

There were frustrations. I remember that after the invasion of Kuwait in 1990, I was sent to Amman in Jordan where most news reporters were based. I made a number of trips to Baghdad where Irish workers were, in effect, being prevented by the Saddam regime from leaving. On several occasions, I was indebted to the BBC for access to camera crews and editing facilities. Reporters like John Simpson and Kate Adie were always generous. They had worked in Belfast and had a good rapport with RTÉ staff. BBC Northern Ireland had an interest in the story I was covering, so I would willingly share material with them. But the BBC was not always able to help. I recall one Saturday morning in Baghdad when I got a decent story about the Irish workers but I had no filming or editing facilities. Simpson was up to his eyes with BBC commitments, and there was no way the BBC could help me out. It was hugely frustrating. I had travelled halfway around the world, had got a really good story, and now I had no access to the necessary equipment to do my job. 'Why couldn't we just send our own camera crew like everyone else?' I asked myself.

This 'seat-of-the-pants' approach was also very evident in April 1988 when a Kuwaiti Boeing 747 airliner took off from Bangkok in Thailand. There were 122 people—crew and passengers—on board Flight 422. About three hours into the journey, half a dozen men, armed with hand grenades and guns, took control of the jumbo jet. Many passengers were tied up. The flight captain was ordered to fly to Mashhad in northern Iran. The hijackers had a single demand—the release of 17 convicted terrorists being held in Kuwaiti prisons.

I watched the hijack drama unfold from the security of the RTÉ newsroom. I was just back from Killarney where I had reported on one of the annual teachers' union conferences. As the Kuwaiti aircraft was on the tarmac at Mashhad, I did a television story on the *Irish Press* changing from broadsheet to tabloid format. But the hijack was the real big news—over the previous few years, a number of similar hijacks had ended in bloodshed. These hijackers were believed to be linked to pro-Iranian Islamic groups who had been holding westerners hostage in Beirut. They warned that they would blow up the plane if anyone tried to approach it. A failure to accede to their demand would, they warned, provoke them to kill passengers. But the government in Kuwait refused to release the 17 prisoners. Despite that decision, hopes of an early end of the hijack came when some passengers were freed. But three days later, the hijackers went their way when the Iranian authorities agreed to refuel the aircraft. The plane took off, its next destination Cyprus.

By now, the hijack was a huge international news story. RTÉ sent news reporter Leo Enright to Larnaca in Cyprus. The decision to send one of the station's own reporters was a big deal at the time. RTÉ tended to shy away from foreign stories where there was no obvious 'Irish angle'. I had been sent to cover the Fr Niall O'Brien story because it had a very clear Irish angle. The hijacking of a Kuwaiti aeroplane was an international story. Still, Cyprus wasn't too far and the costs would be minimal. It was also assumed that the drama would conclude in Cyprus with either the release of the passengers or a storming of the aircraft as had happened previously. But endgame to this hijack was not so straightforward. Two passengers were killed as the hijackers sought extra fuel. The authorities approved the demand. Then, after almost four days on the tarmac at Larnaca, the hijackers ordered the pilot to fly to Algeria.

As the hijack story was ongoing, a very different little drama was unfolding in the RTÉ newsroom. Leo Enright was now stuck in Cyprus while the aircraft was in Algiers. RTÉ had committed to the story, and there was now pressure to follow the story to its natural conclusion. I was told there was a possibility I would be going to Algeria. But before committing any money, RTÉ wanted to see where the story was going. 'Go to Dublin Airport, get a ticket but don't board the flight until we say so,' I was instructed. RTÉ was trying to play a game of 'guess what the hijackers will do next'. If the plane landed and stayed in Algiers, there was justification in getting me on the flight to Paris, where a connecting flight to Algiers could be got.

Just before boarding for the Paris flight closed, I again rang the newsroom. 'Go,' was the decision. But I was to travel only as far as Paris. The situation would be reviewed again after I had landed in the French capital. It was still unclear whether the aeroplane would stay in Algiers; with Leo Enright stranded in Cyprus, the last thing RTÉ wanted was for Charlie Bird to be stuck in Algiers. So I ended up booking into a hotel close to Charles de Gaulle airport. I had a seat provisionally booked on an early-morning flight from Paris to Algiers, and I spent the night tossing and turning, not knowing whether or not I was going to get close to my first really big foreign assignment. I rang the newsroom early looking for a decision. Naturally I was chafing at the bit to get going.

'What's the story?' I asked.

'The plane is still on the runway in Algiers,' was the news from Algeria

'So what will I do?'

'I suppose you'd better go then,' was the almost disappointed response.

I spent over a week at Algiers airport. Almost 300 reporters from all over the world had descended on the hijack scene. It was my first experience of being part of a big international story, and I loved every minute of it, even if I was living in a tent on a busy airport runway. Initially the media were based in the VIP suites at the airport but after a couple of days, the authorities put up eight large army tents on the tarmac. From there, we kept a 24-hour watch on the Kuwaiti airliner.

I got to know most of the British reporters, many of whom had been to Northern Ireland at some stage. While RTÉ was a tiny broadcaster, the name was well known. The BBC had over a dozen people there, with four reporters alone devoted to radio coverage. RTÉ had me. I borrowed a sleeping bag from ITN and an airbed from a BBC colleague. The BBC sent out dried food in special containers to which boiling water was added to make instant meals. It was like war rations and I know I ate those terrible-tasting instant meals a couple of times. When things were really bad, we used to get local taxi drivers to go into the centre of Algiers for bread and bottled water.

One British newspaper reporter complained to his office back in London about the lack of decent food. Surviving on cheese and crackers was an ordeal for him. His editor obviously took the hardship seriously because the next day, a wicker hamper basket arrived, filled with jars of Darjeeling and Earl Grey tea, baby tuna in virgin oil and tins of oyster soup. Some of the French media were totally unimpressed by their British counterpart. 'I suppose you'll be playing cricket next,' one said sniffily.

Another consignment raised our spirits even further. We were hijack-watching during Ramadan so there was no drink in the airport terminal. The British Embassy sent over beer and lager for the thirsty troops! The arrival of the alcohol was immortalised by one British reporter who wrote: 'The only moment of real crisis came when it was realised that the reporter unloading the booze from the embassy Land Rover was a thirsty Irish television presenter called Charlie Bird.'

This was 1988—long before the widespread availability of mobile phones. Talking with the office in Dublin involved a queue—there were only four public telephones in the airport. Without my own facilities, filing for radio and television was heavily dependent on the goodwill of colleagues. The BBC—once more—made my life so much easier by allowing me to use their satellite phone when their journalists had filed their reports. The 'sat phone' came in a huge suitcase and was a considerable weight. One of my biggest problems was finding a quiet spot in which to record reports. I would lie on the ground in the army tent with a blanket over my head to try to drown out some of the noise of the aeroplanes taking off and landing.

The Algerian hijacking has top ranking for me in terms of the stories I have covered. It is up there with the release of Brian Keenan in 1990 and reporting from Rwanda at the time of the genocide in 1994. My time in Algiers also opened my eyes to just how low journalists will stoop to get an edge on a story over their colleagues. The hijackers sent out word that they were prepared to allow three journalists to come on board the plane to hear their demands. The Algerian authorities gathered all the reporters together in the airport terminal to explain the situation. Selection would be by way of a lottery. We were all asked to put our IDs cards into a bowl. I was sort of disappointed when my card was not picked out.

A good two hours of bickering followed. The French journalists complained to the Algerian authorities when it seemed the BBC was going to be included. They were demanding that a French speaker be included in the journalists selected to go aboard. The 300 passengers were not sure whether their plane was going to be blown up and here was the assembled media engaged in a petty row. Some reporters were even up on tables shouting about the unfairness of the selection method.

The weather in Algiers was extremely hot; it was warm from very early in the morning. I had spent most of the week watching the Kuwaiti Boeing 747 airliner. Watching and waiting. And then, shortly after dawn—at about six o'clock—the doors to the jumbo opened. After 16 days in all—and over a week in Algiers—the passengers started to come off the plane. We regarded them a little as our friends after the tension and drama of the week-long stand-off. Some passengers looked bewildered. Some waved at the assembled media. I waved back. The hijack was over. It was time we all went home.

———

I was still a general reporter on the news desk and therefore liable to be assigned to any story, although increasingly I was covering bigger news stories. My foreign exploits seemed to matter little to some in the newsroom. There was one memorable row with Patrick Kinsella who after several years as Economics Editor had been given a programme editor's job in television. I came in one morning to discover that he wanted me to cover a story about dog licences in Dún Laoghaire. I was really annoyed. Having worked my way up through the newsroom, I felt that by now I was a reporter with some seniority. It wasn't about jumping up and down to do the biggest story of the day or the lead item and I wasn't being big-headed but I believed the story was beneath me. Voices were raised and I let Kinsella know that I was really unhappy but I did the story and then didn't come back into the newsroom for a day or so. I'm glad to say, those days were increasingly becoming fewer and fewer.

Another high-profile foreign assignment came about in the summer of 1990 and I think it cemented my position as one of the main news reporters in RTÉ. It was the middle of an August afternoon, and I was working in the Middle East where it was stiflingly hot. The dust was getting to my throat. I had some lozenges but they didn't seem to be making any difference. I was running out of time as I stood before yet another border guard, waving my passport in the air. 'Irish passport,' I repeated, as I had already done to several of the man's colleagues. The border crossing from Jordan into Syria is no place to be when you're the only English-language speaker for miles around.

'Irish passport. Do you understand?' The conversation—if it could have been called that—had been going on for well over an hour. There had been little progress with the various guards who had come and gone from the cramped border office without anyone acknowledging that they understood anything I was saying.

'Look, I'm from Ireland. I have an Irish passport. I'm on holidays in Jordan and I want to go to Damascus to meet a United Nations soldier. He's a friend of mine,' I said slowly, with each word clearly stressed.

I had rehearsed this story several times earlier in the day as I sat in the back seat of a taxi en route from Amman to the Jordanian–Syrian frontier. The 'white lies' were meant to smooth my passage as the clock ticked. I had decided that there was no point in mentioning Brian Keenan or saying anything about the release of an Irish hostage in Beirut. That type of information would certainly have ruined whatever slim chance I had of getting the border guards to allow me to cross the frontier between Jordan and Syria, especially when I had no visa.

My journey had begun several hours previously. The foreign desk in the RTÉ newsroom in Dublin had heard rumours that Brian Keenan, a teacher from Belfast who had been held hostage in Beirut for almost four-and-a-half years, was about to be released. This was not the first time there had been speculation about Keenan's release. A few weeks earlier, the official Iranian news agency had reported—prematurely, as it turned out—that Keenan was close to gaining his freedom. But now, in August 1990, the Irish government seemed confident that a deal was close to securing an end to the hostage situation.

Keenan had gone to Beirut in December 1985 to teach English. He was looking for adventure but soon got caught up in the conflict in Lebanon. Fundamentalist Shi'ite militants wanted to make a point about the Israeli occupation of the Lebanon. So they took foreigners hostage.

In April 1986, Keenan, who was 35 years old, started out on a ten-minute walk to the university campus in Beirut where he worked. Four armed men were waiting, and they bundled him into the back of an old Mercedes. He was held in various locations in Beirut until the middle of 1990; at times, he was kept in complete darkness, chained, and had to endure cockroach- and rat-infested cells. I got to know about Brian Keenan from covering news conferences organised by his two sisters, Elaine Spence and Brenda Gillham. It was never clear whether their brother was dead or alive. Several hostages had been executed by their captors shortly after their abduction. But somehow there was a glimmer of hope that Keenan was still alive. His sisters certainly thought so and, at several news conferences in Buswells Hotel in Dublin, they kept Brian Keenan's name in the headlines. I remember trying to get a visa for Beirut sometime in 1988 but all requests for media accreditation for the war-torn region were turned down.

In August 1990, I arrived in Jordan just after Saddam Hussein had sanctioned the Iraqi invasion of Kuwait. I filed reports from a variety of locations as the prospect of an American attack on Iraq intensified. Near the end of the month, Katie Khan Carl from the RTÉ foreign desk rang me with news about the Keenan release rumours. I was sitting in a hotel room in Amman.

'They're saying he'll be released in a day or so in Damascus. Can you get there?' she asked.

'It's only a couple of hundred miles,' I replied. 'But I've no visa to go to Syria. That's going to be a problem.'

'Please try,' Katie said.

I was on my own in Amman, having travelled without a camera crew. Those were the days before portable communications equipment enabled reporters in the field to be nearly permanently in contact with the newsroom in Dublin. The only assistance Katie could give me was the names of some Irish soldiers who were working with the United Nations in Damascus. 'They might be able to help you out with some information,' she said.

RTÉ had already spent huge resources on its coverage of Keenan's release. Several reporters and crews had been sent to the Middle East on the back of earlier release rumours. But the Belfast man was still in captivity. I wasn't sure why this time would be any different but the office in Dublin seemed to think there were strong grounds for the speculation. The Iranian government had played a crucial role in the release of two Americans the previous April. There had been contact between the authorities in Dublin and Tehran. The Iranian who had some influence over the hostage-takers had been putting pressure on them to free Keenan. It seemed that the Belfast man was being held in Beirut, but if he were freed, he would reappear in Damascus. Getting to Damascus was not going to be easy, but getting there in time for Keenan's release—if the speculation were accurate—was going to be a huge challenge.

I went into the centre of Amman and found some taxi drivers who specialised in travelling the road from Amman to Damascus. It was a popular trading route but I didn't know how I was going to cross from Jordan into Syria without a visa. The driver had little English but, with the help of others on the 'rank', we agreed a price for the journey—about $400. This man drove an old American Cadillac, a big rust-bucket of a vehicle. I sat into the back seat. I had no way of staying in contact with home. It was a bizarre set of circumstances—here I was being driven by a guy who had broken English and I was heading for a border frontier without any proper documentation.

The journey took about four hours. When we got to the border pass-port office, the driver sat in the Cadillac as I tried to negotiate my way into Syria. I had rehearsed my lines as we drove: 'I'm Irish. Look, an Irish passport. I'm on holidays and I want to go to Damascus. My friend—he works with the UN. I have plans to meet him.'

The one-way conversation went on for what seemed an eternity. I did all the talking. The border guards nodded, smiled and spoke about me in their native tongue. I'm not sure what provoked them into action. Maybe they got fed up with my persistence and wanted to get rid of me. Whatever it was, after about an hour and a half, a guard waved his hand towards the border barrier. 'Go,' he said simply.

I was on my way again. There was a chance that Keenan would be released that evening. So time was of the essence. I didn't want to arrive in Damascus only to find that Keenan was on a flight back to Ireland. Time had been lost at the border crossing but, at least, I was now closing in on Damascus. Then more trouble. About twenty minutes into Syrian territory, we came into a decent-sized town. As we drove along the main street, the traffic lights turned red. The driver stopped his car. Then suddenly, there was a loud bang, and I was thrown around the back seat of the car. I had an immediate pain in my neck—a dart-ing pain—and I was somewhat dazed and shocked. Another car had run into the back of the taxi.

After a few moments, my driver jumped out of the car. A huge scene developed. I stepped out and the sight that greeted me was the considerable damage to the rear of the taxi. The car was, literally, a write-off. The taxi driver and the large number of locals who were now on the scene were arguing. There was much shouting, most of it directed at my driver. I had no idea what exactly they were saying because nobody uttered a word in English.

Some order was eventually placed on the crash scene when a local police officer arrived. He had a little English, not much, but enough to understand my plea—'I must get to Damascus.' My driver did not like the sound of what I was saying. 'No, Damascus. No, Damascus,' he shouted at me. But the policeman was interested in restoring order to the main street, and moving the foreigner on was a good start. He spoke to the driver of another car, now in the traffic jam behind the accident scene. The road was a well-travelled route, so it was not unsurprising that another car was also going into Damascus. 'You,' the police officer said to me, pointing to another American-manufactured vehicle that had also seen better days, 'You, go there.'

My original driver was furious that I was heading to Damascus without him. But he quickly got over his huff when I gave him another $200 to sort out the damage to his car. Our business was completed even if our journey had ended somewhat earlier than planned. Taking my belongings with me, I left the policeman to resolve the various disputes, and I was once more on my way. I was now squashed into the back seat with three travelling companions, none of whom had a single word of English. My neck was very sore but all that mattered was that my destination was Damascus.

It had been several hours since I had last had contact with the office back in Dublin, and I had no idea whether Keenan was a free man or whether his captors were still holding him. I eventually arrived at the Hilton Hotel in Damascus sometime before eight o'clock in the evening.

I had a contact number for an Irish official who was monitoring the Keenan situation. He would tell me nothing. Fortunately, I was helped out by local Reuters staff. I made my way to their office, and when I arrived, they were on the phone to Beirut. The news was the best I had received after a day of several calamities. Keenan was going to be released that evening in Beirut and would be brought immediately to the relative safety of Damascus. His two sisters, Elaine and Brenda, were also en route to Damascus, travelling from Ireland with Foreign Minister Gerry Collins and staff from the Department of Foreign Affairs.

There was, however, another problem. The Syrian authorities were prepared to allow Keenan to talk to the media but they were insisting that no material from the news conference could be transmitted from Syrian territory. Back in Dublin, a solution was eventually sorted out. Dermot Mullane, a programme editor, did a deal with the BBC who were in the same predicament as RTÉ and, with Keenan's links to Belfast, just as keen to get the pictures. Both stations agreed to share the cost of hiring a private jet. It would land in Damascus, take possession of the Keenan interview tapes, and then fly on to Cyprus where satellite facilities were available to get the material sent back for broadcast. There was huge international interest in the story, especially as individuals of several nationalities were still being held hostage in Beirut. The pictures would be in demand, so Dermot Mullane decided for the first and only time in his RTÉ career to sanction the hiring of a private jet.

I made my way to the Syrian Foreign Ministry building where Keenan was due to be handed over to the Irish government representatives. The Syrians were being really prickly about which journalists would have access to Keenan. RTÉ was way down the pecking order. I was standing outside the main gates of the Ministry, not certain of getting access. Gerry Collins arrived, along with several senior officials from Iveagh House. They had been centrally involved in the negotiations which had resulted in Keenan's release. Just as the Irish delegation was walking into the Foreign Ministry and the big iron gates were closing, Michael Collins—the minister's press officer—stretched out his hand and literally grabbed me, pulling me along with the minister and his officials. 'No media,' a Syrian security guard shouted angrily. But his words were too late. 'He's with us,' Michael Collins shouted back as we kept going.

We were waiting for about ten minutes before Brian Keenan appeared. He had spent more than 1,500 days in captivity, mostly in terrible conditions: blindfolded and chained, often beaten and assaulted. The man who came into the room was pale and tired. Seeing him was a little bit like when you pick a rock up from the ground and see the whites of the plant roots. He was a man who had enjoyed so little natural light in such a long time that he was ghost-like. And, despite his own release, Keenan wanted to talk about the other men still being held hostage, especially English journalist John McCarthy—'quite the comedian'—who had been captured a week after Keenan.

Being in Damascus to witness Brian Keenan speak after his release was one of the most amazing experiences of my career in journalism. There was genuine warmth in the applause he received from the media and officials who were in the room. The whole atmosphere was charged with emotion. I had tears in my eyes, and I wasn't the only person in the room overcome by emotion. Although I was the only Irish journalist there, Keenan had no idea who I was. I asked a question and blurted out 'Brian, Charlie Bird from RTÉ. Can I ask you what it feels like to be free?

There was a pause. It seemed like minutes but I suppose it was just a few moments before Keenan responded. A smile crossed his face. He looked directly at me. 'What do you think?' he asked me. What was I thinking—'What does it feel like to be free having been chained to a radiator for the best part of four years?' It was a silly question and I knew it.

We left the Foreign Ministry for the Dutch Embassy which was where the Irish delegation had set up base. Keenan read a statement. We had been told that there would be no questions but after four-and-a-half years in captivity, the Belfast man, while obviously overcome with emotion, was in the mood to talk.

When asked what he would do next, Keenan delivered one of the most brilliant sound bites I have ever heard. For all I know, he may have been rehearsing it for years, but it perfectly summed up the exhilaration of being handed his freedom once more.

'I'm going to visit all the countries in the world, eat all the food in the world, drink all the drink in the world and make love, I hope, to all the women in the world,' he said. And then he added, 'And maybe I'll get a good night's sleep.'

We clapped and cheered. He had us laughing and crying. And then, within minutes, he was whisked away to the Irish government jet which was waiting to take him back to Ireland. I was left to edit my report for the news at home. It had been an amazing time since I had left Amman. In all the commotion, the Syrians relented on the transmission of pictures of Keenan's meeting with the media. Pressure from Irish government officials may have had a part to play in this change of position. So we finally got the pictures out of Damascus—and, I think, RTÉ got a bill several months later for half the cost of an unused charter jet!

I later purchased *An Evil Cradling*, Keenan's memoir of his time in captivity. It's a difficult book to read, emotionally charged and brutally honest, and it took me two attempts to get into it. But I have to say, I found it one of the most rewarding books I have ever read.

I have met Brian Keenan only twice since that dramatic evening in Damascus in the summer of 1990. Several months afterwards, in Dublin Castle, we were introduced at the inauguration of Mary Robinson as Irish President. I am not sure whether or not he knew that I was the reporter from Damascus. Funnily enough, the second occasion on which we met was in the summer of 2005. I was in my car, stuck in traffic outside the Mater Hospital in Dublin's north inner city, when I saw this figure walking on the footpath, coming in my direction. I said to myself, 'I know that guy,' before realising that the man was, in fact, Brian Keenan. I rolled down the car window.

'Hello, Brian,' I shouted.

'Hello, Charlie,' he responded.

'I've been thinking about you recently,' I said.

'Have you, yes?' he replied in his slow, measured voice.

'I'm thinking of writing a book—and, if it happens, you're going to be in it,' I said with a laugh.

He stared at me. It was a look I recognised from Damascus all those years previously, and then he said, deadpan, 'Well, Charlie, I'll buy it.'

Chapter 4 ∾

LEINSTER HOUSE: PLINTH LIFE

'You're wasting your time,' P.J. Mara said. I wanted Charles Haughey to tell his story. The controversial politician had left office in early 1992 but the tribunals of inquiry and ongoing revelations about the source of funds for his private life had kept him in the news headlines. I approached Mara, who had been Haughey's long-time press officer, about the possibility of setting up a meeting with the now-retired Haughey.

I had done numerous interviews with Haughey during his time as Taoiseach and Fianna Fáil leader. Sometimes when I doorstepped him outside Government Buildings, he would fix me with a steely-eyed stare, 'Right, Mr Bird, what can I do for you?' On the night the Fianna Fáil National Executive decided to expel Des O'Malley from the party, Haughey greeted me at the steps to the Fianna Fáil headquarters with the words: 'My favourite reporter.' In the rush to get the interview onto the nine o'clock news, the greeting was not edited out and I had some explaining to do!

Mara was not the only person I contacted about a Haughey interview. I also approached Haughey's friend and accountant, Des Peelo, looking for suggestions about how best to get in touch with Haughey. Other journalists were engaged in a similar exercise. 'It's pointless. He'll never talk,' was the response I continued to receive.

My mobile phone rang. 'So you want to meet me,' the instantly recognisable voice said.

'Yes, but I'm out of the country at the moment,' I replied.

'Where are you?'

'I'm in Bogotá. In Colombia,' I said.

'I was there once. Ring me when you get back to Dublin.'

64

THIS IS CHARLIE BIRD

The line went dead.

I was familiar with Charlie Haughey's Kinsealy home in north County Dublin, although more from the vantage point of the roadside entrance. I had done numerous pieces-to-camera outside the house during the various controversies of the Haughey leadership years and, in more recent times, when the tribunals had been examining his financial affairs.

Haughey answered the front door. I had been invited for lunch. 'We're having pâté de foie gras, some smoked salmon and wine—how does that suit you?' the former Taoiseach asked. I couldn't believe my luck. Maybe he was in the mood to agree to an interview.

Haughey had been retired from politics for just over a decade. On the day I visited him in Kinsealy, he looked old. But he was in good spirits and there was no rush as, over the following three hours, we talked and managed to polish off two bottles of wine. My mission that day was to talk about a possible interview. Haughey, however, had other things on his mind. The main topic of conversation was Fianna Fáil's treatment of his son, Seán. A TD since 1989, Seán Haughey was apparently under threat in his Dublin North Central constituency. Fianna Fáil headquarters—encouraged, it was said, by Bertie Ahern— was rumoured to be backing another candidate in an attempt to remove the embarrassing Haughey name from the ranks of the party's TDS. Haughey, the father, was vicious and disdainful about Ahern. I got a real sense of animosity throughout our conversation. 'They're trying to screw Seán,' Haughey remarked.

At one stage, he leant back in his chair and asked, 'So, tell me, why should I do an interview?' I explained why I thought it was important, stressing the need to put his side of the story for historical purposes. To get Haughey to talk, all options were open for discussion. I thought I was reeling him in but, in truth, he had no interest in going before the camera. I left Kinsealy knowing that he would never talk about his contentious political career and equally controversial private life.

There was no mention of the tribunals during that lunchtime visit. I was at the tribunals every day Haughey was in Dublin Castle. When the abuse was shouted—and the catcalls uttered—it was obvious that the public had turned on him. What was revealed at the McCracken Tribunal, in particular, was stunning. I have never accepted Ben Dunne's assertion that everything about Haughey has reached the public domain. Haughey received enormous amounts of money from so many people that I suspect the tribunals uncovered only a fraction of the money. I have long thought that the tribunals should have tried to cut a deal with him—make it worth his while to provide information on his donors. It would have been interesting to have seen his response if he had been offered some sweetener to talk. But there was some justice in getting him to attend the tribunals.

Haughey remains undoubtedly the most controversial politician I have reported on during my time in journalism. His time as Fianna Fáil leader, from 1979 to 1992, was always exciting. I covered many of the heaves against his leadership. During one of the first heaves in the early 1980s, I was given access to the Fianna Fáil offices in Leinster House to monitor the letters and phone calls that were being received in support of Haughey. For every person who strongly opposed the Haughey leadership, there was always a loyal supporter with equally passionate feelings. As we filmed the offices, word came through that a Fianna Fáil backbencher had been involved in a car accident. Fionnuala O'Kelly—who later married Fine Gael's Enda Kenny—came into the office with the news. Clem Coughlan, a Fianna Fáil TD from County Donegal, had been killed in the accident. The tragic news cast an air of gloom over the two sides in the leadership heave.

I also remember in April 1989 when Haughey came back from a visit to Japan. I was at Dublin Airport when his plane touched down. His minority Fianna Fáil government was set to lose a Dáil vote over opposition demands for £400,000 to help haemophiliacs infected with the AIDS virus. I asked Haughey about the impact of a Dáil defeat—it would have been a sixth defeat in the short life of that government. He was visibly furious and left open the possibility of a general election.

There was no need to go to the country but Haughey gambled on winning an overall majority. On his way to Áras an Uachtaráin in May 1989, he told his driver to stop the car as they approached the front gates. The passenger window was wound down and Haughey said 'hello' and did a short interview for the cameras. For all the criticisms levelled at him, he was always willing to say a few words, even if he ultimately lost his gamble in 1989.

Haughey was often crude and had a terrible tongue. My first real encounter with this side of the Fianna Fáil leader came during the June 1981 general election. I was working for the *This Week* radio programme and was sent to report on his campaign. He was travelling to Kerry in a small light plane, along with P.J. Mara, and there was space on board for a couple of reporters. The plane was cramped and I was sitting opposite Haughey as it took off from Dublin Airport. Years later, there was some controversy about his taste in expensive handmade French shirts but what I recall from that day in 1981 was his socks—they were the finest socks I had ever seen.

We were treated well. At the end of the day, an ice bucket with a bottle of brandy was produced. 'We'll have a drink now,' Haughey insisted. Naturally throughout the trip the conversation was all about the election campaign. 'What do you think of Garret FitzGerald?' Haughey was asked. The Fine Gael leader had been disparaging about Haughey on the day he was elected Taoiseach, and their leadership rivalry captivated the media and the public for most of the 1980s. Haughey looked directly at the reporters on the plane and then proceeded to make the most derogatory remark about FitzGerald's wife, Joan. I couldn't believe it.

He could also be totally disparaging of colleagues and often didn't care who heard what he said. In the late 1980s, I covered a constituency visit Haughey made to County Wicklow. One of the morning engagements was at a factory in Arklow, after which he was travelling on to Wicklow town. Broadcast journalists are always looking for opportunities to get some 'actuality' which was on offer that day as the state car was travelling from Arklow into Wicklow town. I was in the back seat, alongside Haughey—a rare enough concession—as we were leaving the factory driveway. One of the local Fianna Fáil TDs, Dick Roche, was walking out to his car. Haughey rolled down the passenger window. 'See you in Wicklow,' Roche said to his party leader.

Haughey nodded and rolled up the window. Then, with Roche out of earshot, but with me sitting beside him, Haughey turned and said, 'That little fucker.' It was a typical comment.

There were so many rumours about Haughey that sometimes it was hard to know what to believe. I had heard the stories about his affair with the gossip columnist, Terry Keane. I particularly liked the story about Haughey rowing with Keane in the back seat of his state car. The story goes that Haughey, in a fit of pique, took her handbag and threw it out the window into the canal. I often wondered about the gossip. I asked P.J. Mara if there was any truth in what people were saying about an affair with Keane. 'No way. Those stories never happened,' Mara ventured.

So the night when Keane was a guest on the *Late Late Show* and started to tell her story, I was totally gobsmacked. I was sitting at home watching the television when Gay Byrne introduced Keane. It was amazing to watch and listen to what she had to say. What Haughey probably discounted is that there is always someone who wants to get a story out. The trick is getting to the person who wants to talk.

One Sunday morning, in September 1985, I was on an early reporting shift. The routine for the early reporter begins with check-calls to the gardaí and the other emergency services. News of car crashes, house fires and late-night/early-morning street brawls are generally gathered in this way. 'Charlie Bird from RTÉ here. Just checking if anything is going on?' It had been a quiet night. There was little news to contribute to the 8 a.m. radio bulletin which was read by Colm Murray. I was talking with Colm when the phone on the news desk rang. I answered the call.

'There's been a big story overnight. Have you got hold of it yet?' a man's voice, at the other end of the line, said.

'It's all quiet here. What are you talking about?' I responded.

'It's a big story. It's to do with a yacht.'

Before I could ask any more, the phone line went dead. I immediately rang Marine Rescue. 'We've had a few minor incidents but nothing newsworthy. One boat ran aground off Mizen Head but nobody was injured.'

A few minutes passed before the news-desk phone rang again. The same voice as before. 'Did you get the information?' the man asked.

'Listen, I've been on to Marine Rescue. They say they've had a quiet night,' I responded. Something told me this man was not wasting my time. 'Let's see,' I said. 'You're telling me there's been an incident involving a yacht but Marine Rescue say nothing has happened. You'll have to give me something else to go on.' We were now playing a game of hot and cold.

'Was someone famous on the yacht?' I asked, somewhat speculatively.

'Yes,' was the reply. My brain was now doing overtime thinking of possible names. The leader of Fianna Fáil was a well-known yachtsman.

'Would this have anything to do with a politician?' I ventured.

'It would,' the man responded.

There was only one name on my lips. 'Are you telling me Charlie Haughey's been involved in an accident?'

There was a short silence before the caller said, 'You're going in the right direction.' And then the line went dead again.

It was 8.50 a.m. I put the phone down and rang Marine Rescue again. They were able to confirm that four people had been rescued from a yacht off Mizen Head during the night. But they had no other details. There were no mobile phones in 1985 to get straight through to senior advisors and government officials. I was up against the clock and decided to go with the story. The man who had phoned wanted this story out but was not prepared simply give to it to me. I decided to trust my gut and to trust the man.

We put the story out on the 9 a.m. radio bulletin. 'RTÉ understands that Charlie Haughey has been rescued from his yacht' was the top line in the bulletin. Within seconds of the broadcast, the phones in the newsroom started to ring. One of the callers was my mysterious voice.

'I see you got the story out,' he said, deadpan.

'Well, you didn't make it easy for me,' I said, jokingly.

'We were sworn to secrecy,' the whistle-blower responded. It turned out that this man had been involved in the lifeboat operation which had brought Haughey to safety.

The fact that there is always one person willing to tell a story—somebody who wants the truth to emerge—meant that Haughey's maritime adventure was not released in the controlled manner in which, I expect, he wanted. It was the same human characteristic that ultimately led to the exposure of Haughey's financial improprieties.

He was, without doubt, a complex man. Over the years, I got a glimpse of various aspects of his personality. When he was on form and in good spirits, he was the best of company, as I discovered one Saturday afternoon in the summer of 1988. I was doing a routine report from Dublin Airport on the departure of a Saudi prince at the end of an official visit. Haughey was at the airport. On the same day, Ireland was playing Holland in the finals of the European Championships. As we finished a brief interview with Haughey, I asked him where he was watching the soccer match. The possibility of filming Haughey watching the crucial match in his north Dublin mansion would have made a great television story. 'Can I come back to Kinsealy?' I asked, more in hope than expectation. The idea of a reporter getting into Haughey's

Abbeville home was fantasyland. I was stunned, therefore, when he agreed. None of us had to think twice and, a short time later, the camera crew—Denis Devane and Michael Lee—and I were sitting in the kitchen of Haughey's home as Jack Charlton's team walked out for the match.

'If we're watching a match, we'd better have some beer,' Haughey told us, as he went to the fridge to get some cans of beer. He even allowed us to film him watching some of the match which Ireland ultimately lost. As the players trooped off the pitch, Haughey brought us into another reception room in which he had built his own personal bar. He was pouring beer when the phone rang. The caller was P.J. Mara, looking to confirm a comment from his boss about the heroic Irish effort, for the newspapers the following day. 'Ask this fellow,' Haughey said as he handed the phone to me.

'Hello, P.J.,' I said.

'Who is that?' the baffled Government Press Secretary asked.

'Charlie Bird here,' I said with a big laugh.

'What the fuck are you doing there?' was Mara's response.

Haughey had a love–hate relationship with the media. He could be charming but, as quick as a flash, he had no difficulty in letting his vicious tongue loose on those who were critical of his leadership. I experienced some humorous moments with him, such as the invitation to watch the Ireland soccer match and also a gift of a feathered duck. Haughey had arrived in RTÉ for a radio interview and afterwards he agreed to talk to me for the television news. It was a fresh spring day so we decided to record the interview outside the Television Building where, at that time of year, a family of ducks always made an appearance. And on that day, the mother duck and her young ones crossed the path where I stood, about to ask my first question. The birds caught the attention of the Fianna Fáil leader. 'Have you ever eaten duck, Mr Bird?' he asked.

I said I had not.

'Well, I have some duck in Kinsealy. I'll send you one,' he responded.

I thought no more of this remark as we proceeded to record the interview. A week later, however, one of Haughey's staff approached me in Leinster House. 'I have something for you,' the Fianna Fáil press officer said. I was handed a bag with a dead duck inside. Haughey had been true to his word.

I presented the duck to my local butcher in Bray, asking him to take the feathers off and make it ready for cooking. I don't think he believed me when I said it was a gift from Charlie Haughey.

The Haughey years were controversial, and, as the end of his time as Fianna Fáil leader approached, it seemed as if one scandal followed another. The late 1980s and early 1990s were filled with allegations that a 'golden circle' of business people and politicians were rewarding themselves nicely through their overlapping connections in the private and public sectors. I recall interviewing the businessman Michael Smurfit at the time of the controversy over the Johnson Mooney and O'Brien/Telecom site in Ballsbridge in Dublin. Haughey surprised everyone by calling on Smurfit to stand aside as chairman of the state-owned telecom company when it emerged that he was involved in an aspect of the property transaction.

The businessman opted to make no comment on the controversy. A statement was issued by Mary Finan, his public relations advisor, who stressed that her client would not be giving any media interviews. Ironically, many years later, Finan was appointed as chairperson of the RTÉ Authority.

More in hope than anything else, I decided to position myself outside the Telecom headquarters—maybe I would get lucky if Smurfit arrived. I am sure he was surprised to see me and a couple of other reporters on the footpath when his chauffeur-driven car pulled up outside the front door. He stepped out of the red Bentley with Finan at his shoulder. It was a bizarre scene. I had never spoken to Smurfit before that day—and I will probably never speak with him again. I asked for a few words but he simply walked past me, shaking his head. I made another attempt, referring to Haughey's comments that he should resign as chairman of Telecom Éireann.

'Do you think you've been badly treated?' I asked.

Smurfit stopped. The question obviously threw him because he turned back towards me and started to talk. He spoke for the first time. 'I'll leave that to the Irish people to decide,' he volunteered.

'Have you a message for the people of Ireland?' I enquired. Some people later said it was a soft question but if I had put what these people might consider a 'hard question', I would have got nothing.

Smurfit, however, had a message and I had a story. 'Let the record speak...not to give up hope...to continue to be prepared to serve in the public service and to try to ensure what happened to me won't happen to somebody else.' Significantly, he also added that he had not benefited from the land transaction.

It was a strong news line and he had delivered it for the cameras.

The controversy involving Smurfit was just one of a number of business-related scandals that increased the pressure levels on Haughey who was losing support within Fianna Fáil. The final heave against his leadership came in November 1991. At times of high political drama, much of the action takes place on the plinth outside Leinster House, on the side that faces onto Molesworth Street where Buswells Hotel is located. TDS and senators are always coming and going, and there is rarely a shortage of politicians willing to say their bit. The task for a reporter like me is to get the right politician on camera at the right time.

It is often through pictures and sound bites from the plinth that the public sees the story unfold. In the days leading up to the crucial Haughey vote, as TDS and senators arrived at Leinster House, there was an opportunity to ask questions about ongoing developments. The politicians would carefully try to pick the time when they came out to reveal publicly who they were backing. During the final heave against Haughey, one undecided backbencher—who was always somewhat scattered—approached me on the plinth. 'Charlie, I want to talk with you. I'm declaring for Albert,' he said. It was another twist for my report for the evening news. The politician—who later became a minister— had a small piece of paper in his hand, which he was consulting as we got into position to do the short interview. He put the paper into the top pocket of his suit jacket.

'Ok, I'm ready to go,' he said, but halfway through answering my first question—'So who are you supporting?'—he stopped talking.

'I've lost it,' the TD admitted. He took the piece of paper from his top pocket. After he had consulted it for a few moments we started again, and again he fluffed his lines.

Taking the paper from his pocket once more, he said, 'Don't worry. Don't worry. I'll get it this time.' But when he tried to explain that he was voting against his party leader, he stumbled again. He was a bag of nerves and I'd had enough.

'Look, go away and learn your lines. Come back when you're ready,' I said.

Members of the Fianna Fáil parliamentary party started to arrive early on Saturday morning for their crucial meeting at which the Reynolds-led faction was seeking to topple Haughey. 'Is it a divided Fianna Fáil at the moment?' I asked Albert Reynolds as he arrived.

'Certainly not,' he responded.

As events unfolded in the Fianna Fáil party offices, I paced the path outside Leinster House in the cold sunshine throughout that Saturday and, as the clouds darkened, well into the early hours of Sunday morning.

Word was reaching the assembled media that Reynolds had delivered an 'angry attack' on his party leader and that there were allegations of phone tapping and mysterious white vans spying on TDs. As the evening drew on—and the pubs closed—the crowd outside Leinster House grew larger. I had been doing 'lives' into news bulletins through-out the day but as I started to file another update for the late television news, the crowd responded as if at a soccer match. 'There's only one Charlie Bird, there's only one Charlie Bird,' they chanted. There was plenty of good-humoured banter.

I waved, which only encouraged the revellers. 'Ooh Ah, Charlie Bird,' they sang, adapting one of the chants made famous by Irish soccer fans during the World Cup in 1990.

Then news came that the meeting had concluded. The TDs and Senators had voted on the confidence motion. 'It's 55 to 22,' someone said. 'Haughey's won'.

A huge cheer went up from the assembled crowd. Haughey had survived one more time. The chants now turned to 'Albert's in a Lada', in a pointed reference to Reynolds's loss of his government Mercedes with his resignation from Haughey's ministerial team. I recall a smiling Gerry Collins leaving the building sometime after 3 a.m. 'The meeting was very friendly,' he said.

Politics is a funny business. Haughey may have emerged victorious in the November 1991 vote but, within three months, he was forced to resign. I walked through Leinster House on budget day in late January 1992. One Fianna Fáil TD turned to me and grinned. 'Charlie,' he said, 'you'd better get back to work before the weekend or else the other Charlie will have gone and you'll have missed the big one.' I couldn't believe it. I had spent years reporting on Haughey and now it did indeed look as if I would miss covering his final exit.

Along with many of my colleagues in RTÉ, I was on strike! The dispute had its origins in technological and work-practice changes involving camera crews. When their absence left a news studio unmanned, newscaster Anne Doyle had declined to read a bulletin. One of RTÉ's best-known faces, Anne Doyle had a genuine sense of fairness with a strong commitment to trade union values. Not for the first time in her RTÉ career, she found herself in the firing line. She was duly suspended and the NUJ was brought into the industrial dispute. I was not too happy to be going on strike but accepted that a suspended colleague deserved support.

The strike crippled RTÉ's output but did not put the station off-air, as management and others provided a skeleton news service. As we picketed outside the gates of RTÉ, one of the biggest political stories in years was unfolding. Seán Doherty, a controversial former justice minister, revealed new information about the illegal tapping of two journalists' home telephones in 1982. Now, a decade later, Doherty claimed that he had shown transcripts of the conversations to Haughey while he was Taoiseach. Haughey denied the allegation but it was the final straw for many in Fianna Fáil, and led Des O'Malley and his PD colleagues to threaten to withdraw from their coalition arrangement with Haughey's party. The strike led to RTÉ missing Haughey's departure from office. I couldn't believe that we were in such a situation. The industrial action was a disaster which achieved very little and left considerable resentment between colleagues.

Haughey had been a huge political figure. As an observer, I had watched his fall from grace after the Arms Crisis. And yet, a decade later, by the time I started as a reporter in RTÉ, he had achieved a remarkable political comeback. His tenure as Fianna Fáil leader and his time as Taoiseach were never dull. The revelations from the tribunals of inquiry meant that his retirement years were no less dramatic than his years in political life. The historians will argue about his legacy and, for that reason, I am glad that I got to see the man up close. In June 2006, as I reported on Haughey's funeral, I was astonished at the small numbers who came to pay their final respects. In that way, I suppose, the public gave its verdict.

Political controversy did not end with Haughey's retirement, I'm glad to say. Albert Reynolds in his two short-lived governments—first, with Des O'Malley and the PDs and then with Dick Spring and the Labour Party—kept the media very much on its toes. My long-time RTÉ colleague, Seán Duignan, was appointed Government Press Secretary. It was a time of high political drama as Reynolds within months of becoming Taoiseach in early 1992 fell out with O'Malley. A general election was called in November 1992. It was the first time I was assigned to cover the campaign of a sitting Taoiseach during a general election.

Reynolds had a very different style from Haughey, and in some ways he was more approachable and far more available. On the first day on the campaign, I travelled to Killarney with Reynolds by helicopter. There was a poor turnout of Fianna Fáil activists to greet their party leader. There was even less enthusiasm among the public when Reynolds went on a walk around the town. Some people came over to meet the group. I signed a few autographs. 'Christ, Charlie, you're more popular here than Albert,' Duignan said, 'How do you think it's going?'

I didn't want to be mean to my former colleague but equally I didn't want to lie. Truth was the best approach. 'Albert's fucked,' I speculated.

The 1992 campaign taught me a valuable lesson about how a political party—especially when its campaign is in free fall—will attempt to use the media to shore up its position. Despite the opinion polls in the national newspapers, the Fianna Fáil team would each day tell us that their 'tracking polls' were showing the party doing far better. However, it subsequently transpired, in a report by Gerald Barry in the *Sunday Tribune*, that this was a bare-faced lie. There were no tracking polls. It was a big con trick and even the advisor recruited from Saatchi and Saatchi in London could not salvage the Fianna Fáil campaign. He joined the Taoiseach's tour in Bandon in County Cork and I recall the poor man being cornered by local farmers to talk about headage payments.

On the night of the election count, as the disaster for Fianna Fáil unfolded, I was in Longford, still reporting on Albert Reynolds. To his credit, Reynolds did not hide from us. He even invited us into his Longford home. 'You don't look well,' he said to me. A bottle of brandy was produced. The results were continuing to arrive in from around the country. Fianna Fáil was losing seats in every region. Reynolds's future was on the line. But he still had time to sit and talk with the RTÉ crew. Perhaps we were a distraction.

'The family would love to meet you,' he said at one point and proceeded to bring me down to a bedroom where one of his daughters was lying in bed, recovering from the flu. 'In what other country in the world, would this happen?' I thought.

Reynolds was well beaten but, over the following few weeks, he managed to salvage his political career by forming the first Fianna Fáil–Labour coalition. Relations between Reynolds and Dick Spring, his counterpart in Labour, were often tetchy. I was increasingly in contact with the IRA and watched with more knowledge than most as Reynolds and Spring invested huge political capital to deliver the August 1994 republican ceasefire. Whatever else, the Reynolds years were entertaining, although no event was as amusing as when Boris Yeltsin came to visit—or not to visit, as it turned out.

Albert Reynolds had just flown into Shannon Airport from an official visit to Australia. He had timed his arrival back in Ireland to coincide with Yeltsin's brief stopover. I wanted to get some reaction from the Taoiseach to a growing controversy about the appointment of Harry Whelehan as President of the High Court but the big story that day was the Yeltsin visit. The Russian President was returning from a trip to the United States. A two-hour stopover in Ireland was scheduled. We were waiting to capture images of the official handshakes on the tarmac. Then word came through that Yeltsin's plane was running late. A lunch engagement between the two leaders at Dromoland Castle had to be cancelled. Instead, they would hold a meeting in the VIP area in the airport terminal at Shannon.

Yeltsin's plane eventually landed an hour late. Reynolds, his wife Kathleen, several cabinet ministers and a host of other dignitaries were waiting on the red carpet. A military band was on alert and a group of local children were holding flower bouquets for Yeltsin's wife, Naina. Twenty minutes passed. Nobody was too sure what was going on. When the door of the plane eventually opened, a senior Russian politician emerged but it was the First Deputy Prime Minister, not the President of Russia. We were told that Yeltsin was 'extremely tired' after a couple of days in the United States. 'When a man is ill, a man is ill,' Reynolds said. I said in my television report that three reasons had been given for the Russian President's non-appearance—he was tired, he had high blood pressure and he was indisposed. It was all shorthand for, 'The man is drunk'. It was a huge embarrassment although it was not the only one in the short life of the Reynolds–Spring coalition.

———

My phone rang. 'Nothing. I'm not sure there will be an interview,' I said to the editor of the *Six One News*. It was almost 6 p.m. There was only one story that day, 7 March 1994. A junior minister in the Fianna Fáil–Labour coalition was on the verge of confirming that he had been stopped by gardaí with a man in his car in the Phoenix Park in Dublin.

Rumours about the incident had been circulating in political and media circles for some time. But most newspapers and RTÉ had chosen for a variety of reasons not to pursue the story. Then the *Sunday Press* put the story on its front page. 'More than one politician in seedy rent boy sex racket' was the *Sunday Press* headline. The newspaper claimed that unnamed political figures were involved with young male prostitutes in the Phoenix Park. The story went beyond the Leinster House gossip because, if true, a criminal offence had occurred. The following day's *Irish Press* took up the story, referring to a 'coalition politician'.

Emmet Stagg was the as-yet-unnamed politician. Stagg was a fairly senior Labour Party figure who had battled with the party establishment throughout the 1980s. He wanted Labour to pursue a more left-wing agenda but his views were among a minority and so he had accommodated himself to the leadership of Dick Spring. To the surprise of many people, Labour agreed a coalition government with Fianna Fáil after the 1992 general election. Albert Reynolds was Taoiseach and Dick Spring was Tánaiste. Stagg accepted a junior ministerial job. In early 1994, relations were already tense between the two government parties without the added complication of a sex scandal.

I had a phone call early on the Monday afternoon from one of the Labour Party media handlers. 'Emmet will do an interview,' I was told. 'It's the only interview he's doing.'

Most people now knew that Stagg was the Phoenix Park politician although his name had not been reported in the media. He was now in Government Buildings with senior Labour figures and his own legal representative. A statement was being drafted. I was promised the interview in time for the main evening news. The pressure was on—I knew it would be a very tight turnaround to get the interview done, to get back to RTÉ, and to have time to edit the best parts for transmission as the lead story on the *Six One News*. It was a tight schedule but manageable. That was at 4 p.m.

The crew set up the lights and camera equipment in a room on the ground floor of Government Buildings. There was no confirmation

Togged out for Sandymount High rugby team in my teenage years.

Speaking from the back of a lorry at a Young Socialist rally outside the GPO in Dublin in 1969/70.

Contentment in the early 1970s came from my pipe and a pint of Guinness.

At the podium at a Labour Party conference, most likely in 1970.
Source: RTÉ

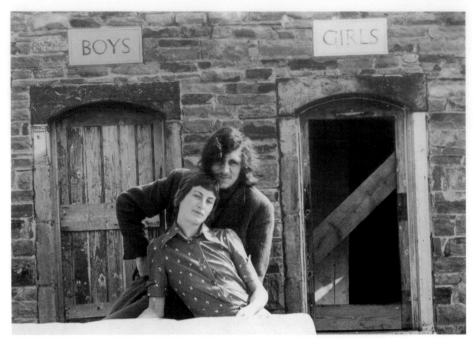

With Mary O'Connor in County Kerry in the early 1970s. We married in 1974.

With documents discovered in a dump in Ringsend in Dublin while working as a researcher in RTÉ in the mid-1970s.
Source: *Charlie Bird, originally from RTÉ*

When I joined the RTÉ newsroom in 1980 I worked as a radio and television reporter. While I was nervous at the start, it didn't take me long to start asking questions of politicians like Neil Blaney.
Source: *Tony O'Shea*

At a Fine Gael press conference during the February 1982 general election. Note the Garret FitzGerald poster on the back wall.
Source: *Derek Speirs*

Chasing after Jim Gibbons during a leadership heave in Fianna Fáil in October 1982. Aengus Fanning, later editor of the *Sunday Independent*, is to the right of Gibbons.
Source: *Derek Speirs*

Journalists sweltered in the heat at the airport in Algiers during the 1985 hijack drama.

Reporting on the trial of Fr Niall O'Brien in the Philippines in 1984 was my first big foreign assignment.

The humanitarian crisis for the Kurds who fled Saddam Hussein's regime after the first Gulf War left a huge impression on me.

Reporting on the plight of the Kurds, who were sheltering on a mountainside in southern Turkey, meant travelling considerable distances on foot.

Inside Nelson Mandela's prison cell on Robben Island. I am fortunate to have met Mandela on several occasions, including during his visit to Dublin in 1990.

Talking to Des O'Malley on the plinth outside Leinster House in 1985 as he prepared to announce the establishment of the Progressive Democrats.
Source: *Photocall Ireland*

I interviewed Charlie Haughey on many occasions. This photograph was taken on his final day as a member of Dáil Éireann ahead of the 1992 general election.

As we waited for the results of the final heave against Charlie Haughey's leadership, in November 1991, the crowds started to sing 'There's only one Charlie Bird'. I gave them a wave.

In September 1990, while on holidays on Inis Oírr, I met Brian Lenihan down on the beach. The Fianna Fáil minister was his party's candidate in that year's presidential election. He had travelled to the island to have his election photographs taken, away from prying eyes.

Currie makes closing appeal for vote transfer with Robinson

By Christine Newman

MR AUSTIN Currie has adopted a new slogan "Make Your Vote Count Twice", as he called on the electorate to give their number two to Ms Mary Robinson.

At his last press conference before the election, the Fine Gael candidate sat beneath a poster carrying the slogan, his name and in slightly smaller type, Ms Robinson's name. Mr Currie said he and Ms Robinson disagreed on some things; for instance, he thought both she and Mr Lenihan had made errors of judgment. Indeed, there would be no need for two candidates if they agreed on everything.

"But we have more things in common that are more important," Mr Currie said. The President was a symbol of our nationality and would represent the people in the way they had a right to be represented — with credibility, integrity and dignity.

"Mary Robinson will do that, I will do that. That is the matter on which we are united," he said.

Mr Currie was joined at the conference by his wife, Anita, the Fine Gael leader, Mr Alan Dukes, TD, the party's director of elections, Mr Jim Mitchell, TD; and Mr John Bruton, TD.

Mr Dukes said the majority of people did not want to see Mr Brian Lenihan as President and the party had to look at the voting strategy to ensure the people got what they wanted. The clear way was to vote number one Currie and number two Robinson. At this, he stood up and made his point by writing the numbers by the two names on the banner behind him.

It was vital to use the PR system to full effect, he said. He was not talking about Gallup polls, he was talking about voting. The Presidential office meant dignity and a good name, and the best way to ensure that was to make the votes count.

Mr Currie was the only candidate who had not had to reinterpret anything he had said and for that reason this country would be in a "safe pair of hands", Mr Dukes said.

He was asked if his leadership of the Fine Gael party would be called into question if Mr Currie received a poor vote. "Nothing will affect my position as leader," he said.

Mr Currie said that he had been the first to raise the issue of the independence of the Presidency. The Brian Lenihan affair had highlighted matters which he had been trying — without much success — to bring to the attention of the public. He had raised the issue of Mr Lenihan's independence, from the beginning, but it was not picked up.

Mr Currie said many people believed that Mr Lenihan's long and close association with Mr Haughey meant that he was not sufficiently independent. As a result of the disclosures, the independence issue was clearly seen by everyone to be important, he said.

"I am the only candidate who has not made a major error of judgment. During this campaign, I have indicated that the country would be in a 'safe pair of hands'," he said.

Mr Currie paid tribute to President Hillery. He said that he thought Dr Hillery was much underrated. The Lenihan affair had shown how good a President Dr Hillery was. He thought that he, too, would have the safe pair of hands that President Hillery had during his terms of office.

Mr Currie said his Irishness had been questioned, but his answer to that was that he was proud to be a Tyroneman, proud to be an Ulsterman and proud to be an Irishman.

Mr Brian Lenihan campaigning in Tralee, Co Kerry, yesterday. — (Photograph: Jerry Kennelly).

When Mary Robinson started to emerge as a serious contender for Áras an Uachtaráin in 1990, Fianna Fáil resorted to negative advertising. I got Robinson to sign this advert which today hangs on the wall in my kitchen.

Labour leader Dick Spring had convinced Mary Robinson to contest the 1990 presidential election. This press conference given by Spring and Robinson took place two days after she had won.

Source: *Photocall Ireland*

I spent a great deal of the Robinson presidency reporting on the activities of Ireland's first woman head of state. This photograph was taken as we filmed material for an RTÉ documentary on Robinson. Her trusted advisor, Bride Rosney, is in the centre.

By the summer of 1997, Mary Robinson had decided to bow out as President at the end of a single seven-year term. RTÉ was given unique access to the private quarters in Áras an Uachtaráin where I interviewed the President and her husband, Nick, about the highs and lows of those seven years.

At a trade union protest outside Leinster House in 1986, against the controversial Section 31 ban which prevented RTÉ from broadcasting interviews with IRA and Sinn Féin members. Source: *Derek Speirs*

Broadcast journalists were free to interview republican figures like Gerry Adams following the lifting of the Section 31 ban, in early 1994, as part of the emerging peace process.

Recognising the potential of the current situation and in order to enhance the democratic peace process and underline our definitive commitment to its success the leadership of Oglaigh na h-Eireann have decided that as of midnight, Wednesday, August 31st, there will be a complete cessation of military operations. All our units have been instructed accordingly.

At this historic cross-roads the leadership of Oglaigh na h-Eireann salutes and commends our volunteers; other activists; our supporters and the political prisoners who have sustained this struggle, against all odds, for the past 25 years. Your courage, determination and sacrifices have demonstrated that the spirit of freedom and the desire for peace based on a just and lasting settlement cannot be crushed. We remember all those who have died for Irish freedom and we reiterate our commitment to our republican objectives.

Our struggle has seen many gains and advances made by nationalists and for the democratic position. We believe that an opportunity to secure a just and lasting settlement has been created. We are therefore entering into a new situation in a spirit of determination and confidence: determined that the injustices which created this conflict will be removed and confident in the strength and justice of our struggle to achieve this.

We note that the Downing Street Declaration is not a solution, nor was it presented as such by its authors. A solution will only be found as a result of inclusive negotiations. Others, not least the British government have a duty to face up to their responsibilities. It is our desire to significantly contribute to the creation of a climate which will encourage this. We urge everyone to approach this new situation with energy, determination and patience. ENDS

In August 1994, the IRA called its first ceasefire of the peace-process era. I was told by my IRA contact to destroy the statement but decided to do otherwise. The piece of paper was tiny, as this same-size image shows.

about what Stagg was going to say, and there was still a possibility he might resign. There was even some speculation that he might be sacked.

Fergus Finlay, a senior advisor to Labour leader Dick Spring, stuck his head in to the room on more than one occasion. 'He'll be down to you in a few minutes,' Finlay said. But the minutes just kept ticking away. I was pacing the interview room for not far off two hours. We missed the top of the *Six One*, and, by 6.30 p.m., I had decided we should cut our losses and bail out. There would be no interview.

Then, Finlay came in again. 'Just hold on. The statement is nearly finished. He'll be with you then,' he said.

My phone rang again. 'Is there any chance this will happen in time for the nine o'clock news?' a colleague back in RTÉ asked, half in jest.

At about 7.30 p.m., a posse of Labour Party figures came through the door. Finlay was there, along with John Foley, the Deputy Government Press Secretary, and John Rogers, a former Attorney General and one of Dick Spring's close confidants. Stagg was smoking. He looked shattered. His eyes were puffy. He nodded towards me. As I remember the scene, Finlay did all the talking. I was handed a typed statement in which Stagg set out the events of early November 1993. He had been sitting alone in his car in the Phoenix Park in an area which he knew was frequented by gay men. A man in his mid-twenties, cycling a bicycle, approached the car. He stopped his bicycle beside the car and, through the open car window, he started a conversation with the Labour Party minister. 'He then sat into the car and we were talking. No wrongful act occurred,' Stagg confirmed.

The difficulty for the junior minister started, however, when a garda car pulled up. One of the officers shone a light into the parked car. Stagg got out. The garda asked for his name. The statement did not say how the officer responded when he realised he had a well-known politician in front of him. Stagg did admit that, 'The gardaí spoke to me in no uncertain terms about the nature of the area in which I was parked and told me to leave in vigorous terms.'

From a quick read of the statement, I knew that this was a powerful story which would divide the public. Forty-nine-year-old Stagg was married with two children. He was not resigning and his resignation had not been sought by his party leader, but the fallout over the subsequent days could change all that.

'Go easy on him,' Finlay said, not looking for a soft interview but

rather that I appreciate Stagg's huge personal tragedy. There was no
stipulation on the questions I could ask.

Time was now very much the issue. Stagg sat down. I saw a beaten man
in front of me. He still had a cigarette in his hand. Just as we were about
to start recording, he broke down in tears and had to leave the room for
some minutes. When we eventually started the interview, we went
through the material in his written statement. It was dynamite stuff.
'What have your family and your party leader been saying to you?' I asked.

The guy was choking in front of me. 'I'm not making light of what
occurred,' he said, adding, 'It was certainly indiscreet and it shouldn't
have occurred. I regret it most sincerely.'

And then, as I was about to ask another question, Stagg broke down
again. Tears were running down his face. We stopped filming. He left
the room for a few minutes as he composed himself. The break in
recording meant more time lost. 'Thank you very much,' Stagg said as
the interview concluded. He immediately lit a cigarette and moved into
a far corner where Finlay and Foley were standing.

While Stagg, Foley and Finlay quietly accessed the interview, Rogers
asked could he look back at it before I left. There had been no agreement on questions so I was somewhat taken aback. But Rogers wanted
only to review the material. Another delay. It was well after 8 p.m. There
would be no time to do a proper edit so the interview got more time in
the news bulletin than it would have if circumstances had been different.

Since that night in 1994, I have never spoken to Emmet Stagg about
the interview or any of the events surrounding the whole episode. We
have passed on the corridors of Leinster House, and I have interviewed
him a few times about different matters out on the plinth, but neither
of us has mentioned that night in March 1994. I'm not sure he ever
again discussed the episode in public. I really believe that the interview
saved Stagg's political career. The strategy of doing only a single interview was hugely successful. There was considerable public support for
the Kildare man. Fianna Fáil opted not to make an issue of the controversy. Stagg's colleagues in the Labour Party rallied around him.
Dick Spring said the whole episode was a 'very unfortunate personal
tragedy'.

Indeed, much of the anger was directed at the Garda Síochána as it
seemed that the story had been leaked from a source within the force.
There was a furious political response. Mary Harney talked about a

breach of the Official Secrets Act. Her then colleague in the Progressive Democrats, Pat Cox, said that the person responsible was a 'merciless bastard'.

The Stagg interview was probably the biggest I had done in several years. Some people said I was too soft on him. Others felt my questions had been too personal and that I had no business asking them. During my career as an RTÉ journalist, I have been praised and criticised in equal measure. It comes with the job. A lot of the complaints have come from politicians. Over the years, all the political parties have claimed that reporters in RTÉ are out to get them. They seem to believe that the journalists in RTÉ sit down and decide as a group that they will have a go. Indeed, each party when it is in government becomes extra critical of RTÉ. It doesn't matter if it's Fianna Fáil, Fine Gael, Labour or the PDS—when it's their turn to be in government, they start complaining about how RTÉ is covering them. I've always found this suggestion very strange because the reporters in the RTÉ newsroom are like a microcosm of Irish society. They come from every town and village in Ireland. I laugh at the idea that RTÉ journalists wear their political colours on their sleeves. It's just not true. Equally, when the newspapers are criticising RTÉ for its coverage of say, Sinn Féin—saying we're too soft on them—there will be complaints coming in from Sinn Féin claiming that we're too hard on them. That's just the way it is.

I've had reason on a few occasions to complain myself. A handful of politicians have made allegations against me that I found unacceptable. Usually they have trotted out the line about my involvement in the Labour Party in the early 1970s, insinuating that this long-past association somehow influenced how I did my job as a reporter. I remember one Fianna Fáil minister complaining when I hadn't included an interview clip of him in a news report. 'Fuck off. You're only a Labour Party hack,' he told me. I was not impressed with this attitude and I later got an apology.

It was not just Fianna Fáil politicians, however, who attacked me in this way. Not long after the formation of the Fianna Fáil–Labour coalition in late 1992, I was walking out of Leinster House from the Merrion Square side. A senior Fine Gael TD was coming towards me. I went to ask him a question but, before I got too far, he lost his cool. 'You're so far up Dick Spring's backside that you'll probably disappear up there,' he remarked before walking on. The outburst was offensive in itself but again it was the insinuation that I was compromised in how I did my job that really made me mad. I rang the Fine Gael press office, and some days later, a note arrived in RTÉ from the Fine Gael leader, John Bruton. He was apologising on the TD's behalf.

As a working journalist, I have spent a fair amount of time outside Leinster House, looking for politicians to say their bit on whatever is the big story of the day. There's always banter which I enjoy. It's the suggestion that I go easy on some politicians or favour some parties that makes me angry. Some complaints directed against me stick in my mind more than others. Labour's Dick Spring had another way of getting his message across. As I discovered in 1986, he wasn't shy about telling you when he didn't like a question. I didn't know him particularly well at the time. The life of the Fine Gael–Labour coalition was coming to an end. There had been huge difficulties at cabinet over the state of the national finances. And it wouldn't be long before Spring and his colleagues walked out over cutbacks proposed by Garret FitzGerald's Fine Gael.

On that particular day, Spring was on Merrion Street, just outside Government Buildings. He was answering questions about the economy and the latest political row in government. Several reporters, including myself, were huddled around Spring with microphones and Dictaphones, recording his comments. I asked a question and it was obvious that Spring was not too pleased with the continued probing about another political crisis.

Suddenly I felt a dart of pain in my shin. Someone had kicked me. The man in front of me had kicked me. And that man was Dick Spring, Tánaiste and leader of the Labour Party. I wasn't sure if the kick was intentional or not. He kept talking, although, looking back at the tape later, it seemed to me that he was somewhat distracted for the length of time it takes to kick someone on the shin. When the questions finished, I let my feelings be known. I was totally taken aback by his answer. 'I didn't kick you,' he responded. I let the matter go. My leg was sore but no more than that. It was one of those bizarre episodes which are nearly impossible to explain.

In later years, I reported on Dick Spring a great deal more, especially when he was Minister for Foreign Affairs in the 1992–97 period. I travelled on many overseas trips, reporting on his role as a government minister. Sometimes he would joke before an interview—'Be careful now, Charlie, or I might kick you.'

Spring was often tetchy and he could be grumpy. I put this down—in part—to the discomfort he suffered from a back injury he had acquired in a serious car crash in the early 1980s. I remember one trip with Spring in the mid-1990s to southern Lebanon. The media and ministerial entourage were all staying in the same hotel in Beirut, partly for security and safety reasons. The hotel was overlooking the sea and, if you ignored the burnt-out buildings that surrounded the area, it was the perfect holiday destination. One evening, I went down to the hotel's outdoor pool for a swim. There I found Spring alone in the pool, and all I can say is that he was trudging up and down the water. He looked a forlorn figure trying to ease the discomfort from his back injury.

There was another side to the Labour leader, too. I had one of my strangest nights-on-the-town courtesy of Spring who, by the mid-1990s, I had got to know somewhat better. In his final Christmas as Minister for Foreign Affairs, I was invited along with other journalists to festive drinks in Iveagh House. My plan was to drop in for a short while before moving on to the RTÉ newsroom Christmas party at a nightclub in central Dublin. There was a good atmosphere in Iveagh House. Spring was in good form. 'Come upstairs for a nightcap,' he said as the official reception neared an end.

The minister's expansive office had a good view out over the gardens at the back of Iveagh House which were still visible with the office lights on that dark December evening. 'Let's open the bar,' Spring declared as a handful of reporters who had travelled with him on some foreign trips settled into the ministerial suite. We all had a few more drinks.

A senior official who was involved with policy on Northern Ireland started up a sing-song with a ditty that poked fun at the British. It was that sort of night. I think I sang a few verses of 'The Auld Triangle'. It's the only one I sing and I sometimes miss some of the verses, but I love it. Many of Spring's advisors had already left for home so they weren't to know that their boss was on a serious night out. We cleared out every drop of drink in the office.

'So, where to next, Charlie,' the Tánaiste asked, not long after 11 p.m. 'I'm going to the RTÉ Christmas party,' I replied. 'Okay, let's go,' he replied, gathering up his coat and scarf. We trooped down the main stairs in Iveagh House and out to the ministerial car. And there I was, sitting in the back of the state car, being chauffeur driven to the RTÉ newsroom party. There were more than a few turned heads when I got to the nightclub with the Tánaiste alongside me. It was one of those nights. All I remember is that the ministerial car drove us back to Spring's Dublin apartment where I slept in the spare bedroom. The next morning, I ventured out to the living room with one hell of a hangover. Spring made coffee. 'What collar are you?' he asked, offering me a change of shirt. It had been that sort of night.

Spring led the Labour Party into government with Fianna Fáil after the 1992 general election. He had capitalised on the Robinson victory two years earlier. There were over 30 Labour TDs, the largest number the party ever had. Many in Labour—and some of Spring's own staff—had private misgivings about their alliance with Fianna Fáil. There were ongoing tensions in the coalition with Albert Reynolds, especially in the summer of 1994, over the proposed appointment of Attorney General Harry Whelehan to the position of President of the High Court. There was a huge stand-off—Reynolds wanted to give Whelehan the job but Spring was opposed to the appointment. I had asked Reynolds about the controversy while we waited for Boris Yeltsin at Shannon Airport. A few days later, on a different story, I interviewed Spring at Dublin Airport. In conversation afterwards, I predicted that Whelehan would get the job. 'Absolutely not,' was Spring's reply.

'I bet you Albert will go ahead with it,' I said.

'Not over my dead body, Charlie. It won't happen,' he responded.

'What do you bet?' I asked, jokingly.

But Spring challenged my confidence. 'Let's wager a fiver,' he responded.

'Done,' I said, taking a five-pound note from my wallet. John Foley had been listening to the conversation as it developed into a betting match. He took a £5 note from each of us, then put the two notes into an envelope and wrote the nature of the bet on the outside.

Three months later, I ran into Foley in Leinster House. He was still working for Spring, but the government had changed. Out had gone Albert Reynolds as Taoiseach and Fianna Fáil leader. In had come John Bruton as head of a Fine Gael–Labour–Democratic Left coalition. Foley laughed as he reached into his suit pocket. 'I believe this is yours,' he said, handing me the envelope with the two fivers sealed inside. Whelehan had been appointed but his tenure had been short-lived. The controversy over his appointment was one of the factors leading to the collapse of the Fianna Fáil–Labour coalition. It was good to have been proven correct.

But I wasn't going to see Spring out of pocket! So I went to a picture-framing shop and got them to mount the two fivers and the envelope with Foley's handwritten explanation of the bet. And when I met Spring at some stage early in 1995, I handed him the framed fivers and envelope. I'm told he has them hanging on the wall in his Dublin apartment.

Just after Spring had taken Labour out of government with Fianna Fáil in late 1994, negotiations had started about forming the new coalition led by John Bruton of Fine Gael. The talks were held in secret. 'No point hanging around here today,' John Foley said on one particular day when it became clear that contacts between Bruton and Spring were likely but well away from the view of the media.

There was little happening in the environs of Leinster House. I knew that Spring was in the building, but Bruton had not been seen. I was like a dog with a bone as I stood on the path opposite the Merrion Square entrance to the Leinster House car park.

Regardless of what Foley had told the media, if Bruton did arrive, it might be worth my wait. It was a cold winter's day and I know on that particular afternoon I paced the footpath for about two hours. Suddenly John McGlinchey, an RTÉ cameraman who was working with me, spotted John Bruton being driven in his Mercedes car down Mount Street. He jumped into his own car and started to follow the Fine Gael leader. A few minutes later, I caught sight of Spring but not in his car I later learnt he was driving his secretary's car. I raced to my own car and, not really sure whether I was doing the right thing or not, I followed the Labour Party leader. It was the nearest I've ever come to one of those high-speed chases from a Hollywood movie. Through the Dublin traffic, I followed Spring to a house on Ailesbury Road in Ballsbridge where John McGlinchey was now outside, sitting in his own car. As I saw Spring going in the front door of this house, I noticed that John Bruton's car was parked in the driveway.

I didn't know who owned the house but I now knew that this was the secret location where the programme for a new government was being finalised. I rang John Foley.

'John. It's Charlie Bird. You'll never guess where I am,' I said teasingly.
'Where?'
'I'm outside a house on Ailesbury Road.'
There was a brief silence before Foley responded, 'How the fuck did you find out?'

The house on Ailesbury Road was the home of lawyer Dermot Gleeson. I am not sure John Foley ever believed that I got that story by simply hanging around a street corner!

Over the years, I have spent a lot of time on the plinth outside Leinster House. Sometimes when waiting for a story to happen or an interviewee to arrive, I used to sit down on the metal chairs and talk with colleagues or other politicians. I was very fond of the late Gordon Wilson, whose daughter was killed in the Enniskillen bombing in 1987. He had been nominated to the Seanad as a Taoiseach's nominee by Albert Reynolds in early 1993. He was a lovely man but I think he was a bit lonely and out of place in Leinster House. Politics was not his forte but he had a certain presence despite the awful thing the IRA had done to him. The emotion was never far from the surface. He would often sit down beside me on the plinth and we'd chat. I really liked Gordon Wilson and I was shocked when he died unexpectedly in 1995, although it was probably only appropriate that I first heard the news of his death while standing outside Leinster House.

Over the past quarter of a century, there have been many changes in how politics is reported, and the Leinster House plinth, facing onto Molesworth Street, has played an important role in those changes.

When I joined the RTÉ newsroom, the political correspondents' room on the top floor in Leinster House was the centre of political reporting. The so-called lobby system was how the government delivered its message to the media. The Government Press Secretary, irrespective of what parties were in power, would arrive in the political correspondents' room at a set time each day to brief the journalists on the story of the day.

The political correspondents were undoubtedly the doyens of news reporting. The first of these characters whom I met were newspaper people like Dick Walsh, Michael Mills, Chris Glennon and Liam O'Neill, and, of course, RTE's Seán Duignan and Donal Kelly. In the 1980s, Geraldine Kennedy and Emily O'Reilly broke into what had been a male-dominated business. Olivia O'Leary was another exceptionally talented reporter who smoothly moved between print and broadcast journalism. These women brought a new dynamic to political reporting at a time when there was the start of a shift away from the political correspondents' room—and, indeed, from the Dáil chamber itself. Increasingly, political drama was unfolding for the cameras and microphones out on the plinth.

The introduction of new technology in television reporting in the late 1980s and early 1990s gave news reporting a new immediacy. Political controversy in Leinster House could for the first time be delivered to the public almost as it happened. It was, in fact, a two-way process. Politicians also realised that they could get greater exposure on RTÉ News by talking to news reporters outside on the plinth than from speeches delivered in the Dáil chamber. A whole new area of political coverage was being delivered from the Leinster House plinth, and this was even before there was live broadcasting of the proceedings in the Dáil chamber

Radio reporters had for many years successfully gone beyond the political correspondents' room to try to get news stories. One of the classic moments came in early 1982 at the end of Garret FitzGerald's first coalition government. Mary Flaherty, a junior minister, was getting into her ministerial car when she was approached by a young reporter by the name of Seán O'Rourke. Pushing his microphone forward, O'Rourke asked, 'Minister, do you think this is going to be your last ride in the back of a state car?' The infamous question was broadcast on radio a short time later.

A deliberate decision had been taken in RTÉ to change the direction of the station's political coverage. I eventually adapted to a routine of spending my working day in the environs of Leinster House when there was a big political story. More often than not, I was working on the plinth along with my colleague, Caroline Erskine. We got used to people like Liam Skelly, a controversial Fine Gael backbencher, who was one of the early exponents of the plinth. Skelly was somewhat of a maverick and was a frequent critic of the 1982–87 Fine Gael–Labour coalition. To the annoyance of his party colleagues, he would often arrive out on the plinth to let fly at some decision or other of the government's with which he disagreed. Others, like the late Jim Kemmy and Fine Gael's Michael Lowry, were also frequent occupants of the plinth as they attempted to get their messages across.

The advent of commercial radio and television has also changed the way politics is reported. Until his appointment as Deputy Government Press Secretary in 2005, Mark Costigan of Today FM was also a focus of attention for politicians as he paraded up and down the plinth. Colour writers like Miriam Lord, for so long with the *Irish Independent* before her move to *The Irish Times*, have also become a staple component for reporting on big political events. Increasingly, the 'doorstep' is how news is gathered. In a way, it's a development of what can be called 'plinth reporting', where a group of reporters from national and local media outlets surrounds an interviewee at an impromptu media conference. In this way, news is gathered and stories filed.

Not everyone wants to talk, however. One Fianna Fáil politician took great pleasure in telling me where to go. In all my years working in Leinster House, I never had any reason to look for an interview with Willie Farrell from County Sligo. He was a Fianna Fáil senator in the early 1980s and again after 1987. He had hardly any national profile until the mid-1990s when it emerged that he had signed property developer Tom Gilmartin into Leinster House. Gilmartin, who was also originally from Sligo, had made a number of serious allegations about politicians looking for bribes in return for planning favours. There was controversy about a meeting the developer said he attended with several Fianna Fáil figures in Leinster House. When it emerged that Farrell had got approval for Gilmartin to visit Leinster House, I went looking for the Sligo senator.

I was on the plinth when I saw him coming in from Molesworth Street. 'Willie, I'd like to talk to you about Tom Gilmartin,' I said.

He stopped and looked straight at me. 'Charlie,' he said, 'will you ever fuck off.' There was a smile on his face. He was enjoying this. 'It's as simple as this. You can fuck off. For years, I've been coming in and out of Leinster House, walking across this plinth, and never once have you stopped to ask me anything. And now you want to talk to me about Tom Gilmartin.' He paused, and then added, 'Well, I'm not going to talk about it. So you can fuck off now.' He laughed heartily as he walked on.

A few days later, I got a slap on the back from Farrell as he passed me on the corridor in Leinster House. 'Charlie, I was never going to talk about Tom Gilmartin,' he said with a wicked smile across his face. He had taken some measure of satisfaction from having one up on me. Fair enough, I thought.

Many people have told me to get lost when I've gone looking for a comment or an interview. Sometimes they were right. I believe a television camera is like a loaded gun, the most powerful weapon we have. I also believe that an RTÉ journalist is in a very privileged position. If we abuse the position that we have, it has a huge effect on people. Mistakes can be made, and in television they get exposed very quickly.

Sometimes the outcome can be funny. I recall the floods in Dublin and Bray in 1986. We took to a small boat to get up some water-filled streets. One man who was stranded on the roof of his house wasn't too impressed with my arrival. As I pointed the microphone in his direction, about to ask a question, he shouted, 'You're too late, Charlie. Go away or I'll put your head under the water.'

Often the person who is central to a story refuses to talk. One just has to accept that and get on with the story. But on one occasion that attitude led to an unseemly row outside the Burlington Hotel in Dublin. I have never experienced anything like the winter's morning in early 1995 when I was trying to doorstep John Bruton outside the Burlington Hotel. It was a bizarre episode. The fallout from the Harry Whelehan appointment had led to Bruton's becoming Taoiseach just before Christmas in 1994. Bertie Ahern was the new leader of Fianna Fáil, and a row had developed between the two politicians. I wanted to get a response from Bruton who was speaking at a function in the Burlington. Bruton's new press officer was a former RTÉ colleague, Shane Kenny, who had presented the News at One on Radio One for many years.

I arrived at the Burlington and told Shane that my hope was to get a brief reaction on camera from the Taoiseach when he was leaving the function. 'That's not happening,' was his response. I suppose he was only doing his master's bidding although there was probably a certain tetchiness between us given that we had been colleagues as recently as a few weeks earlier.

My attitude has long been that if someone, a politician or anybody else, does not want to do any interview, that is their choice. However, if a legitimate story comes up, as a journalist I have a right to ask the questions and a right to 'doorstep' the person involved. They have the right to say nothing. So, for that reason, I took no notice of what Kenny had said. John Bruton could walk past me and decline to comment but I was still going to ask my questions.

I situated myself at the door where Bruton would leave for his state car. Half an hour passed before he emerged. The camera started to roll. 'Taoiseach, may I ask you about what Bertie Ahern said last night,' I asked. Bruton stopped and looked at me. Kenny did the talking. 'He's not answering that question,' he interjected before repeating himself. 'The Taoiseach is not answering that question.'

I was not going to be put off so easily so I ignored Kenny and repeated my question again. Bruton had moved closer to his car and was about to get into the passenger seat when he hesitated. I saw the opportunity and so put the question a third time. But again Kenny interjected. 'You can't ask that question,' he ordered me as his voice grew louder and more agitated.

The Taoiseach was now standing by the door of his car, watching the Government Press Secretary and RTÉ's Special Correspondent engaged in fierce verbal exchange. I was really annoyed with Kenny's attitude. 'That's fine,' I said. 'If he doesn't want to answer the question, that's up to him, but I have to ask.'

Then Kenny threw a verbal grenade. 'You wouldn't have treated Charlie Haughey like this,' he shouted at me.

I saw red immediately. I took great exception to the remark. I was insulted: I was there to do my job, to put the questions, irrespective of who was in government. Bruton sought to bring the stand-off to a conclusion. 'Look,' he said, 'I'll do the interview.'

But by now I was so mad at what had been said and, to be honest, I had lost my cool. 'No, forget it,' I replied. 'Shane has made an allegation about me. I would have asked the question regardless of who was Taoiseach.'

Now the three of us were involved in a heated discussion. Bruton kept saying, 'Look, let's do the interview. I'll answer the questions.'

From the corner of my eye, I could see the doorman from the Burlington looking on, gobsmacked. 'The camera has been rolling. All of this is recorded,' I said. 'So when I go back to RTÉ, my bosses will see it.' Kenny had overstepped the line but I was being petulant.

Eventually Bruton and Kenny got into the state car and left. The entire episode lasted for about five minutes. 'I've never seen anything like that in my life,' the hotel doorman ventured.

The cameraman, Michael Lee, was also looking at me in amazement. 'Let's get out of here, Charlie,' he said.

During the short drive back to RTÉ, I wondered briefly if I had gone too far. But back in the office when they viewed the tape—with Shane Kenny's voice clearly audible—there was agreement that the new Government Press Secretary was the one who had gone too far. Nobody said it directly but I knew myself that I had probably been silly. It was not the first time that I had had cross words with government press personnel and it would not be the last. These types of verbal exchanges are just part and parcel of the cut and thrust of how reporters, politicians and their media handlers operate. The row did not sour my relationship with Shane Kenny who, a couple of years later, was back working in the RTÉ newsroom. A few days after the incident outside the Burlington Hotel, I found myself down at the Royal Hospital in Kilmainham. Bruton was attending a conference. Inside the function room, he caught my eye and came over. We shook hands. 'Look, no hard feelings. Let's just forget about it,' the Taoiseach said. And we did.

Chapter 5 ～

THE DANCING PRESIDENTS

The uninhabited part of Inis Oírr, the smallest of the Aran Islands off the Irish west coast, looks out onto the Atlantic and the Cliffs of Moher. Save for the black-and-white painted lighthouse— which stands tall and dark against the sea—the view probably hasn't changed much for over a thousand years. On a winter's day, one might come across an islander out collecting the *slata mhara*, the sea sticks. In summertime, looking towards the County Clare coastline, you might see a tiny currach bobbing up and down as a fisherman hauls in his lobster pots.

Inis Oírr is one of my favourite locations and, in early September 1990, I travelled to the island for a short break after the exhilarating but ultimately tiring weeks reporting in the Gulf region. I am always assured of a warm welcome on Inis Oírr but I also like the solitude that's on offer. You can sit on the rocks and take time out from the madness of the world. There isn't a soul I have met who hasn't come away from Inis Oírr filled with a sense of spirituality.

Over the years, I have become close friends with Bríd and Peadar Póil who run a guesthouse on the island. I stay with them whenever I take a few days' break. They are amazing people, always generous and welcoming. Peadar farms a few acres and has tried at various stages to introduce daffodils and deer farming onto the island. When I'm visiting, he will often give me a lift in his tractor to the local pub in the evenings. The island is also a great location for good brisk walks and plenty of clean fresh air. One morning, shortly after my arrival in September 1990, I was on my way to the beach when I saw more activity than normal on the strand.

There on the beach was Brian Lenihan, posing for photographs against the clear blue water. I am not sure who was more surprised, the veteran Fianna Fáil politician or myself. Lenihan was his party's nominee for the presidential election due in late October 1990. A popular figure, he was still recovering from a life-saving liver transplant operation, and was an opinion-poll favourite to become head of state.

Not unlike myself, Lenihan had come to Inis Oírr for some privacy. His campaign photographs were being taken at various locations on the island. The slogan had already been chosen—'A President with a Purpose'. Now they needed sharp images to accompany that message.

A make-up artist was on hand, along with several members of his campaign team. A former *Irish Times* photographer, Tom Lawlor, was the man behind the camera. Some of his photographs from the Inis Oírr shoot would later appear on billboards around the country as Lenihan sought election to Áras an Uachtaráin.

If the Fianna Fáil candidate was somewhat taken aback to see me strolling towards him, his entourage was completely bowled over.

'What are you doing here?' I was asked. There were a few glances around the beach in search of a concealed camera crew.

'Don't worry,' I laughed. 'I'm not working, just enjoying some downtime.'

Lenihan was his affable self but he didn't look particularly well. We chatted and then Tom Lawlor took some photos of the two of us before I left them on the beach. Later that evening, I joined Lenihan and his colleagues in Ruairí Ó Conghaile's pub for a few drinks.

Ruairí is a big Fianna Fáil supporter and was delighted to have Lenihan as a patron. There was a bit of slagging about my having stumbled upon their private photo shoot. The handlers with Lenihan had lightened up. Ruairí thought the whole episode was amusing and he later got his hands on one of Tom Lawlor's photos of Lenihan and myself. To this day, that photograph is hanging on the wall in Ruairí's pub.

I was back in RTÉ by the start of October and would see a lot more of Lenihan before polling day at the end of the month. He was Tánaiste and Minister for Defence and favourite for the Park. Mary Robinson, however, had other ideas, even if the opinion polls pointed to a credible showing but ultimately a defeat for the first woman to seek election to the office of President. An IMS survey in the first week of October put Robinson on 33 per cent with the Fine Gael candidate on 16 per cent, but Lenihan was way ahead with 51 per cent.

I hadn't had many dealings with Robinson before the presidential election in 1990. Obviously I knew the broad outline of her career—a distinguished lawyer, a Trinity College academic and, for many years, a member of Seanad Éireann. She had been a long-time Labour Party member but resigned in 1986 over the Anglo-Irish Agreement. I don't think I had ever interviewed her before 1990, which was funny in a way as, over the following seven years, I would travel the world, reporting on the Mayo woman.

Robinson had been the first candidate to be nominated for the 1990 presidential election. The fact that there was going to be a contest was a novelty in itself—people had grown used to the presidency being a retirement home for aging political figures who rarely ventured out into the public gaze. In over ten years as a journalist in the RTÉ newsroom, I had only ever reported on presidential functions. A presidential election was a rarity. That was all about to change.

Robinson had been on the election trail since early in May 1990. Like other journalists, I had heard the rumours of difficulties within her campaign team, especially with senior Labour Party figures, several of whom resented her decision to stand as an independent candidate. She was taking their support but not flying their flag, as it were. There was talk that the Labour Party organisation in some parts of the country had been slow to come out and work for her campaign.

After my break on Inis Oírr, one of my first assignments was to spend a day following the Robinson campaign. The pre-arranged meeting place was Ardee in County Louth. It was a weekday and Robinson was scheduled to canvass early morning mass-goers after they left the local church. I will never forget the scene. The Robinson battle bus arrived in the town. The candidate got off the bus. But only a small number of people had turned up to meet her—maybe half a dozen Labour Party canvassers, but certainly there was no crowd and most definitely no razzmatazz. The whole thing was a mess and very embarrassing. The local Labour organisation was blamed and later, when we travelled into Drogheda, there were heated words between Labour members and the Robinson team. After what I had seen, if anyone had tried to convince me that Mary Robinson could win the presidential election, I would have said that they were mad.

The third candidate in the 1990 presidential election was Austin Currie. He had had a long political career in Northern Ireland with

John Hume's SDLP before moving south of the border in 1987. He won a seat for Fine Gael in Dublin West but was hardly a national figure. The Fine Gael leader, Alan Dukes, had struggled to find a high-profile candidate and, from what I was picking up, his party colleagues feared they would be beaten into third place behind Robinson and Lenihan.

Maybe Dukes should have rowed in behind Robinson. However, the Fine Gael leader wanted his own candidate and, after much scratching around, convinced Currie to stand. I reported on the launch of the Currie campaign. He was thrown in at the deep end and never looked like a winner. To my amazement, after what I'd seen in Ardee, Robinson was increasingly looking like a serious challenger to Lenihan.

The growing success of the Robinson campaign became clear to me on the day Fianna Fáil took out advertisements in the national newspapers, bearing the slogan 'Is the Left Right for the Park?' If Fianna Fáil was targeting Robinson in this way, she was obviously perceived as a possible threat to a Lenihan victory. Eugene Murray in RTÉ was very taken with the Fianna Fáil advert and asked me to get Robinson to sign one, which I duly did and, for good measure, I got her to sign an advert for myself. A framed copy of one of the Fianna Fáil attack adverts—signed by Mary Robinson—today hangs on the wall in my house.

As public and media interest in the presidential election campaign increased, Robinson was gaining momentum but it's difficult to say whether or not she would have beaten Lenihan were it not for two monumental gaffes that holed the Fianna Fáil campaign.

Lenihan was responsible for the first mistake. He gave conflicting versions of what had happened back in January 1982 when phone calls were made to the then President, Paddy Hillery, in an attempt to ask him not to call a general election after the Fine Gael–Labour coalition had lost a crucial Dáil vote. Lenihan had told a UCD politics student that he had made calls to Áras an Uachtaráin to try to persuade Hillery to ask Charlie Haughey to try to form a new government, as is permitted under the constitution. But on RTÉ's *Questions & Answers* programme, the Fianna Fáil presidential candidate denied having made any phone calls.

I remember the buzz in the RTÉ newsroom after Lenihan did his 'on mature recollection' interview on the *Six One News*. The Fianna Fáil campaign was all over the place. The next day, I was asked to go to Dublin Airport to interview Bertie Ahern, who was Lenihan's director of elections. Ahern said that they were no longer seeking a meeting

with Hillery to clarify matters, as Lenihan had earlier promised. Ahern
then boarded the plane.

Minutes later, Lenihan arrived and told me he wanted to meet
Hillery. 'Are you sure?' I asked, and then played him the interview clip
with Ahern. The Lenihan camp was not happy. All of this confusion
was captured on camera and I included it in a television report on that
evening's news. The 'calls-to-the-Áras' controversy led to Lenihan's
being sacked from cabinet by Charles Haughey, as the Fianna Fáil
leader sought to protect his coalition with the Progressive Democrats
from collapsing. Several years later, when Lenihan died, I went out to
Haughey's Kinsealy home in north County Dublin to interview him
about his long-time colleague. It was a day for tributes to the deceased
and Haughey was generous in his. But he somehow looked uneasy
when I reminded him about having sacked Lenihan.

'It was extraordinarily difficult for both of us. We had been close
friends but when this matter arose, he knew what he had to do and I
knew what I had to do,' Haughey told me.

I think the truth came in another answer when Haughey—then
disgraced by the various tribunal revelations—admitted somewhat
regretfully about his own position: 'I don't know anyone in modern
Irish life who was so universally loved as Brian Lenihan was.'

Loved or not, in late October 1990, Lenihan was sacked. But he was
still the Fianna Fáil presidential candidate and was garnering considerable
sympathy. Then his cabinet colleague, Pádraig Flynn, attacked
Robinson on RTÉ Radio's *Saturday View* programme. His comments
about her 'new-found interest in family' caused huge offence. There
was no comeback for Lenihan after the Flynn outburst.

I remember feeling sorry for Lenihan. The controversy was wearing
him down. He was obviously not well. Plus there were telltale signs that
some in his party sensed defeat. People peeled away from the campaign,
so much so that, near the end, he really had only his immediate family
around him.

On the day of the count, I was working at the RDS in Ballsbridge.
Thousands of ballot papers were being counted and piled into bundles.
In the early afternoon, Lenihan arrived to survey the scene. I recorded
a short interview with the Fianna Fáil candidate in which he effectively
threw in the towel. All the votes may not have been counted but
the party workers, who were monitoring the counting process, had

preliminary figures pointing to a Robinson win. Fianna Fáil was going to lose its grip on the presidency for the first time ever.

With the Lenihan 'concession' on tape, I worked the phones to see if Robinson would respond. The formal first-count declaration was not likely to come in time to make the top of the *Six One News*. But having the two main candidates talking about the election outcome was a good second best. Robinson agreed to a short interview, so I left the RDS for her home on Sandford Road in Ranelagh.

When we pulled up outside the Robinsons' house, I was struck by how quickly the trappings of the presidential office had appeared. The official result was still some way off but already two gardaí were stationed at the front gate.

There was great excitement inside the house, with lots of people coming and going. People were hugging. Some were punching the air. Phones were ringing. This was the winner's party. Downstairs, in a basement-level kitchen, Mary Robinson and her husband Nick were receiving a constant stream of well-wishers. I told them about Brian Lenihan's as-good-as concession of defeat. She wanted to be sure about what he had said before giving me some remarks. So, along with her husband, Mary Robinson peered into the viewfinder of the RTÉ camera and watched what Lenihan had said in the RDS a little over half an hour earlier. They were both clearly delighted. We then recorded a short interview with Robinson.

When the camera was switched off, the soon-to-be president asked us to join her for a cup of tea before we headed back to RTÉ. Large numbers of people were being fed as a party atmosphere was developing. I laughed to myself when I saw the food set out on the dining-room table—brown bread and smoked salmon! If the Fianna Fáilers could have seen the scene, they would have enjoyed harping on about the smoked-salmon socialist who was about to become president!

In early December, I reported on Mary Robinson's inauguration at Dublin Castle. The great and the good were all invited. It was one of those great historic moments and I would not be telling the truth if I did not admit that I was very excited about the possibilities the Robinson presidency opened up for the country. 'The Ireland I will be representing is a new Ireland, open, tolerant, inclusive,' Robinson said in her acceptance speech. I had long left behind my dabbling in political activism and by 1990 had no party-political allegiance whatsoever but even an impartial RTÉ journalist could enjoy the sense of occasion, especially as the 21-gun salute echoed across the capital.

Shortly afterwards, RTÉ decided that I would prepare a documentary over the course of Robinson's first year in Áras an Uachtaráin. The people had elected her, whereas political deals had guaranteed the elevation of several of her predecessors. She was a liberal woman, whereas elderly Fianna Fáil grandees had traditionally filled the position. There was much to capture on camera. The documentary centred on footage from various functions over the course of the twelve months after the November 1990 election. Robinson had a busy first year—over 800 public engagements and some 700 speeches, covering every county in the Republic.

I recall reporting on her visit to a special-needs school in County Galway. One little boy whose name was Richard took a shine to the army cap of the President's aide-de-camp. The cap was too big but Richard was very pleased with himself. He smiled broadly. 'Will you salute me?' Robinson asked. Richard liked the attention. The President got her salute. We also saw the ease with which Nick Robinson fulfilled his rather unique role as spouse to a woman head of state. Some of the children at the special-needs school were taken by his bushy beard. 'Hasn't he got a great beard?' the President said with a laugh. 'He's a bit like Santa Claus.'

There was genuine excitement everywhere Robinson went and our cameras captured the warmth with which she was received. At a function at the Galway Rape Crisis Centre, it was as if a pop star had arrived in town. People were queuing up to have their photograph taken with their President.

The documentary was broadcast in October 1991 and included a fifteen-minute interview with Robinson. We recorded the interview in one of the reception rooms at the Áras. We sat in two golden chairs. The President had a somewhat wary look in her eye as we started filming. I suppose the interview was a big deal at the time because up to then, presidents had kept their dealings with the media to a complete minimum.

Robinson spoke of a 'challenging year but a very enjoyable one'. Given the restrictions on her office, there was only so much she could say in the interview, so I veered the conversation onto the less political side of the job. I had seen the positive public response to her husband at several engagements. She had been well schooled and gave me a nice sound bite as an answer. They had just celebrated their twenty-first wedding anniversary and Nick was enjoying being in an 'exclusive club of one—the only husband of a democratically elected president in the world'.

Arising out of the first-year documentary, RTÉ took the decision to mark the Robinson presidency with an in-depth television programme that would be compiled over the course of the remainder of her seven-year term and broadcast in the middle of 1997. The idea was very much driven by Ed Mulhall, who was a senior newsroom executive at that time. It was a forward-thinking idea and the type of project appropriate for RTÉ's commitment to public-service broadcasting.

Over the following six years, along with my colleagues, Denis Devane and Michael Lee, I was given unprecedented access to Robinson, although everything went through Bride Rosney, Robinson's formidable advisor who was central to the entire operation in Áras an Uachtaráin. It had become apparent to me during the 1990 presidential election that the two women were very close. Bride kept a close eye on what we were up to with the documentary but was always encouraging and helpful. We established a regular routine of meeting in Bewley's Café in Grafton Street to discuss the work in progress and my requests for more access. We didn't get everything we asked for but the behind-the-scenes access was a first.

It was a slow process and it certainly took time to build confidence but I think that, over the following six years, I established a decent rapport with Robinson. She was a shy person who took time to get to know people. That was just her personality. But on top of that, she was the President of Ireland and was always conscious of the position she held. I think that out of respect for the office of President, she deliberately kept her distance. It wasn't aloofness but more a formality and respectfulness which, I have to say, I admired. Over the course of her presidency, I developed huge admiration for the way she went about the job.

Mary Robinson was not the type of person who, at the end of a day's work, would come, sit down and unwind over a few drinks. We followed her around when she was fulfilling her official duties—in places like South Africa with Nelson Mandela, Washington with Bill Clinton and London with Queen Elizabeth—but there wouldn't be any swapping of stories afterwards. She did her job and we did ours. Her husband, Nick, was certainly easier to talk with and he would make a point of always chatting to us.

There were occasions near the end of her presidency when the more relaxed side of Mary Robinson's personality came out. I remember we travelled to Inis Meáin—the President had gone to the island to learn Irish not long after her election—and, after a day's filming, she joined the crew for a drink in the evening time. It was funny but there was the President buying a round. But it was funnier still when she went to the bar to pay for the drinks and had no cash. However, she saved her blushes by producing a chequebook from her handbag.

There is no doubt that Robinson was President during a period of great transformation in Ireland. She was, I really believe, the right person to be President at that particular time in our history. As we followed her at various stages over the duration of her seven-year term, I was convinced of the genuine warmth that people felt towards her. There was real pride in having this woman as President. She did the job so well from Somalia to South Africa, and all the places in between.

We generally travelled ahead of the main presidential entourage so as to be ready to film her arrival at whatever destination she was visiting. There were a few times when we were all on the same plane, including one particular journey from New York to Washington. It was an afternoon flight on a commercial airline and the Irish contingent was all seated together. As we flew between the two cities, an almighty thunderstorm started, with dramatic lightning filling up the sky outside our aircraft. Then, all of sudden, the plane started to drop. There was total panic in the cabin. It was terrifying. I said to myself, 'If this is it, well at least I'm going to die along with the first women President of the Irish Republic. I'm guaranteed a footnote in history.' My pessimism was, however, overplayed, because we did eventually land safely. When I caught sight of Mary Robinson, I realised that she had also had thoughts of impending doom—her face was totally drained; she was completely white.

I travelled with Robinson to the White House where she met Bill Clinton in the Oval Office in June 1996. As the media pack was escorted in to meet Clinton and Robinson, I remembered Conor O'Clery of *The Irish Times* telling me that Clinton had visited Trinity College in Dublin at the end of the 1960s when Robinson was also a student there.

Robinson and Clinton discussed the peace process in Ireland and they were asked about the possibility of a new IRA ceasefire.

There was time for a handful of questions at the end of the meeting so I decided to ask Clinton about his visit to Trinity. With Robinson by his side, Clinton burst out laughing. 'Have you been checking up my files?' he responded. The moment captured the mood in the Oval Office. While it was somewhat outside the main story of the Robinson–Clinton meeting, I thought it made great television and edited my report that evening to include the hearty Clinton laugh. But the producer back in Dublin had another opinion. When I got back to Dublin a few days later and had a look at the tapes from the various reports I had filed from the US, I discovered that to shave some time off my Oval Office TV package, the Clinton laugh had been cut out. I couldn't believe it.

Mary Robinson was well aware of the limitations of her job. The President has no political power, but Robinson was convinced that symbolism could be a powerful compensation for the things she could not comment on directly. When she first walked in the doors of Áras an Uachtaráin, the peace process in Northern Ireland was still developing in the background. But Robinson was, like many other people, fully aware of the political possibilities that would open up should the IRA end its military campaign. With the visits to Northern Ireland right from the start of her presidency, she was putting down markers; likewise her trips to Britain were about normalising relations between the two countries.

Funnily enough, her eventual visit to Buckingham Palace actually caused less opposition than many people had anticipated. It was nothing like the controversy generated by a visit to Belfast in June 1993. Whenever she went north of the border, she was always conscious of being balanced. So, for every visit, we found ourselves reporting on functions in nationalist areas followed by similar engagements in loyalist areas.

In the summer of 1993, she was invited to a community event in west Belfast. Gerry Adams was one of the local public representatives, and was going to be present. It is easy now to forget just how much of a pariah Adams was back in 1993. The IRA had not called its first ceasefire. As an RTÉ journalist, I could not broadcast an interview with Adams but here was the Irish President going to shake his hand. It was a huge story.

Some people were not too pleased to see Robinson when she visited a women's centre in a loyalist area. There were catcalls. One man yelled, 'You're not welcome here.' But all day in Belfast, as Robinson went through the itinerary of her visit, there was only one question—would she shake Adams's hand? And the obvious follow-on for a television reporter—would we capture the handshake on camera?

I was in the room in the community centre in west Belfast when Robinson arrived. She was introduced to a long line of local community activists and public representatives. And then she was face to face with Adams. To be fair to him, he didn't make a big deal of it. 'Céad Míle Fáilte,' he said as they shook hands. And then it was over. The President moved on to someone else in the hall.

John Major's government in London was furious. I was aware of the deep unhappiness—particularly in the Labour Party section of the then coalition government—with her actions. Relations between Mary Robinson and Dick Spring were tetchy. Spring was Minister for Foreign Affairs for most of the period Robinson was President. I reported on several foreign trips undertaken by Spring and from what I picked up, I understood that they had a strained relationship.

Whatever about the controversy over the Belfast trip and the Adams handshake, there was a real sense of occasion about Robinson's visit to Buckingham Palace in June 1996. She had been to Britain on 14 occasions since becoming President but, unlike previous trips, this was an 'official visit'. There were still political sensitivities to her visit—Robinson was a guest of the British government and not the monarch. There was a protocol dispute about how she would be announced at the various functions and engagements. 'President of Ireland' was politically sensitive and was guaranteed to have unionists up in arms. In the end, the diplomats settled on the title 'President Mary Robinson', with no reference to what exactly she was president of.

There was only one story and one set of images—the trip to Buckingham Place. We had two crews recording every moment. It was one of those occasions when I got goose pimples on a story. The red carpet was out at the front entrance to the palace where President Mary Robinson received a formal welcome from Queen Elizabeth and her son, Prince Edward. I'm not a person for fashion but I still remember the colours that morning. The British Queen wore pink. The Irish

President wore green. John Major described the day as 'a unique and historic occasion'. He was right.

Nick Robinson and Queen Elizabeth stood and watched—like the rest of us—as the President and Prince Edward walked to inspect the guard of honour. The Irish Guards stood tall in their red coats and fluffy black headgear. Then the moment arrived when the military band played Amhrán na bhFiann. We had heard over and over that the President was above politics with no real political power. But for me that day in Buckingham Place was about real politics. The divisions between Britain and Ireland were being healed in a whole variety of ways.

After her lunch with the British Queen, I interviewed Robinson and asked a question that I would put to her on more than one occasion— 'What about a visit by Queen Elizabeth to Ireland?' Robinson's reply never really changed—any visit would depend upon circumstances, but she would welcome it. The visit did not take place during her time in Áras an Uachtaráin and has not taken place yet.

———

In April 1996, we travelled ahead of the presidential entourage to South Africa, so we were ready at the airport to record President Mary Robinson coming off her plane and being greeted by President Nelson Mandela. There was, however, some delay, and we were waiting in a small VIP room in the terminal building near the runway where the red carpet had been rolled out.

I was standing, chatting to Ed O'Loughlin and Nicola Byrne, two Irish reporters who were then based in South Africa. Suddenly the door opened wide and Nelson Mandela walked into the waiting room. He came over, and there were handshakes and a few words for us all. He quickly focused all his attention on Nicola.

'Young lady, come here,' he said. Nicola moved closer to him

'Are you married?' Mandela playfully enquired.

'Not yet,' Nicola quickly replied.

There was some laughter.

'Well, if I was younger, I would ask you to marry me,' he responded with a glint in his eye.

The jovial banter ended with the announcement that the plane carrying the Irish President had touched down and was taxiing towards the terminal building. Mandela bade us goodbye and went to greet Robinson as a military band played the national anthems of Ireland and South Africa.

As I watched the scene on the runway, I received a call from Seán O'Rourke back in Dublin. It was a quiet news day—would I do a radio interview about Robinson's arrival in South Africa for the *News at One*? So, on a phone line from Cape Town, I recounted Robinson's arrival and the words of welcome spoken by President Mandela. Then, near the end of the interview with Seán, I told the story of waiting in the terminal building and of how Mandela had jokingly suggested marriage to an Irish reporter. Within half an hour, the story was running on every international news service, while, back in Dublin, the *Evening Herald* changed its front page to give space to Nicola Byrne's impending marriage! It was a funny example of how a story just takes off. Needless to say, the South African President—who at that time was not long divorced from his first wife, Winnie—went on to marry again but not Nicola Byrne.

There were many highlights of the South African visit in 1996. We visited Robben Island where Mandela had spent 27 years imprisoned during the apartheid era. I recall the heat and the dust in the island's lime quarry where Mandela and other members of the African National Congress had been forced to crush rock. It was a picture event with powerful images for a television report I filed for the news later that day. However, Ed Mulhall, who was on the trip as producer of the ongoing Robinson documentary, decided that the occasion should be marked while we were there. So, I filed a short audio report for 2FM News, signing off—Charlie Bird, 2FM News, Robben Island.

At a state banquet in the Tuynhuy residence of the South African President, Mandela displayed more interest in Irish women when he got Mary Robinson up onto the dance floor. I couldn't believe it: the two presidents, dancing.

Nelson Mandela is, without doubt, the most charismatic person I have met in my entire life. I first met him in June 1990 when he came to Dublin to receive the freedom of the city. He had actually been made a freeman of Dublin in 1988 but was able to receive the honour in person only after his release from prison which had occurred earlier in

1990, following 27 years in captivity. A new era was dawning in South Africa and he was saying 'Thank you' to those around the world who had battled to end the apartheid system. His journey to Ireland was part of that process.

Mandela arrived in Dublin on the same day that Jack Charlton and the international soccer squad were due to arrive back from the World Cup. Two big news stories on the same day—either would have presented all sorts of logistical challenges for the RTÉ newsroom as a single story. Of course, there was an added complication—traffic.

Charlton and his players had reached the quarter finals of Italia '90. On the night before their arrival home, I had done a report for the main evening news on the excitement sweeping the capital. Unfortunately the Irish team lost 1-0 to the Italians in the quarter finals but they had achieved more than anyone had expected. National pride was running high.

Some 300,000 people filled the streets to welcome the team home. The ten-mile route from the airport into the centre of the capital was lined with green, white and orange. There was hardly room to move with all the soccer fans. I had moved on from the soccer story, however, as now I was assigned to the Mandela arrival. To avoid the crowds, RTÉ decided to hire a helicopter, which was waiting at Dublin Airport to get me—and the tape of Mandela's arrival—back to Montrose in time for the lunchtime television news.

We had the helicopter sorted out, but when I got to Dublin Airport, it was not certain that there would be much of story. An official greeting was scheduled for when the ANC leader came off his plane but there was a problem. 'No interviews until later in the day,' was the official line—a few pictures of Mandela, but no sound actuality. 'He'll take questions when he gets to the Mansion House,' we were told.

This left me without a strong story. Suddenly I started to wonder if I would be better off covering the rapturous scenes greeting the World Cup soccer heroes. As I tried to work out what to do, I caught sight of Gerry Collins across the tarmac. Collins was Minister for Foreign Affairs and was leading the welcoming party. I made eye contact with him and he came across to the barrier behind which the media were located.

'Is there any possibility of a few words with Mandela for the lunchtime news?' I asked.

'I'm not sure what the plan is,' Collins replied, which wasn't much use to me.

'Do what you can,' I replied.

There was great excitement when Mandela came down the steps of his plane. Here was a man who had spent 27 years in prison for the right of black people to be treated the same as their white counterparts in South Africa. What I found so amazing was the generosity he showed when he was released from prison. But now what I needed was a few words with him.

Collins was introducing Mandela to a line of dignitaries. They strolled along the red carpet, with Collins guiding Mandela towards the terminal building. I became aware that they were not walking in a straight line; instead, Collins shepherded Mandela towards where I was standing with the RTÉ camera crew. To be honest, I am not convinced that Mandela was sure who I was—another dignitary or diplomat? He actually put out his hand to shake mine. I was overcome and babbled out a question or two—enough for us to get a few words for the television news. We had our story.

I have made several visits to South Africa. Not long after Mandela was released, I reported on the changes in the country as it geared up for a world beyond apartheid. In the Transvaal, I met a white farmer who chillingly told me, 'I will take up arms. It's our land.' And a white taxi driver agreed to be filmed as he openly told me that all blacks were 'shits'. I remember he was blunt and personally very honest. 'There's nothing wrong with being a racist,' he said.

In the early 1990s, South Africa faced a stark choice between anarchy and democracy, I believe. The problems were not just tied up with the strident views of the white farmer and racist taxi driver. Travelling around the country, I saw huge poverty. The conditions in which people were living in the townships were truly awful. Crime was out of control. The country's murder rate was the highest in the world. Every day, around 40 people were murdered.

It is to Nelson Mandela's considerable personal credit that these negative factors did not threaten the emergence of black rule. Nothing sticks in my memory like the first post-apartheid multi-party elections in 1994. I arrived in South Africa as the election campaign was coming to an end, in late April. I filed a couple of news stories on the final days of electioneering and the electoral strength of the ANC.

I remember visiting Gavin and Mary Beck, a white family who ran a fast-food business. In a magnificent setting at Westville, the Beck family home had spectacular scenic views. The couple had two school-going children, and Mary was concerned about maintaining education standards. Gavin was worried about foreign investment. 'We don't want to become another African banana republic,' he told me.

A huge international monitoring operation was in place for when the polling booths opened on 27 April. There were long queues as millions of South Africans went out to vote. As with all the other blacks in South Africa, this was the first time Mandela would vote in a non-racial, free and democratic election. I remember the day very well because I had got accreditation to cover the polling station where Mandela was due to cast his vote. It was going to be the image of the election.

Our transportation arrived at about 4 a.m. International reporters climbed aboard the bus, including myself and my colleagues, cameraman Colm O'Byrne and soundman Jarleth Tierney. We were being taken to the Ohlange High School at Inanda in the Natal province. The location had huge symbolism for the ANC—this was where John L. Dube, the man who established the Ohlange School, had founded the organisation in 1912.

It was still dark when we arrived along the dirt track that led to the schoolhouse. Voters were already in line outside. There was also a large media presence. South African television, CNN and several other rolling news stations were broadcasting live from the polling station. The journalists had formed an orderly queue outside the entrance to the small whitewashed schoolhouse where Mandela would vote.

The media line stretched down a small hill. Most of the foreign journalists, including the RTÉ crew, were at the end of the queue. There was great excitement when Mandela's motorcade arrived shortly after the polling station opened at 7 a.m. The man who was on the verge of becoming President of the new South Africa stepped out of his car. He moved slowly but had smiles for all around him. We had been told that he would go straight to the main door of the polling station. But Mandela had other ideas. He walked slowly around the side of the building to where Dube's grave was located. 'Out of the darkness into the glorious light,' the inscription on the headstone read.

When Mandela had finished paying his respects, he started to walk back towards the polling station, but his route meant that he was walking alongside the media queue, and walking from the back of the queue upwards. Several handlers surrounded him. I saw my opportunity and shouted out a question. He stopped, looked in my direction and came over.

'Can I ask you, who will you vote for today?' I said.

A broad smile came across his face.

'I've been agonising over that question,' he responded. 'When I decide, it will be a secret.'

In his autobiography, *Long Walk to Freedom*, Mandela wrote about voting at Ohlange High School.

> Before I entered the polling station, an irreverent member of the press called out, 'Mr Mandela, who are you voting for?' I laughed. 'You know,' I said, 'I have been agonising over the choice all morning'.

The other reporters were clambering to get near what until a few moments earlier had been the worst position in the queue. I still had an opportunity to put another question.

'What does this day mean for you?' I asked.

'This is a historic day for which our people have struggled. It's the realisation of our hopes and our dreams. And it's an unforgettable moment,' Mandela responded.

South Africa had a new President. Along with Bryan Dobson and Seán O'Rourke, I reported on the inauguration ceremony in Pretoria in early May. It was remarkable how smoothly the elections and transition to ANC rule had gone. It was one of those amazing days. Having filed my new reports, I walked among the crowds in Pretoria. Hundreds of thousands of people were out on the streets. They were singing and dancing. The scenes were a dramatic mixture of a rock concert and a political rally. People were hugging and crying. Two decades previously, I had gone on anti-apartheid marches in Dublin. Many people had grown up with the anti-apartheid movement. The story had come full circle that day in Pretoria—in the midst of the colour and the music of Mandela's new South Africa. I was very moved by the occasion. South Africa was in transition and the poverty in the townships showed just how much work the new ANC government had to do, but with the presence Nelson Mandela radiated, I felt that something special was happening; it was amazing to experience even a little of that.

At the start of 1997, I was aware of the hard decision Mary Robinson was facing. Did she want a second term? We recorded some material for our documentary while walking along a beach in County Mayo. She talked about 'stocktaking'. Throughout the previous year, there had been continuous speculation about her moving on to a big international position. The top job in the United Nations had been mentioned.

On 12 March 1997, Robinson confirmed that she would not be seeking a second term as President. 'I have made my contribution,' she said. I think there was some annoyance in John Bruton's coalition that I had an interview recorded with the President about her decision before it had been conveyed to the government. The minute the Áras confirmed her decision not to seek re-election, RTÉ was able to broadcast the audio of the interview.

The documentary now had a natural ending. Her final day of engagements was very emotional. There was a function in Abbeyleix in the morning. Schoolchildren lined the streets of the County Laois town. I remember asking some of them what they thought of her. All the responses were glowing. When I asked who had been President before Mary Robinson, there was silence. It was confirmation that she had done her job well. Later that same day, we travelled to an event in County Wicklow. But what I remember most was the final interview I did with her as President.

We were invited into the family kitchen in Áras an Uachtaráin. The Robinsons were incredibly private despite the high profile that went with the job of President. I had seen them up close over a number of years but there was still a distance. They valued their privacy, the little they had of it. The presidency was 'a bit like being in a goldfish bowl on top of a pedestal,' was how Robinson once described the attention to me.

They kept their children out of the spotlight. I said 'hello' to them once or twice in the Áras but there was never any question of the children featuring in a prominent way on camera. So, because of this strong divide between the public and private, it was interesting to be invited into the family area where there were family photographs on the walls. The famous light to the Irish community abroad was positioned in the kitchen window. Over the previous six-and-a-half years, it had been one of the powerful symbols of the Robinson presidency.

I got to interview Mary and Nick as they sat at the Robinson kitchen table. She was far more relaxed than at any time on camera over the previous seven years. There were more laughs and she even ventured into the political arena with a very interesting observation about modern Ireland:

> I think there is a widening divide in Irish society as we become more prosperous. It's widening because for some people life is looking very good and our economy is developing; if you have a job, you have very good prospects and your tax position is probably better off. But then that makes others more left out—they may not be worse off materially but they feel more left out.

———

Robinson may have departed Áras an Uachtaráin—and the RTÉ documentary chronicling her seven years been broadcast—but our paths crossed on another memorable occasion. As United Nations High Commissioner for Human Rights, Robinson had pressurised the Chinese authorities into giving her permission to visit Tibet.

I was starting an assignment covering Bertie Ahern's visit to China when Robinson arrived in Beijing. I filed a couple of stories during her visit, including a meeting with the country's President. Her trip to Tibet promised to be controversial as it was expected that she would use the opportunity to raise the issue of human rights abuses of the local population by the Chinese authorities. I put in a request to accompany Robinson on the trip as did Conor O'Clery who was at that time his newspaper's Asia Correspondent based in Beijing and, as always, had been very welcoming to me in the time since I had arrived in the Chinese capital.

Word came back that I was to be given accreditation for the Tibet trip but Conor O'Clery was refused permission to travel. It was a very unusual decision which I found difficult to understand. Conor was, however, firmly of the view that Robinson was score-settling for his critical coverage of her visit to South America when she was President of Ireland. The South American trip certainly left its mark—the controversy makes its way into both Robinson's official biography and Conor Brady's memoir of his time as Editor of *The Irish Times*.

Paddy Higgins was the RTÉ cameraman on the trip. We were accompanied as we had been during all our time in China by a government minder. He was an official from the Foreign Ministry who knew a little bit about Ireland and had met us as we first came off our flight in Beijing. Now, on our way to Tibet, he was again keeping a watchful eye on me and 'Mr Paddy Higgins' as he called the RTÉ cameraman.

Tibet is sometimes known as the Roof of the World, and for very good reason. In places, the height is some 16,000 feet above sea level in this elevated region in central Asia. We arrived in the city of Lhasa early in the morning, conscious of warnings about the impact of altitude sickness which hits most visitors to the region. The sickness is caused by breathing the rarefied air at such a high altitude. The lack of oxygen hit me like a thunderbolt. I got this almighty headache and felt totally short of breath. I smiled when I first came into the hotel bedroom to see an oxygen bottle beside the bed. I needed it. The advice was to stay awake to help the acclimation process, and it worked, with the splitting pain in my head gradually easing as the day went on. Lhasa was stunning. It was one of the most amazing places I had ever visited. Flags, ribbons and scarves were tied to every lamppost. Prayer wheels were positioned at the entrance to the Potala Palace which dominates the city. People touched these wheels as they passed, in acts of meditation. Candles were burning everywhere. It was a deeply spiritual place.

The Chinese kept a tight grip on the visit. Robinson was walking straight into the longstanding dispute over the legitimacy of Chinese rule and claims that traditional Tibetan culture and identity were being deliberately destroyed by the authorities in Beijing. The Dalai Lama, the spiritual leader of the Tibetan people, had been in exile from his country since the late 1950s. Robinson had no serious interaction with ordinary Tibetans. We visited some magnificent temples and palaces, including the Potala Palace, one of the most important sites in Tibetan cultural history, which had once been home to the Dalai Lama. Robinson surprised her hosts by asking to meet one of the leading Tibetan monks who had previously been jailed by the Chinese. The response came the following day—she was politely told that the monk could not be found.

The Chinese authorities were responsible for all our movements. Monks sympathetic to the Chinese took us around the city. They were expecting Robinson to raise the issue of human rights abuses but we were warned that we would not be allowed to film Robinson making her remarks. The visit was never going to be easy. 'I'm not a comfortable presence for the Chinese,' Robinson told me.

The news that our filming was to be limited produced a bit of a stand-off between the government minder and myself before it was agreed as a compromise that we could film Robinson's opening comments at her meeting with local dignitaries. Robinson then surprised her Chinese guests by mentioning the controversial subject right at the start of the speech. Paddy Higgins had his camera on his shoulder, filming Robinson. But not for long.

Our minder from the Foreign Ministry intervened. He literally started to pinch Paddy all over his body. 'You're pinching me,' Paddy shouted as he jumped out of the man's way.

'You're not meant to be doing this,' the minder said as he continued to pinch the RTÉ cameraman. The strategy worked because eventually Paddy could not hold the camera and we were both forcefully manhandled out of the room. Despite the commotion, and to her credit, Robinson succeeded in delivering her points about the human rights abuses in Tibet.

Meanwhile, a blazing row ensued. 'You pinched my cameraman,' I shouted.

To my amazement, the minder responded, 'I didn't. I didn't touch him.'

He was denying to our faces what had happened only a few short moments earlier. The pinching strategy was obviously one that had been thought up previously and, on that day, it worked successfully for the Chinese.

Chapter 6 ～

FOREIGN TRAVELS

For a time in 1990, the phrase 'Charlie Bird, A-man' became a bit of a joke. I arrived in Amman—the capital of Jordan—in early August 1990 just after the Iraqi invasion of Kuwait. I spent most of the following month reporting on the growing crisis in the Gulf region, regularly ending news reports with the sign-off, Charlie Bird, RTÉ News, Amman'. The joke stuck.

Amman was the closest location for broadcasting purposes, so the entire media world descended on the Jordanian city. The country was officially neutral and would remain so throughout the crisis. I booked into the Marriott Hotel. The tourists were departing as the media sought out every available room. The man behind the check-in desk handed me my room key and a roll of Sellotape. All residents were advised to tape up the windows in their rooms in case Saddam Hussein approved a chemical attack. While Jordan was neutral, it was a country centred between Iraq and Israel, and there was no knowing what Saddam had planned.

It was a time of considerable tension. Iraqi troops easily overwhelmed the small pockets of resistance in Kuwait. The United Nations speedily passed a resolution condemning the invasion and demanding a withdrawal of Iraqi troops. American soldiers moved into Saudi Arabia on 7 August as the long build up to the first Gulf War commenced.

While the diplomatic manoeuvrings were going on, Saddam Hussein detained thousands of westerners working in Iraq. They were, in effect, hostages and a potential bargaining chip for the Iraqi regime. A number of Irish people working in Baghdad had not been allowed to leave Iraqi. They had an unusual status—they were not prisoners in the conventional sense as they could move around but they were being prevented from leaving Baghdad. They were 'guests of the nation'—Saddam's nation.

During this period, I made two trips to Baghdad, a city waiting for the Americans to attack. Getting a visa was not easy. Up to 100 journalists queued every day at the Iraqi Embassy in Amman. RTÉ would not normally be high up the accreditation list at such times but because of the Irish workers, I was granted a visa.

I arrived in Baghdad on an old Iraqi Airways 707 jet. With restrictions on air travel, there was a three-day turnaround in flights. One of the Irish workers met me at the airport. As we drove into the centre of the city, all the famous images of Saddam were in front of me. His face adorned buildings, and statues were prominently placed at many junctions.

Baghdad was a city filled with tension. There was a government minder with me for the entire time I was in Iraq. It was the first time I had experienced such close monitoring. Each report I filed had to be shown to the official censor before it was sent back to Dublin. Every image and every word was being monitored. Despite this, I never had any difficulty, but the atmosphere was intimidating.

Many of the Irish workers were living in what was known as Apartment Block 34. They were being well looked after but they wanted to go home. 'Guest is a polite word,' one man said in an interview for one of the many reports I filed on their situation. They were key medical personnel who were under contract. The authorities kept saying that the Irish workers would be released only when replacements were available. I interviewed the speaker of the Iraqi parliament. 'Why won't you release these Irish nurses and doctors?' I asked. He shifted around in his chair and grew more uncomfortable when I told him that I had spoken to nurses who had cried because they could not go home. It was one of those occasions when it was obvious that the man in front of the camera deeply regretted having agreed to an interview.

There was limited freedom to move around the city, but I did take a walk through one of the main market areas. I bought a small, dark red carpet and ran into John Simpson of the BBC who was haggling over the price of an old gramophone player. But even in the market, there was no opportunity to talk with ordinary Iraqis. My minder was at my shoulder and, in any event, the local population was particularly cagey about dealing with foreigners.

I made a second trip to Baghdad a few weeks later when a delegation of TDS, including Michael D. Higgins, Paul Bradford and David Andrews, visited the city to lobby on behalf of the Irish workers. When I was leaving the city, having covered the visit, I ran into some difficulty at the airport. My baggage and belongings were checked by Iraqi soldiers who pulled out my stash of dollars—the only currency to get around in Baghdad. I was afraid that the money—about one thousand dollars in all—was going to be taken from me. 'It's my money,' I said firmly. Having listened to me repeating this sentence over and over for about ten minutes, the soldier eventually waved me through along with my hard currency.

As the build-up to war continued, thousands of people fled Iraq and Kuwait, and for many of them the disputed border region between Iraq and Jordan offered a form of safety. The Jordanian authorities opened the desert border crossing but they were totally unprepared for the numbers arriving. Three hundred kilometres outside Amman, a makeshift tent city appeared like a mirage in the desert.

When I first travelled out to the hastily erected refugee camp, there were about 50,000 people trying to survive in sweltering heat. The conditions were terrible. There were only half a dozen makeshift toilets for all these people, while food and water were in short supply. International aid agencies were arriving in a frantic attempt to limit the scale of the unfolding tragedy. From what I could see, many of these people had fled their homes with a single suitcase containing their most precious belongings. Jordanian soldiers used sticks to try to keep order. Most of the people just wanted the conflict to be over so that they could return to their homes and a peaceful life.

I came and went from the region over the latter half of 1990. With Saddam Hussein ignoring the resolutions passed by the United Nations, the threat of war never left the Gulf. In mid-January 1991, a massive air operation, led by the United States, began; it was called Operation Desert Storm. A few reporters were based in Baghdad as missiles reigned down on the Iraqi capital city. Maggie O'Kane from the *Guardian* was one of the last to leave. She had started her career in RTÉ and, like another Irish journalist, Orla Guerin, blazed a trail as an exceptionally talented foreign correspondent. They were two of the bravest reporters produced by RTÉ and I had huge admiration for them as they carved out very successful careers in British journalism.

Many reporters had left the city. Peter Arnett of CNN, a veteran news reporter, was the last journalist in the city, and the world watched his dramatic reports to find out more about what was happening to Saddam's regime.

By the time the US attacked Baghdad, I was back in Amman, staying again at the Marriott Hotel. The BBC's John Simpson arrived from the Iraqi capital and was booked into a room two doors down from me. Simpson was a story himself, having been expelled by the authorities in Iraq. I was on air continuously, doing live reports for television and radio. I experienced a mixture of fear and excitement. Amman was deserted. The Sellotape was now very much up on the windows in our bedrooms. We had been told that Saddam would use chemical weapons but I am thankful that never came to pass. However, we were not to know that, when the sirens sounded and there was a mad rush down to the basement of the hotel.

On foreign assignments, I always pack a shortwave radio; it is generally a good source of news from the wider world when there is no local radio service and no access to international newspapers. The radio was in my shoulder bag as I set off, with a group of other reporters, for Israel. With Baghdad closed off to the media, most reporters moved between Amman in Jordan and Tel Aviv in Israel. As the war continued, Saddam launched scud missile attacks on the US-led coalition bases in Saudi Arabia, as well as on Israel, in the hope of widening the war in the Gulf.

Our convoy was stopped about 20 kilometres from the Jordanian border with Israel. The Jordanian soldiers were tetchy with us as they searched our bags. After a few minutes, we were told to move on. But as we climbed back into our car, I discovered that my radio was missing. 'They're after stealing my radio,' I said.

A reporter colleague from Finland was indignant. 'Go back in and get it,' he insisted.

I asked to see the officer in charge but I was getting nowhere.

'I am sorry but you are wrong,' I was told in very hesitant English.

'Your King told us all the journalists would be safe,' I kept repeating as I tried to get my annoyance across to the young soldier.

But my protests were to no avail, and so we set off again on our journey. We were approaching the border itself when our car was again stopped.

'Wait,' the officer said without any explanation and we sat in the car in the desert for about 20 minutes. We had no idea what was going on when eventually a Land Rover sped up alongside our car. A senior officer got out and, without a word, handed over the shortwave radio.

The journey from the Jordanian capital into Jerusalem took about six hours. It was an amazing trip along the Dead Sea. I spent a few days in Jerusalem before moving on to Tel Aviv where I was relieved to have my Irish army-issued special protective suit and face mask to guard against the threat of a chemical or biological attack by Saddam. Any missiles from Iraq would come in over the water. Most of the big television networks had booked out the buildings by the waterside which gave their cameras the best shots in the event of a missile attack. Some of the American stations had even booked apartments that they did not need, just to ensure that the buildings were not available to their main competitors.

The warning sirens went dozens of times when I was in Tel Aviv. It was frightening stuff as we all put on the protective suits and waited. Fortunately, none of the scud missiles did any great damage, but one missile attack on an American army base in Saudi Arabia left 28 US soldiers dead. That attack emphasised the danger posed by a missile attack and stressed the importance of having protective suits in the event of a nuclear or biological attack.

I was glad to have my shortwave radio to keep abreast of developments in the war, which came to an end towards the end of February when a chastened Saddam gave the order for his troops to withdraw from Kuwait. Along with my radio, my travel bag usually contains chocolate and a small medicine pack including plasters and throat lozenges. Sometimes I bring a sleeping bag and a mosquito net. Space is always left for a supply of dollars. In more recent years, RTÉ has become much more professional in its approach to foreign news assignments. The old days when reporters were given bottles of whiskey and forced to beg from the BBC are, I am glad to say, now long gone.

Reporting on the conflict in the Gulf region in 1990 was a huge challenge, but nothing prepared me for the scenes I witnessed a few months later as Saddam Hussein threatened revenge on the Kurds over their lack of loyalty during the war. The Kurds had been encouraged by George Bush senior's administration in Washington to rebel against Saddam's regime. But the Americans never followed through on their encouragement by supporting the Kurds when Saddam turned on them. In a matter of days, hundreds of thousands of people from northern Iraq arrived in southern Turkey. They were fleeing for their lives.

The images of these people quickly filled television screens. In RTÉ, the decision to travel to cover the story at first hand was made at lunchtime on a Friday. I remember it well—the quick dash to the airport and the relief when I made the flight. Unfortunately my luggage was less successful and did not arrive in Ankara. It was supposed to be an assignment of a couple of days, but the story was so dramatic that I ended up spending over two weeks. I made do without my luggage— lost somewhere between Dublin and Ankara—and made some purchases at the local markets.

The refugees had fled into Turkey not because of some crop failure or natural disaster. These were people with jobs and with homes—I remember meeting a man who was a pilot with Iraqi airlines. They had had to leave northern Iraq for fear of being killed. Turkey did not want these people and the international community was very slow to respond. Men, women and children were camped out on the side of a mountain. Their plight was heartbreaking. They were existing in a pitiful state, literally dying from the cold and starvation.

Getting to the area where the refugees were camped out was not easy. I used to hire a battered taxi in Diyarbakir. Some days, I would be unlucky enough to have a driver who had not travelled the route previously and it was a treacherous journey as he negotiated the muddy mountain roads. The car journey took five hours. It was followed by a walk to the foot of the mountain and then a trek of several thousand feet uphill. The other international media organisations had facilities to make their job somewhat easier; the BBC had even hired a helicopter. I was on my own with no facilities, hiring local camera crews every couple of days.

But these were minor complaints compared to what the Kurdish refugees were enduring. The scenes of suffering were incredibly moving. I lost count of the number of people I saw die before my very eyes; I saw little infants die. It was horrendous. One old man was trying desperately to dig a grave on the side of the mountain but without much success. I felt it was right to offer to help him. I took up a shovel and shouted at other reporters and camera crews to help. The old man was burying his daughter who had died from the cold. I lost my composure on a number of occasions. Tears ran down my face as I witnessed the awfulness of what was happening to the Kurds. It was nothing to do with politics; it was an honest human reaction. The people would thrust pieces of paper into the hands of reporters. They had written out the names and addresses of relatives in places like the Netherlands and Australia. They wanted us to make contact with these people to reassure them that their loved ones had got out of Iraq. When I eventually got back to Ireland, I followed up on many of those requests.

The coverage given to the plight of the Kurds brought out great generosity in Ireland. Millions of pounds were raised as people responded to the images in nightly news reports, and to the words of reporters like Deaglán de Bréadún of *The Irish Times*. Covering the plight of the Kurds was the first time I recall working alongside Deaglán. One evening, after we had both filed our separate reports, we took a walk on a mountainside road to see camp fires dotted along the darkened mountain. As we gazed at this truly remarkable sight, the sound of a gun could be heard. Some Turkish guards were keeping an eye on Iraqis coming across the nearby border. Fortunately they chose not to use their weapons on us.

The aid agencies were under great pressure. I remember one day looking for an interview with Paddy McGuinness of Concern. The local cameraman whom I had hired for the day was delayed. McGuinness had a job to do and could not wait for the cameraman despite the promise of publicity; I admired him all the more for this attitude. I filed radio reports from a nearby schoolhouse where many of the inter-national media had based themselves. There were always people coming and going. When I was phoning in reports, I covered my head with an anorak to try to drown out the background noise. On one occa-sion, I firmly but politely shouted, 'Would everybody shut up, please.'

It was while covering the story of the Kurds that I saw at first hand the way the news media move on when a big story is no longer a big story for editors and programme makers back at base. I was sitting in a hotel room used by many broadcasters to prepare their reports that were then sent back home by satellite feed. Jeremy Bowen of the BBC had just sent through a particularly moving report. He was on the phone to his bosses to check they had received it. The response was a signal that the attention of news was shifting away from the plight of the Kurds. 'Another great package, Jeremy, but I think we've had enough of the emotional pornography,' the man in London said.

The phrase 'emotional pornography' haunted me for many years afterwards. All big stories do come to an end but I think in more recent times there has been a greater responsibility about revisiting stories. I think of the Asian tsunami and the earthquake in Pakistan from my own reporting career. RTÉ covered these tragedies when they happened, but each story has been returned to on more than one occasion, to ensure that the public is informed about what has happened since the initial burst of publicity put the suffering of the affected local community onto the television screens. Rwanda is another good example. Stories about massacres in Rwanda began to make the news in the spring of 1994. I was in South Africa covering the first post-apartheid elections when the world started to pay attention to stories of bloodletting in the central African nation. Awful images of bodies hacked to death featured in news reports.

Back in Dublin, the RTÉ newsroom's Foreign Desk arranged a deal with Reuters to share facilities and costs on a trip to report on what was happening in Rwanda. I broke off from the election story and met my travelling companions at a small airport outside Johannesburg. A small plane had been hired to take us up to the Rwandan/Tanzanian border. There were seven or eight passengers—a South African cameraman who was working for RTÉ and a German reporter and his crew. The arrangement was that we would share all the pictures we shot on the trip. Aengus Finucane of Concern joined our travelling party. It was probably the first time I was able to offer him a seat, rather than the other way round.

Since their Belgian colonial masters had departed some 40 years earlier, ethnic violence between the majority Hutus and minority Tutsis had become a feature of life in Rwanda. The Hutus controlled all the levers of power. On 6 April, a plane carrying the President of Rwanda was shot down as it came in to land in Kigali. The President was a Hutu. The Tutsis were held responsible for his death. Violence re-emerged. Between April and June, around 800,000 Rwandans were slaughtered in the space of 100 days. Most of the dead were Tutsis. Television reports showed dead bodies of men, women and children floating in the Rwandan rivers.

The international community was slow to respond to what was emerging in Rwanda. The media were describing the bloodletting as

genocide. Our plan was to visit one of the biggest refugee camps populated by Tutsis who had fled the slaughter. The pilot of our light aircraft
was over 70 years old; as we took off from outside Johannesburg, I hoped
he was up to the long journey. We stopped for fuel at an airstrip outside
Harare in Zimbabwe, but were not allowed to leave the aircraft. By the
time we arrived in Dar es Salaam in Tanzania, it was after 2 a.m. We had
been flying for almost 11 hours. Everyone was totally exhausted and we
were still several hours from our final destination. Before we could continue any further, we needed clearance from the authorities in Tanzania.

We walked towards a small office at the far end of the airport, where
light aircraft landed. In the small hours of the morning, there was little
activity. I lined up with my travelling companions, passport in hand. As
the passport official checked my travel documentation, I heard someone making reference to 'yellow cards'. This documentation contained
details of vaccination records. There had been no need for 'yellow
cards' to get into South Africa, and I had no vaccination information
with me. We passed through passport control smoothly enough but
there was a problem at the 'yellow card' desk. And I was the problem.

'You need to have a yellow card to be allowed to enter Tanzania,' the
guy behind the desk told me.

'Look, I don't have mine with me,' was my honest response. 'My
passport is in order,' I added.

'But you have to have vaccination injections,' the official said.

He repeated this sentence several times as our exchange became
more heated.

I was tired and could see the others from my flight watching and
listening to what was quickly developing into a full-scale row. I could
sense their impatience to get moving after our long flight.

Suddenly the official had a solution. 'I can give you the injections,' he
offered, pointing to a grubby office behind the 'yellow card' desk. The
cramped building was filthy. And, to make matters worse, the official
who held my passport looked decidedly shifty. With images of dirty
needles, and an 11-hour flight behind me, I now completely lost my cool.

The German reporter appeared at my shoulder. 'Let me see your
passport,' he said. He then disappeared with the official, leaving me
fuming at the desk. A few minutes later, they both returned. The
official handed me back my passport and waved me through without
any further mention of yellow cards or vaccination injections.

'Say nothing,' the German advised me. I later learnt that he had slipped a fifty-dollar note into my passport before he handed it to the official. I was so caught up with the idea of dirty needles that I hadn't had the presence of mind to offer the guy a bribe. That, and not my health, had obviously been his priority.

To get to the capital of Tanzania we had travelled up from Johannesburg over Zimbabwe and part of Mozambique. With our travel documentation stamped, the stopover in Dar es Salaam was a short one. Our light aircraft was soon in the air again and we set off for the Tanzanian border area where Rwandan refugees had taken shelter from the massacres in their native country.

I marvelled at the ability and stamina of our septuagenarian pilot. He had just finished a physically draining journey, and now here we were, on a further three-hour flight across Tanzania. The pilot circled, looking for a suitable place to land the aircraft. Looking out the window, I could see tens of thousands of people dotted on the ground below. I could also see another plane at the end of what looked like an airstrip. It was, in reality, a wide dirt path, and the aircraft I was looking down on was actually turned upside down. It had apparently had a difficult landing. Fortunately our pilot got his bearings correct and we had a safe touchdown. My worries about his age were misplaced.

A couple of Concern volunteers greeted us as we climbed off the plane. We had a single day here. The pilot would be taking off from Dar es Salaam in 24 hours, with South Africa his final destination. What met us was a sea of humanity: 250,000 people scattered on the side of a valley with no water or food. They were sleeping under plastic sheets in makeshift camps, having fled their homes in fear of death.

I spent most of the day filming the refugees, hearing their stories of slaughter being translated into English. With my own eyes, I saw evidence of the savagery. One five-year-old boy had had his face mutilated. Like all of us, Aengus Finucane was horrified at the scene. 'Look at these children,' he said. 'How can they be blamed for anything?' There was little response to the horror stories we heard throughout the afternoon.

When the sun went down in the early evening, we travelled to the Cameroon Hotel. A single-storey structure made from corrugated metal, which served a little food and some warm beer, it was the most inappropriately named establishment I have ever encountered. The food was stored in large vats, and I decided to sample what seemed a type of stew. But I gagged when I saw bits of meat and a sheep's head bobbing up and down in the vat. I quickly pushed my bowl aside.

Aengus Finucane produced a bottle of vodka. It was without doubt the best offer since we had left South Africa. As we sat and talked about the awful stories we had heard throughout the day, the discussion turned to God. I felt really strongly about the subject and I know I didn't give Aengus an inch as argument railed within our little group which included the South African cameraman and some Concern workers.

'Please, explain to me why God would allow the slaughter of hundreds of thousands of innocent people,' I said.

Like all of us, Aengus had been distressed by the stories the Rwandan refugees had to tell. Now he was under pressure. 'Man does what man does. This is not God's work,' he explained.

I wasn't so certain about the answer. I had seen death before. The plight of the Kurds was to the forefront of my mind. The sheer butchery in Rwanda made me really angry.

I have never been sure about religion. When it comes to concepts like life after death, I really don't have a clue. I simply do not know the answer. I may die roaring but I am hoping to keep in with anybody who is out there. I honestly feel that nobody has the right to say, 'We know this is it.' Travelling to places like India and Somalia has made me realise that everyone's religion is not what we grew up with in Ireland.

After much heated discussion—and with the vodka polished off—we all tried to get some sleep. The Cameroon Hotel did not offer overnight accommodation. I remember trying with great difficulty to get a few hours' sleep in the back of a truck owned by Concern.

The next day, we returned to the dirt airstrip. The German reporter and his crew who had gone their own way the previous afternoon had not yet arrived. Concern had a separate plane about to take off so I went ahead. The Germans eventually arrived in Dar es Salaam a couple of hours later. We were pooling the material we got—this was a shared enterprise; all the pictures would be used when we got back to South Africa—and we started to compare notes.

As the Germans began to tell me what they had filmed, I became deeply embarrassed. While I was spending time talking to the refugees and aid workers—which was in itself a valid exercise—the German reporter had had the presence of mind to travel up towards the waterfalls. He had the images of mutilated bodies floating in the water. I am not sure why I became embarrassed but I knew that he had made better use of his time.

The bloodletting of the Hutus against the Tutsis was shocking. A number of years later, I returned to Rwanda to a place called Nyamata where, in the view of a local church, Hutus had massacred their Tutsi neighbours. In the space of a few hours, they had hacked around 5,000 innocent men, women and children to death. The local people later gathered skulls together and placed them inside the church as a memorial of sorts. There were still bits of flesh on some of the bones. Personal belongings of some of the dead were still scattered around the grounds of the church. It was difficult not to be moved. Tears filled my eyes. This was real hell. And, thinking back on that conversation with Aengus Finucane, I was still not sure I accepted his explanation about God's role.

As a consequence of the genocide in Rwanda, the country's prisons were full of Hutus. They were being held indefinitely with no prospect of early trials to determine their involvement, or otherwise, in the attacks on the Tutsi community. By the late 1990s, almost 100,000 Hutus were in prison. I remember, in particular, the prison at Butare which I visited in late 1995. What I witnessed chilled me. The prisoners wore a pinkish uniform. They were lifeless, showing no emotion. About 5,000 Hutus were held at Butare. Some of those in the cells were no more than boys. The conditions were inhumane—they were crowded into very small cells with little room to move. They had been there for well over a year, and, at that time, there was no prospect of early trials to determine their fate.

Of course, Rwanda is not alone in having a divided Hutu/Tutsi population. There was also deep hatred in Rwanda's neighbour, Burundi, a country I travelled to in 1995. We were in Bujumbura and shots could be heard in the distance. There was a real sense of anarchy. It was very much a 'get-in, get-out' trip. But as we were about to leave, the locals told us that a South African television crew had been shot dead by rebels on the road we were due to travel on to Tanzania. We were forced to revise our travel plans. Two days later, with gunfire still raging, we eventually set off. On our journey, we passed the place where the shooting had happened. There was still shattered glass on the side of the road. I was glad to get out of the country.

The other occasion when I realised that I was in over my head was during a trip to South Africa in the mid-1990s. I had bumped into

Fergal Keane, who had started his broadcasting career in RTÉ but who was now the BBC's South Africa Correspondent. I have met Fergal on numerous foreign assignments and have long been impressed by his generosity and his willingness to share resources and contacts. On this occasion, he insisted that the RTÉ camera crew and I come to a party in his house on Saturday night. We did and had a very pleasant evening in the company of Fergal and his wife, Anne Flaherty.

As we chatted in the Keane house, it emerged that Fergal had a full diary for the following day. 'We're going to follow Cyril Ramaposa into the Alexander township,' Fergal said, adding, 'Why don't you come along?' There was the possibility of a good story; there had been much violence in the area in the preceding weeks. Ramaposa, a senior ANC figure, was going to try to ease tensions but he was not certain of a warm welcome from the locals.

We had a quiet day planned for Sunday, with no satellite facilities available for sending material back to Dublin, so going into the Alexander township might give us another story. The following morning, we turned up at the BBC offices. 'Are you guys coming along?' a BBC producer asked. 'Yeah, Fergal invited us,' I replied. The producer pulled a face. 'I'm not sure that's such a good idea. If anything happens, you're on your own.'

Alarm bells started to go off in my head. Fergal's invitation was typical of his generosity. I also wanted to get the maximum out of what was a fairly short trip to South Africa, but I was out of my depth. I had to consider my own safety and that of the RTÉ crew who were with me. We had no bulletproof vests. We would be travelling in a hired car. And we really didn't know the situation on the ground. So we decided to give the Alexander trip a miss. We returned to our hotel. Later in the day, word came through of a shooting. A couple of people travelling in Ramaposa's convoy had been killed. Fortunately, I had made the correct decision.

For all its troubles, South Africa is still the beacon of light in the African continent. The years since the ending of apartheid have brought at least some stability. Rwanda and Burundi showed me another aspect of Africa. Somalia was somewhat similar. With a coastline along the Indian Ocean, Somalia has been crippled by years of fighting between rival warlords. After a coup against its Marxist president in 1991, the country descended into further lawlessness and anarchy. A failure to deal with famine and disease threatened the lives of up to one million people.

The worst of the fighting in Somalia took place between late 1991 and early 1992. Irish interest in the plight of the Somali people increased after a radio interview with Fiona O'Reilly from Dublin who was working as a nurse with an aid agency in the country. I met Fiona O'Reilly a few months later. She had a dramatic story to tell:

> It was a nightmare. We woke up every morning to the sounds of shells falling. And then we'd get to the hospital and what you'd meet was men, women and children blown apart. People have the idea that during war it's the fighters with the guns who get killed and wounded but when you see two-year olds with limbs missing because a shell dropped on their hands, it's a nightmare.

At Easter 1991, I travelled to Somalia with the RTÉ camera crew from Belfast, Johnny Coughlan and Paddy MacEntee. Both men were used to working in difficult circumstances in Northern Ireland, and we needed all the experience they could muster. The country's capital, Mogadishu, had been destroyed by indiscriminate shelling. Most people had already fled. Thousands of displaced people were on the verge of starvation. But this was a hidden hunger. People were not in the familiar refugee camps so much a part of this type of humanitarian disaster, but were instead in urban areas, hiding from the gun battles going on all around them. 'We are living in a dark world,' Omar Sabrie, a university lecturer, told me.

I was genuinely scared in Mogadishu. The first night in the city, we stayed with a young American student, Herby Ludwig. He had bizarrely remained behind as the sole representative of one of the United Nations organisations which had already left because of the fighting. He travelled with local militia members for protection. Within minutes of our arriving at the house where Ludwig was staying, a major gun battle erupted between two rival factions. Within moments, Johnny Coughlan, with his training from Belfast, was on the roof of the house, filming the battle. I was crouched down for safety inside the house as bullets bounced off the marble walls of this once-fine residence. Eventually a calm of sorts was restored but the next morning we left Herby and his gunmen protectors behind. It was just too dangerous.

We swapped Herby's house for the relative safety of the local building where the Red Cross had set up a makeshift hospital. For the next few nights, we slept on the roof of this building. It was a strange environment. From the roof you could see the majestic blue of the Indian Ocean, while below us injured people just kept on arriving.

The difficult security situation in Mogadishu placed huge pressure on Geoff Loane, the County Tipperary man who was working with the Red Cross and who had the task of minding the visiting RTÉ crew. Loane was a remarkable individual. Today, he is the representative of the International Committee of the Red Cross in Washington and one of the few people to have limited access to the prisoners held by the United States at Guantanamo Bay in Cuba.

Thousands of the victims of the civil war in Somalia needed help. The aid agencies faced a desperate battle to get food, water and medicine to the people. I remember, we travelled to a prison which had been converted into a makeshift hospital. The wounded were arriving every day, nearly all needing treatment for gunshot wounds. One person remains in my memory—Jerry Hayward-Karlsson, a nurse in her late thirties from Somerset in England. She had been working with the Red Cross. Somalia was not her first job for an aid agency. Jerry had been married six weeks previously. She had returned to Somalia and her husband to Afghanistan. I interviewed Jerry in a makeshift hospital. 'We get the cases who survive enough to get to a hospital,' she told me. A short time later, news came from Kabul that Jerry's husband had been shot dead.

I travelled with the Red Cross north of Mogadishu close to the border between Somalia and neighbouring Ethiopia. The Hercules aircraft, which was carrying grain, circled to warn off people and animals walking along the dirt strip where we intended to land. A large group of locals was waiting to receive the grain. There was evidence of the drought that threatened to leave thousands facing starvation. Dead livestock were scattered along the roadside. In a nearby village, the grain was boiled in large vats. The children were the first to be fed. Despite its best efforts, the aid agency was not able to cope with the numbers in need of assistance.

A young Irish nurse lost her life in Somalia. Valerie Place was a staff nurse at St James's Hospital in Dublin. She had volunteered to work with the aid agency, Concern, at the feeding station in Mogadishu. In late February 1993, the convoy she was travelling in near the Somali capital was fired upon. Valerie was killed. Her death was a reminder of the danger many young aid volunteers enter into when they agree to work abroad. I have seen the work of these people in so many countries and, while I am often critical of the organisations themselves, and especially of the unnecessary competition between them, I have nothing but admiration for the individuals involved.

Mary Robinson helped introduce Somalia to the Irish people. The crisis had been raised by the Irish aid agencies. Having recorded material for a separate story at Áras an Uachtaráin, I was told by Bride Rosney, the President's advisor, not to leave too quickly. So I waited for the outcome of a briefing Robinson was receiving on the situation in Somalia from representatives of the aid agencies. Aengus Finucane from Concern asked her, 'Why don't you go there yourself, President?' Finucane had, in fact, been prompted to ask the question. Robinson had a carefully worked-out answer; and I had a story.

Robinson's decision to travel to Somalia in 1992 was brave and helped to put the international spotlight on what was happening in that African country. The visit was marked by her dramatic reaction during a media conference when, struggling to contain her emotions, the President talked about being 'shamed and diminished when you see fellow citizens of this world so deprived of a right to life.'

Even today, I feel ashamed about the way the international community has neglected Somalia. The American media were actually waiting for the US troops as they arrived dramatically on the beaches to restore law and order not long after Bill Clinton was elected President in 1992. The Americans, however, failed miserably, and today, nearly 15 years after I first visited Somalia, the country and its capital city are as lawless as ever, while innocent people continue to suffer the consequences.

During my travels to various countries, I have witnessed truly awful suffering. The Kurds who fled Iraq for the mountains in Turkey after the first Gulf War come to mind as do the victims of the tsunami in December 2004. But alongside the devastation of wars and the havoc wreaked by natural disasters, I have also seen the terrible conditions in which our fellow human beings are forced to live. Making the documentary 'Slaves Without Chains'—along with my RTÉ colleague, Caroline Bleahen, and Caroline Lynch from Trócaire—opened my eyes to the poverty millions are locked into in countries like India and Brazil. Like most people, I thought that slavery was a concept from the nineteenth century. But here in the so-called modern world, some 20 million people were classified as slaves.

There were no dramatic images of people in chains. But the stories were really powerful. At a quarry in India, we met people for whom slavery was a generational inheritance. Some were paying off loans that had been taken out by their grandparents. Six days a week, they worked from 8 a.m. to 5.30 p.m. Their payment—rice. We travelled to one school in India where the young children—some as young as six or seven—worked from 6 a.m. to 4 p.m., cutting stones. They were working to pay off the debt incurred by their parents or grandparents, and they had no prospect of ever clearing the outstanding amount even though many of these loans were as low as $10. The system was structured to work against repayment. Slavery was legally outlawed but the loan system allowed wealthy landowners to prosper on the back of these unfortunates. After work each day, the children went to school for two hours. Under wicker shading, about 100 children sat in front of a blackboard. I got them to shout out, 'Hello, Charlie.' We practised a few times for the camera. Their energy was incredible as was their cheering when I said to the teacher, 'Maybe, I should give them a day off.'

We trekked into the mountains to a remote Indian village where the people lived in absolute poverty. These tribal people owed everything to the local landowner. They didn't own even the clothes on their backs. They lived a life of debt, and many had never handled money. The highlighting of this bonded slavery by non-governmental agencies like Trócaire was forcing some change. An official from the Indian government was present on the day we visited the village to present some of the villagers with a cheque which would buy their freedom.

From India, we travelled to Brazil, a country with more slaves today than at any time in its history. The poor and unemployed in urban areas are targeted with promises of decent incomes and prospects from work on landed estates. But these promises are never delivered. Instead, the workers are held by armed guards under threat of being shot if they attempt to leave. We heard about one landowner, Carlos Barbosa, who had been accused of mistreating his employees and treating them as slaves. So we travelled to his ranch to get his side of the story. Barbosa was out on his horse when we arrived at the entrance to his estate. He was somewhat surprised by the arrival of a television reporter and his entourage, to say the least. The translator put to Barbosa my questions about bonded slavery. 'He says, "I have been here for 30 years and I treat the people like a father would treat his children"'. That was all we got from Mr Barbosa who grew annoyed at my continued questioning. 'He won't talk any more to us,' the translator said, suggesting we keep our distance as the man on the horse actually had a gun that was visible in his jeans back pocket. It was time to leave.

During my career, I have seen the work of probably all the Irish aid agencies. On occasion, I have travelled with representatives of individual agencies. This can be a good way to do one-off reports, especially when it's important to get ready access to parts of the world where facilities are poor and travel is difficult. One trip to Africa with GOAL will long remain in my memory. Maura Lennon from GOAL met me at Dublin Airport. 'You're a man. Would you take this for me?' she asked as she handed me a rucksack. I saw nothing unusual in the request and took the bag on board the flight to Paris where we had a nine-hour wait before transferring to a flight to Nairobi in Kenya. There was time to travel into central Paris for a meal. I decided to put Maura's bag with my own hand luggage into a left-luggage safe in the airport.

'Better not do that,' Maura said.

'Why not? What's in it? I asked, not thinking twice about my question.

'Money,' came her reply.

'What?'

'There are no banks we can deal with in some parts of Africa. We carry cash. That's how we operate,' Maura explained.

I wasn't sure I wanted to know the answer but decided to ask the obvious question. 'How much is in the bag?'

Maura drew closer to me. 'A quarter of a million dollars,' she whispered.

My grip tightened on the bag as I felt a sweat break out on my forehead.

The following couple of hours were among the most nervous of my entire life. I was particularly uncomfortable when we got onto the flight to Nairobi. 'This is crazy,' I was telling myself. 'If I get caught at immigration control, what will RTÉ say? I'll be sacked and thrown into prison.'

I never walked through passport control as quickly, and I was one relieved man when the Kenyan official stamped my documents and waved me on. GOAL could have their dollars back.

There was, however, a sequel to this story. Almost a year later, the *Late Late Show* decided to do a tribute programme to the founder of GOAL, John O'Shea. I was invited to appear and was seated in the audience. There was plenty of laughter when I told my dollars story. Two days later, however, John O'Shea rang me. 'Look at the problem your little yarn has caused us,' he said. It seemed the Garda Síochána had been watching the *Late Late Show*, and an officer had duly been sent out to O'Shea's GOAL office, to express concern over the safety implications of carrying around that amount of money. I laughed and reminded John that I had also been concerned when in Paris and Maura Lennon had whispered to me, 'A quarter of a million dollars.'

That particular trip was memorable for other reasons. We flew from Nairobi into the famine areas of southern Sudan. The pilot of the small aircraft, a white South African who operated a travel business out of Nairobi, was named Charlie Fish. We had a few laughs at our respective names but the smiles were wiped off my face when Charlie Fish announced that he was switching off all the aeronautics equipment for fear that Sudanese rebels would target us with a heat-seeking missile. On the ground, we saw scores of bodies, victims of the civil war in the region. Concern and GOAL had organised the flight to assess the level of need in the area and also the safety situation if they were to set up aid operations. A few hours later, Charlie Fish had us all on board again, but the engines on the aircraft would not start. We were parked on a dirt airstrip in the middle of nowhere and the security situation meant that it was too dangerous to remain after dark. Charlie Fish worked on the engines for about half an hour. He eventually got one engine working and it was enough to get us into the air.

I also remember travelling to the border area between South Africa and Mozambique with representatives of another Irish aid agency and Seamus Rushe, an affable and easy-going cameraman, from the RTÉ offices in Sligo. Refugees were coming across the border from Mozambique. An Irish missionary priest—a young man in his early thirties—was working in the area and helped take us around. The night we arrived was actually his final one before moving on to some other position. Two local aid workers from County Cork had organised a small going-away party for this priest, and we joined them for a few bottles of beer. It soon became apparent that the two women were hatching a plan that involved the priest and his particularly beautiful housekeeper. They were actually taking bets based on their knowledge that the housekeeper and the priest had got on well together over the previous few months. Did they win their bet? All I will say is that the following morning, the young priest had a very happy smile on his face.

Chapter 7 ~

| THE POLITICAL CLASS

Eoghan Harris, my old friend and former colleague, was in flying form as a guest on Vincent Browne's radio programme. He was lavishing praise on me. 'Charlie Bird's style is brilliant. It's ebullient, it's fantastic, it's chutzpah and it's got power,' Harris enthused. I have been criticised enough in my career that I take the compliments when they come my way. Unfortunately, this praise in the summer of 1997 came with a serious caveat.

I had been asked to follow Bertie Ahern for the duration of the 1997 general election campaign. It was his first general election as leader of Fianna Fáil. He had got the job at the end of 1994 and was the first Fianna Fáil leader not to become Taoiseach on the same day he got the party position. Now, after almost three years in opposition, Ahern was seeking to knock Fine Gael's John Bruton out of Government Buildings. It was a crucial campaign—failure to become Taoiseach could have had serious implications for his future as Fianna Fáil leader.

As the campaign unfolded, it was clear that Ahern was having a good election, and I was to blame. It seemed I was too good at my job, and that was why Eoghan Harris was praising me. He had left RTÉ in the late 1980s and carved out a new career as a controversial newspaper columnist. He had also made his mark as a political advisor to Mary Robinson during her 1990 presidential election campaign, and later to John Bruton during his time as leader of Fine Gael. Many people in Fine Gael shared Eoghan's opinion that somehow my reporting on Ahern's campaign was helping him in the election.

I had known Bertie Ahern for many years but not in any personal way. I had interviewed him on many occasions but the 1997 campaign was the first time I saw him up close. He was hugely successful at the glad-handing and handshakes. The public responded to him. The simple truth was that he was leaving Bruton in his wake.

Fine Gael had been annoyed from the outset about the allocation of reporters. While I was shadowing the Ahern campaign, my colleague, Joe O'Brien, was following Bruton and, whereas Ahern was out and about meeting people, Bruton was having a more low-key campaign. Fine Gael made a formal complaint to RTÉ about the prominence Ahern was getting on the television bulletins each evening. But blaming the allocation of reporters or the different styles was ridiculous— Eoghan Harris had Joe O'Brien down as 'an analytical reporter' against my 'ebullience'. The reality was that these criticisms could not avoid the fact that Ahern was simply having a better campaign than Bruton. It was bizarre that seasoned political figures and media-watchers could seriously think that two RTÉ reporters could, on their own, influence the outcome of the general election. The comments made about Joe O'Brien were not only unfair but they were also untrue. Joe is a top-class professional and he's been one of my closest colleagues for many years. He has been a really good friend who helped me through some of the most difficult days of my personal life.

If Fine Gael criticisms were not bad enough, Ivan Yates, the party's Minister for Agriculture, opted to attack me on RTÉ's *Questions & Answers*. I was furious when Yates accused RTÉ of putting out 'video promotional material' about Ahern. He alleged that I had not asked the Fianna Fáil leader 'a single hard question' and that my interviews with Ahern were like 'a fireside chat'. The implication was that I was biased in my reporting, and I took huge exception to this allegation. Yates and his colleagues in Fine Gael would have been better served looking at how the two parties and their respective leaders managed and organised their campaigns. If they had undertaken such an exercise, they would have discovered why the campaigns were getting different treatment in the nightly television reports. I reported what I saw and Joe reported what he saw. We were just doing our jobs.

The morning after the *Questions & Answers* programme, Ahern travelled by helicopter from Dublin to Galway. I thought it better not to give Yates and Fine Gael any ammunition. Given their state of frenzy, an image of me climbing into a chopper with Ahern could have been seized upon to say, 'Told you so'. My job was to give a flavour of each day's campaigning, but the pictures we would have got during the journey with Ahern were not worth any more hassle. So, instead, the camera crew and I drove by car to Galway.

That was the day when a young woman approached Ahern on the street in Galway and planted a big kiss on his lips. The Fianna Fáil leader was getting that type of reaction and, despite what Ivan Yates believed, Ahern did not need me to help him out. In truth, it was hard not to do a good job reporting on the Ahern campaign in 1997.

I was really angry at what Yates had said, and in no uncertain terms let him know how I felt. To his credit, the Fine Gael politician did have the good grace to apologise. A week after the television attack, he wrote to me at RTÉ. 'It was never my intention to in any way impugn you personally or professionally,' he acknowledged.

While Bertie Ahern was popular with people on the hustings, he also had a different approach from other party leaders in that he would take time during the day to talk with the reporters. I spent three weeks covering his every move. I knew from conversations with him that if he won the election, there would be immediate efforts to get the IRA to restore its ceasefire. Talks with republicans were already under way. I had seen some evidence of this myself on the very night that the IRA bombed Canary Wharf in London in early 1996. I later discovered that senior Sinn Féin figures including Rita O'Hare had gone to meet Ahern—then leader of the opposition —at his constituency office in Drumcondra. On one of the last days of the election campaign, I said to Ahern, 'Make me one promise. If you do become Taoiseach and the IRA is going to restore its ceasefire, you'll keep me informed.' He said he would and, a few weeks later, he duly rang me on the eve of the cease-fire restoration.

After the 1997 general election campaign, when my reporting was over, Ahern put a question to me. 'Would you be interested in becoming Government Press Secretary?' he asked. I was flattered but my immediate reaction was to say 'no'. A few days later, one of Ahern's advisors rang me about the offer. I knew it wasn't the right move at that time. I actually suggested Donal Kelly's name. Donal had been a colleague for many years in RTÉ and, as Political Correspondent, he was an extremely solid character whom I respected deeply. During the various periods of industrial strife in RTÉ, Donal could always be relied upon to provide a more realistic assessment of events. Despite the attractive position, Donal was not keen to leave RTÉ, so he too decided to decline the offer.

The job went ultimately to a man much better qualified for the position. At that time, Joe Lennon was press officer at the Department of Finance, working with Ruairí Quinn. A career civil servant, Lennon went on to great success as Government Press Secretary and enhanced his own reputation as one of the highest-regarded officials in an era when spin-doctors generally had a bad name.

I have spent most of my working life in RTÉ and my entire career in journalism as a reporter with RTÉ News. There have been opportunities to leave, some of which have been tempting. The *Sunday Independent* made me a very attractive offer at one stage in the 1990s. There was a certain irony in the approach given that the *Sunday Independent* had, on more than one occasion, been sharply critical of my reporting, particularly in relation to the peace process in Northern Ireland. It was at a time when my basic salary in RTÉ was unexceptional and was a million miles—and several hundred thousand pounds!—from the financial packages approved for people like Gay Byrne and Pat Kenny. I decided ultimately that print journalism was not for me and passed on the six-figure sum and the possible carrot of shares in the Independent Group. Bizarrely, a few days later, the driver's window of a car I was walking past was rolled down and Tony O'Reilly's son, Gavin, stuck out his head. 'Sorry you didn't join us,' he said.

The closest I came to leaving RTÉ was when Willie O'Reilly from Today FM asked me to replace Eamon Dunphy on the station's drive-time current affairs programme. We met in the Avoca shop on the way to Wicklow town. Negotiations on a new contract with Dunphy had been unsuccessful and he was about to move on. 'You're the ideal replacement—will you consider it?' O'Reilly asked.

The offer on the table would have doubled my RTÉ salary. My interest, however, went beyond money. The prospect of making my mark in journalism in a completely different way was hugely attractive, even if I was somewhat nervous about ending a three-decade association with RTÉ. I was, and I suppose continue to be, really keen to re-invent myself, to have a new challenge. RTÉ tends to put people into a box and leave them there. In that way of thinking, I'm a news reporter. Today FM was offering something very different.

I met O'Reilly for a second round of discussions and I talked the offer over with a number of people whose judgment I trusted. I was considering turning down the offer when O'Reilly rang me to say he had to withdraw the proposal as Dunphy had agreed to stay. I was disappointed but just got on with my own job. When Dunphy did eventually leave Today FM a number of years later, there was no contact from the station. I think the moment had passed.

Not long after he was elected Taoiseach—and I had turned down his job offer—Bertie Ahern followed up on a remark I had not given much thought to when he had made it after the general election campaign. 'We must have a drink,' he had said. So, several weeks later, I arrived at the appointed time at his constituency office in Drumcondra. 'Will you have something to eat?' he asked. We drove to a small pub over by Dalymount Park where the two of us, without any fuss from the staff or the handful of regulars, sat in the corner. Over steak and chips, we talked about the election and the situation in Northern Ireland.

I doubt if I would ever have found myself in such a situation with any of the former Taoisigh on whom I have reported for RTÉ. Bertie Ahern has a very different style and approach in comparison with Charlie Haughey, Garret FitzGerald, Albert Reynolds or John Bruton. As a politician, Ahern is fairly open and I have always found him affable and friendly. I have met him for background conversations, mainly about Northern Ireland; sometimes we've had a cup of tea and a few slices of toast as we talked in his constituency office. He can also be surprising.

One evening, I was reporting on a story about the possibility of IRA decommissioning. There was speculation that a deal had been done. My mobile rang. It was Bertie Ahern. There was no small chat just a warning that the situation was not as positive as some had been saying. Over the years, I have seen Ahern's passion to resolve the conflict in the North. He has left no stone unturned in that regard and, while the phone call to me about decommissioning was a small gesture, it illustrated that commitment. It was clear that he was interested only that I was on the right path about what I was reporting. On another occasion, I actually had Ahern knocking on the window of my car.

There had been controversy about the proposal for a state-funded national stadium with which Ahern was closely associated. But under pressure from his PD partners in government, Ahern had been forced to revise his plans. I was reporting on the announcement that the soccer and rugby authorities were to row in behind the idea to redevelop Lansdowne Road, with the government having a central role in the project. John O'Donoghue, as Sports Minister, had confirmed the news at a press conference held in Government Buildings. There was no sign of Ahern. Afterwards, RTÉ was almost prevented from interviewing rugby and soccer representatives in the grounds of Government Buildings, despite the fact that these individuals were involved in the project and had actually been at the press conference.

I had a heated exchange with some of the officials in Ahern's office as RTÉ was forced to move its facilities out onto the street outside Government Buildings after the early-evening news bulletin. The story about the changed plans for the sporting stadium was reported on the *Six One News*. Sometime after seven o'clock, I was sitting in my car—which was also parked outside Government Buildings—writing up my notes for the nine o'clock news. There was a knock on the window. I looked up and was totally taken aback to see the Taoiseach peering in at me.

'Were you looking for me to talk about Lansdowne Road?' he asked. I hadn't been, but I was delighted to have an opportunity to do a short interview with him. There is probably no other country in the world where a political leader would come looking to do an interview like that. It was typical Bertie Ahern. He had taken a bloody nose with the coverage earlier in the evening. Now he wanted to regain some influence over the story.

Ahern saw John Bruton off at the general election in 1997 and, five years later, Michael Noonan went the same way. Because of the previous controversy, RTÉ decided that I would not stick with a single party leader during the 2002 general election. I found myself reporting on the big developments during each day's campaigning. It was obvious from early in the contest that Fine Gael was in trouble. Even the mood at the party's daily press conference lacked any sense of confidence.

Fine Gael started the campaign with its election headquarters in a run-down building on Tara Street, before the unsuitability of the building became obvious and the team was forced to relocate back to party head office on Upper Mount Street. I attended most of the morning media briefings and could see the ramshackle nature of the whole Fine Gael campaign. Most mornings, Mark Costigan of Today FM and I were among the first to arrive at the Fine Gael offices and we would bizarrely find ourselves almost helping to set up the room for that morning's press conference. Fianna Fáil, on the other hand, ran an amazingly professional campaign in 2002, straight out of a textbook about how to run an American presidential campaign. Walking into the foyer of the party's election headquarters in the imposing Treasury Building on Grand Canal Street in Dublin, one was greeted by a massive portrait banner of Bertie Ahern.

Away from the press conference rooms, in the background, Fianna Fáil had assembled a large team of helpers to monitor every media outlet in the country. This practice, which was known as rebuttal, was borrowed straight from New Labour in Britain and the Clinton campaigns in the US. It meant that, within minutes of any radio or television report, the rebuttal unit was able to issue a statement countering any negative comment on Fianna Fáil. The party had also assigned key officials to stay in daily contact with all the main journalists from all media outlets. In my own view, Fianna Fáil's daily media conferences succeeded in setting the agenda for reporters and for politicians from all the other parties.

The Fianna Fáil campaign was going so well and Fine Gael's was in such disarray that an overall majority for Bertie Ahern's party became a real possibility. Senior Fianna Fáil figures, however, were very keen to dampen the overall majority speculation. One morning, in the middle of the campaign, Charlie McCreevy, in his own distinctive fashion, was selling this message. It was after the early-morning press conference and McCreevy was sitting on a sofa talking with reporters Emily O'Reilly and Katie Hannon and myself. The Minister for Finance promised that if his party won an overall majority, he would strip naked and don the underwear of the two female reporters present, to climb the front of the Treasury Buildings. It was one of the strangest pledges I had ever heard from a senior politician, but I suppose only Charlie McCreevy could have got away with it. I suspect he was thankful that the election result turned out as it did, with Fianna Fáil just short of the magical majority figure.

Michael McDowell was one man who was responsible for making the voters think twice about giving Fianna Fáil a majority of Dáil seats. The PD politician literally went up a pole to hang his famous 'Single Party Government—No Thanks' posters. I was there for the so-called photo-opportunity. It was a stunt but the image was really powerful and probably changed the voting intentions of enough people to have had a real impact. One of my most vivid recollections of that election campaign was the reaction of Mary Harney to a story in *Magill* magazine, alleging that she had taken corrupt payments. The potential impact of the story, if it was true, was so huge that I decided to ring the PD leader myself. Although her press office had been contacted by *Magill*, she was not personally aware that the magazine was about to publish the story. I read the contents of the article to her and it was obvious from her response that she was totally taken aback. As it emerged that there was no substance to the claim, I could hear the emotion in her voice. The following day, the PDs provided another great visual image of the 2002 campaign when Harney and her colleagues binned a copy of *Magill*.

On election night, the inevitable Fine Gael implosion happened. I ended up doing a very strange interview with the Fine Gael leader. When I arrived at Noonan's apartment in Sandymount, he had tears in his eyes. He was presiding over an electoral disaster which just kept getting worse as the evening wore on. 'What's the story with Brian Hayes?' he asked me.

I made a quick call to the election-results centre back in RTÉ. The news was not good for Noonan—Hayes, an outgoing TD in Dublin South West, was going to lose his seat. As I relayed the news, Noonan just shook his head. A few minutes later, we were recording the interview in which he announced his resignation as leader of Fine Gael.

If Noonan was the beaten man of the 2002 general election, Ahern was the big-time winner. The contrast between them was unbelievable. Half an hour after I'd left a dejected Noonan in his Sandymount apartment, I arrived at the Treasury Building and the Fianna Fáil election headquarters. The mood was upbeat and the celebrations were well under way. Ahern had already made his 'victory' speech for his election workers. But I needed something for the cameras so, without a quibble, Ahern actually re-did part of the speech and the Fianna Fáilers present re-did the cheers. It was an unusual situation which I doubt would have been facilitated anywhere else in the world, but it was a good example of the media professionalism of Fianna Fáil in 2002. In subsequent years, under the leadership of Enda Kenny, Fine Gael improved its approach to organisational matters, as well as the presentation of its public image, and the party once more became a match for Fianna Fáil.

The media have changed a great deal in my quarter of a century as a news reporter. When I joined RTÉ, it was still the only serious broadcast news outlet in Ireland. The main point of comparison was the BBC which probably had an influence on how RTÉ reported news. It certainly raised standards in RTÉ. Compared to two decades ago, the competition is now huge. The rush to be first with the news is real, while stories don't seem to last as long on the news agenda. Sometimes what is news at 11 a.m. is simply history by 12 noon. Every story is now a big media event and, to some extent, the increased number of broadcast news outlets means that RTÉ is no longer the only place people get their daily news. Despite these changes, I still think the quality of journalism is high in Ireland.

I have been fortunate that the people who have been in charge of the newsroom in RTÉ have all aspired to achieve the highest of journalistic standards—people like Wesley Boyd, Mike Burns and Rory O'Connor. I suppose I emerged as a news reporter while this powerful group of managers was in charge of the newsroom. From being a general reporter, my wide-ranging role was recognised, with new titles such as Special Reporter and Special Correspondent. When Wesley Boyd stepped down, his replacement was an individual with a very different personality. I knew Joe Mulholland from my days in current affairs. I had worked as a researcher on a few programmes produced by him. During the 1980s, he was a very successful but highly controversial editor of *Today Tonight*, the award-winning current affairs programme. In his long RTÉ career, Mulholland produced some of the most dramatic programmes, which, irrespective of their ultimate targets, never pulled their punches.

Given his history in RTÉ, it was no great surprise that controversy was never far away in the years when Joe Mulholland was Director of News. There were varying opinions about him. He was a man who generated very little neutral reaction. Neither was he afraid to take contentious decisions. He had a passion for news, and he also loved politics, be it in the office or in Leinster House. He would on occasion produce a bottle of whiskey in his office. 'Tell me how you're getting on,' he would say in his dry Donegal drawl as he poured the drink.

To his credit, Mulholland sought to expand the ambition of the newsroom. Foreign travel became more frequent and foreign coverage became more comprehensive. He was also prepared to take risks as I discovered when he decided that RTÉ needed to develop contacts with the IRA. His personal views might have told him to continue maintaining distance from republicans but Mulholland was driven primarily by a news rationale of having a better understanding of what was happening within the IRA. When Joe Mulholland left RTÉ in 2000, I was flabbergasted. I had been surprised when he missed out on being appointed the station's Director-General. He was probably the brightest recruit of his generation, and he would have had a very ambitious agenda for the station. But he was overlooked for the top job and, not long afterwards, he left RTÉ. I was left scratching my head on both counts.

During all this time, as the personnel changed and RTÉ News became more ambitious, the wider media world was changing, too. For one thing, standards are very different today—no better or no worse, just different. Certainly the types of stories that drive the news agenda have changed. There is no way the controversy surrounding Roy Keane during and after the 2002 World Cup would have led the news agenda 25 years ago. Technological developments have played their part. Pictures are now available instantly. It's possible to edit broadcast reports at the scene of a story and get them live on air almost immediately.

There is also less trust in authority. The various political and business scandals have undermined public confidence in an array of institutions. The political parties have first-hand experience of this dilution in public confidence. The sexual abuse scandals have left the Catholic Church exposed like never previously in its history. Compared to the child-abuse scandals, the initial church revelations now seem so tame and, in a way, innocent. I can remember in May 1992 being asked to go to Dublin Airport to doorstep Cardinal Cahal Daly. The fallout from a variety of revelations about priests breaking their vows of celibacy had been dominating the news agenda. There was considerable debate about married priests. I am not sure what Daly was expecting but it was clear he did not like my questions.

'Is the church facing a particular problem at the moment over this particular issue about priests who are finding it difficult to stay celibate and having relationships with women?' I asked. It was a changed world when cardinals and bishops were asked to account for themselves although I don't think the Cardinal was too impressed.

His face displayed anger. I was told that it was, 'grossly irresponsible to parade rumors of that kind' and that in his 51 years as a priest and 25 as a bishop, he had never experienced anything like it. 'Grossly offensive,' was the phrase he used. Looking back now, priests having relationships with women was the least of the church's worries.

The treatment of cardinals and bishops just like any other interviewee is one example of how much less respect for authority there is in the media, and among the public, today. There is also a more personality-type attitude to news coverage. Personal lives are now part of the story. In a way, Charlie Haughey and Bertie Ahern best represent these different worlds. Haughey had a long-time mistress and nobody in the media considered it a story to be reported, whereas Ahern has had his relationship with his former wife and subsequent partners discussed openly in the newspapers and on television and radio. It's a big change in a quarter of a century.

Bertie Ahern was one of the first senior political figures to speak openly about the breakdown of his marriage. I knew a little of what he had gone through as my own marriage ended in the mid-1990s and, like Ahern, I maintained a good relationship with my wife. Celia Larkin, Ahern's new partner, accompanied him to many functions after his election as Taoiseach. There was some comment but, in general, their relationship was accepted. Ireland was a changing country. However, there were some difficulties when the couple travelled abroad, as I saw at first hand when they visited China in late 1998.

It was amazing to see Tiananmen Square decked out in the Irish colours. The tricolor of green, white and orange hung from every lamp-post in the vast square. The Irish national anthem was played when Ahern and his entourage arrived in the Great Hall of the People. We had been warned by the Chinese authorities that we would have no reporting access at the function. 'No cameras. No microphones,' they said. Bizarrely, however, it was possible to get a signal for my mobile phone inside the building, which allowed me to do a live piece on the ceremony for the Pat Kenny radio programme. It was a report I could never have done from inside Leinster House.

While the visit continued at a pace, it was obvious that behind the scenes the Chinese were having difficulty with Celia Larkin's status. They wanted to know what her official title was. 'First Lady' was not an option while the idea of her being the partner of the Irish head of government was something they had a problem comprehending. The diplomatic upheavals in the background did not, however, appear to distract Ahern and Larkin who both seemed particularly relaxed, especially on the day when their itinerary included a visit to the Great Wall. We got some amazing shots, and when all the work was done, we all took photographs. I even got a picture taken with Ahern and Larkin.

The Chinese had responsibility for internal travel during the visit, so when moving from Beijing to Shanghai, the Irish delegation travelled on an aircraft owned by the Chinese government. Ahern and other dignitaries were seated at the front, with the handful of travelling media at the rear of the plane. I remember, Celia Larkin came down and spoke to us for a few minutes. She didn't give any indication that the background noises from the Chinese were getting to her. In fact, she was very relaxed.

Less relaxed, however, was Tom Kitt, the junior minister who was also on the trip, and the person responsible for a most extraordinary outburst during a visit to the Shanghai Stock Exchange. We were following the Taoiseach as he was led to the viewing gallery overlooking the trading floor. I could see Ahern at the top of the entourage when suddenly and abruptly Tom Kitt came bounding up to me. 'You fucker,' he shouted. I was flabbergasted. 'You put Conor O'Clery up to it,' he continued, without any attempt to lower his voice. The Fianna Fáil politician had his say and eventually moved on. I was furious at this unwarranted attack. I spoke with Joe Lennon, the Government Press Secretary, making it clear in no uncertain terms that I found Kitt's outburst to be way out of order.

The cause of Kitt's anger was a report in that morning's *Irish Times*, written by Conor O'Clery, the newspaper's Asia Correspondent and a very generous journalistic colleague. Conor had written an article on the Taoiseach's visit to the Foreign Affairs College in Beijing where he had spoken and taken questions. The Irish Ambassador to China, Joe Hayes, was on the podium with Ahern but, when it came to having photographs taken, he stepped down to allow the junior minister take his place. I had seen what Conor reported—Kitt signalling to the Irish Ambassador that he wanted his seat at the top table. Kitt took exception to this report which he had either read on the internet or had relayed to him from home. I'm not sure why he decided to attack me—maybe he thought I passed the information to Conor—but in any event he did get a clarification in the following day's *Irish Times* which noted that 'Mr Hayes invited Mr Kitt for protocol reasons to take his place on the platform.' The minister was not the only person getting a clarification. A few hours after my complaint about his outburst, Kitt rang me and apologised.

———

I will always look back on Bertie Ahern's years as Taoiseach as the time when the peace process in Northern Ireland, through many twists and turns, was eventually bedded down. Another association I will always make with the Ahern years will be Drumcree, a picturesque location outside Portadown in County Armagh which greatly exercised the minds of Ahern, and his counterpart in London, Tony Blair.

I covered the controversial Orange Order parade for a number of years in the 1990s. I was first asked to cover the Drumcree weekend in July 1996 although there was no indication that it was going to emerge as a big news story. I travelled to Portadown a couple of days before the Drumcree march. Johnny Coughlan, RTÉ's cameraman in Belfast, did the driving. I wanted to get an impression of the area and see for myself what was going on. We drove around the whole town and the surrounding areas. I was very taken by the small Protestant Church at Drumcree which is set in a quiet rural area. But not far away, two communities were very much intent on shattering any illusion of tranquillity.

As Johnny Coughlan was driving thought the loyalist Corcoran housing estate in Portadown, I saw a group of tough-looking young men hanging around one corner. 'Let's see if any of them might talk to us,' I said.

They looked fairly relaxed as I approached them. 'Do you think there will be trouble with the parade at the weekend?' I asked.

'Who are you?' came back the reply.

I made a nondescript response: 'Charlie Bird, from Dublin.' I knew that mentioning RTÉ might bring an immediate end to our conversation. 'Is there anyone prepared to say a few words for me?' I enquired.

A guy with shaved hair and an earring stepped forward. 'I'll talk to you,' he said. We did a short interview.

Back in the car, Johnny Coughlan said to me, 'I think that was King Rat.'

My response best illustrated how Drumcree and its cast of characters had yet to become national news. 'And who the hell is King Rat?' I asked.

It seemed we had just interviewed Billy Wright, the leader of the Loyalist Volunteer Force. I decided to check, so I got out of the car and walked back to the group on the street corner. 'I need names for identification purposes on the TV,' I explained.

'My name is Billy Wright,' the man replied.

When we got back to Belfast, I told Gary Honeyford from Sky News who we had got talking on camera. Sky News has offices on the floor below RTÉ in Fanum House in Belfast. The two broadcasters often swap footage. Gary was impressed with my minor scoop. 'I'll have some of that,' he said. Wright was a notorious loyalist paramilitary who was later found dead inside Maghaberry Prison in December 1997, having been murdered by a republican prisoner.

Drumcree was a powder keg of a story. The unionist protests at not being allowed walk down the nationalist Garvaghy Road brought much of Northern Ireland to a standstill. It was very strange travelling down from Belfast to Portadown over those few days. It was the height of the summer and, even during daylight hours, the motorway was empty. As the sun went down during the 1996 Drumcree stand-off, the loyalist hardmen would emerge with petrol bombs and stones which would rain down on police officers and members of the British army. I went across to the field alongside the church where the Orangemen were congregated, but they were not happy to have an RTÉ reporter around, so, after a very uncomfortable ten to fifteen minutes, I decided it was advisable to get out of there.

I caught sight of the local MP, David Trimble, arguing loudly with the police. Trimble was later elected leader of the Ulster Unionist Party. My dealings with him were few enough and confined to doorstep interviews and press conferences. His ire was always raised with reporters from RTÉ and I always found him cold and hostile in a way not even Ian Paisley was towards reporters from south of the border. That said, I also saw the huge risks Trimble took which helped to secure the peace process in Northern Ireland.

The Orangemen were eventually forced down the Garvaghy Road. I climbed up on a garden wall backing onto the road and had a good vantage point as I recorded live pieces into a series of programmes.

Drumcree has not been easily resolved. Compromise has been a difficult commodity in Portadown. The tension was never as bitter in the years after 1996, although the events in July 1998 left an indelible mark on me, and, I suspect, on many others.

I was actually assigned to cover events in Derry but on the morning of Drumcree Sunday, the news desk in Dublin asked me to travel to Ballymoney. Initial reports suggested a house fire had cost three children their lives. Shortly after midday, the police officer in charge of the investigation came to speak with reporters. Richard Quinn was ten years old. Mark Quinn was nine. Jason Quinn was eight. They had been murdered when loyalists petrol bombed their home in the small hours of the morning. The Catholic family had just moved into the pre-predominantly Protestant area and had been targeted in a sectarian attack.

As the handful of reporters stood on the footpath outside the Quinn home, a police officer confirmed the terrible news. As discussed previously, I am not a religious person but there was something about the deaths of those three little boys that suddenly put Drumcree, and all it was associated with, into perspective. The protests lost their momentum as most Orangemen went home. I have been back to Drumcree many times. I have even visited the church during wintertime. It is a stunningly beautiful place which has been sullied by so many people.

Blair and Ahern have had to deal with more than Drumcree in their attempts to get a deal in Northern Ireland. I was in France when the Omagh bomb exploded in August 1998. Like all journalists, my first reaction was to go with the story and, if I had been at home, I would have immediately travelled to the County Tyrone town. It's the reporter's instinct. I did go to Tyrone in early September to cover the visit of Blair and Ahern, and I did an interview with Michael Gallagher, one of the relatives who lost loved ones in the explosion caused by dissident republicans in the so-called Real IRA. As I was leaving his home, he handed me a memorial card containing a photograph of his son. The Gallagher family and the other Omagh relatives suffered a terrible wrong and one can only admire and be impressed by the doggedness with which they have pursued their campaign for truth and justice.

Alongside the peace process in Northern Ireland, the Ahern years have been dominated by various revelations about political and business corruption. For a period after 1997, I spent as much time in the court-yard of Dublin Castle as I did on the plinth outside Leinster House. The various tribunals threw up a whole series of dramatic stories and characters, and few of those characters were as controversial as the late Liam Lawlor. The Fianna Fáil politician was always a bit of a maverick. Before he came to the attention of the tribunal investigating planning corruption in the Dublin region, I had had very little contact with him. I knew that he drove a big car and I used to see him around Leinster House, sometimes in the company of another controversial figure, Ray Burke. Our paths eventually crossed over stories I did relating to the planning tribunal. I got a good tip-off about Lawlor's involvement in a land deal near his Lucan home in west Dublin. The deal involved the then Fianna Fáil TD and the reclusive businessman, Jim Kennedy, who was refusing to co-operate with the tribunal and who seemed to have left the country rather than answer questions about alleged planning corruption.

I approached Lawlor about the story. He emphatically denied that he had had any business dealings with Jim Kennedy and he refused to do an interview. I started digging a little more. A former employee in Kennedy's amusement arcade in Westmoreland Street in Dublin pro-vided some very interesting information. It seemed that Lawlor was a regular visitor to the amusement arcade. He would park his car at the back of the building before joining Kennedy and George Redmond, the leading planning officer in the Dublin region, in a nearby coffee shop. My story was standing up despite Lawlor's earlier denial. I also obtained documentary proof of the Lawlor–Kennedy involvement in the contro-versial Lucan land deal. John Caldwell, a solicitor in Dublin, was also involved. My source—an influential businessman—was impeccable.

With Lawlor in denial, and Kennedy on the missing list, John Caldwell was the key to getting one of the parties to confirm the story. I decided to approach Frank Dunlop, the former Fianna Fáil advisor turned business lobbyist. For many years Dunlop had been a leading figure in business and political circles in Dublin. But in April 2000, his world fell apart. He had denied any involvement in planning corruption but Fergus Flood's tribunal of inquiry was on his tail. The tribunal had evidence that Dunlop had been a middleman in paying bribes to local councillors for their support with planning decisions. They were among the most dramatic days I could remember. Dunlop was his usual confident self in denying any wrongdoing. Flood told him to go home and think about his situation. By the time Dunlop returned, he was a changed man. Reality had struck and the bravado was gone.

While not condoning Dunlop's actions, I had some sympathy for him. His world had collapsed; his public relations business was gone; and some time earlier he had also lost one of his children through illness. I met him every few months in a small basement coffee shop near his Mount Street offices. 'I've told my solicitor I'm meeting you,' he would always say, in case he was ever accused of passing confidential tribunal information to me.

Dunlop had had connections with Lawlor, Kennedy and Caldwell. I asked him if he could set up a meeting with the solicitor. We met in Dunlop's office in central Dublin. I wasn't sure what Caldwell would tell me so I decided to give him a flavour of what I knew. 'I heard there was a falling out between Lawlor and Kennedy over money,' I said.

Caldwell looked genuinely surprised. Only a handful of people knew this story. 'How did you know that?' he asked.

I was happy that I could stand over the Lawlor–Kennedy connection. A few days later, outside Dublin Castle, I again put the story to Lawlor. He looked me straight in the eye. 'I'll see you in court, Charlie,' he hissed.

The late Fianna Fáil politician never followed through on his threat although there was a certain irony in it, in that I would a short time later report on his dealings before the courts when he was sent to Mountjoy Prison for failing to co-operate with the planning tribunal. There was obviously a great deal of information that people like Liam Lawlor wanted to hide. He had lied to me in denying a business relationship with Jim Kennedy who was still refusing to deal with the tribunal of inquiry. I rang Kennedy's amusement arcade looking to contact the elusive businessman, but to no avail. I also wrote to him about the planning stories I was covering, in which he featured prominently. I put a series of questions in the letter and hand-delivered it to his Westmoreland Street arcade, but it was returned to me at RTÉ.

I then got a fortunate break in my search for Kennedy. A colleague in RTÉ was contacted by somebody who used the gym facilities at the exclusive Merrion Hotel opposite Government Buildings on Merrion

Street in Dublin. The information was passed on to me—Jim Kennedy worked out at this gym. I discussed the next move with my boss, Ed Mulhall. We decided to keep watch for Kennedy. But after a few days there was no sign of him at the Merrion Hotel gym or at his amusement arcade. He had a house on the Isle of Man. I travelled there and spent a fruitless couple of days watching for this man whose photograph had never been published.

It seemed our investigation was going the way of the planning tribunal as far as Kennedy was concerned. A couple of months passed. Then, unexpectedly, a source who cannot be identified called. 'Charlie, your man is back in town,' she said. The following evening, the source rang me again. 'He's at the gym now.' A mad scramble ensued as cameraman John 'Rocky' Curtis and I rushed into central Dublin. Kennedy's wife later blamed staff at the upmarket hotel for blowing the whistle on her husband. She was wrong. The source was another business figure who had had a run-in with Kennedy some years earlier.

There was a real air of excitement as we stood under a streetlight on the pavement across from the main entrance to the Merrion Hotel. My source was on her mobile to a contact who was inside the building. 'He's about to leave,' she predicted. A few moments later, a small stocky man wearing a black leather jacket and a black hat emerged. He had a kit bag slung over his shoulder. 'That's our man,' she said.

We followed the controversial businessman onto Merrion Row and caught up with him outside the Shelbourne Hotel on St Stephen's Green. Kennedy must have known this situation might one day arrive, but as I introduced myself and asked to speak with him, there was a look of total shock on his face. For a moment or two, I actually thought he was going to collapse right there in front of us. But he regained his composure and was clever enough not to talk. He just kept putting up his hands to wave me away. We walked towards Grafton Street and the whole way to the amusement arcade on Westmoreland Street. Rocky did a wonderful job of keeping focus on his mystery man who was now no longer a mystery in terms of his appearance, whatever about the tribunal's ability to unravel his complicated and allegedly corrupt business deals. It was a real scoop.

Most of Kennedy's—and indeed, Lawlor's—land deals involved George Redmond. I knew from my sources that the former local government planning official was a regular visitor to the amusement arcade.

Redmond denied any wrongdoing in his relationship with Kennedy although evidence I obtained showed that they had known each other for many years.

The tribunals have uncovered hugely important information and put the spotlight on corrupt practices that previously went without punishment. Not long after the planning tribunal was set up in late 1997, I was stunned to see the very deliberate attempts that were made to collapse the inquiry which was being chaired by Fergus Flood. These people knew exactly what they were doing and they used some journalists to leak information which was damaging to the tribunal's work. These stories were not scoops in terms of how most reporters would view 'exclusives'. Documentation was being deliberately leaked prematurely for malevolent reasons. I honestly believe that a number of leading members of the legal profession should hang their heads in shame at their unscrupulous behaviour.

Despite the initial successes of the planning inquiry, the McCracken Tribunal into the links between Ben Dunne and Charles Haughey and Michael Lowry probably remains the best of the tribunals of inquiry. McCracken's report reads like a good thriller. What is strange is how some individuals have escaped having their reputations tarnished. One leading Fianna Fail figure told me the story of a former minister whose children's school fees were paid by business people. The money was not given without something being provided in return. Unfortunately I could never get enough evidence to run the story which I believe is true. I suspect there are plenty more stories out there which we'll never get to hear the truth about.

If there is any consolation, it is knowing that some of those involved in wrongdoing have been caught. Ray Burke is a good example. For many years, I saw Burke as part of Charles Haughey's gang. He was always well turned out. He wore the best of suits and—why I noticed I don't know—his hands were always immaculate. I did the doorstep outside Leinster House in the autumn of 1997 when Burke 'drew a line in the sand'—as he put it—over the series of revelations that had emerged, linking him to corrupt payments. It was a powerful performance but a good example of how a famous phrase can come back to haunt an individual, especially if that individual is not telling the truth. Burke did not remain long in his position as Minister for Foreign Affairs and it was amazing a few years later to see him being escorted to a garda van to be taken off to Mountjoy Prison.

Just after the publication of the report of the planning tribunal which damned Burke, I went out to his house in north Dublin to see if he would do an interview. The former Fianna Fáil minister came to the front door but there was no question that he would talk to me with the camera on. We had a brief conversation. 'If I'm going down, then other people will do so as well,' he predicted. I took the 'others' to refer to Bertie Ahern. It was a threat that the late Liam Lawlor also made in private against Ahern. But neither man ever delivered any evidence to support the insinuations.

The 1990s were dominated by stories of political and business corruption. Michael Lowry was another of those characters to dominate the agenda of one of the tribunals at Dublin Castle. I had seen the Tipperary North TD rise up the ranks within Fine Gael. Anyone reporting on the activities in Leinster House during the leadership of John Bruton could not but have noticed the important role played by Lowry. He was a serious player in Fine Gael. He was crucial to everything the party did, and when Fine Gael got back into government in late 1994, Bruton appointed him to a senior ministerial position. I was at the press conference when Lowry announced that the licence for the second mobile phone operation in the country had been won by the Denis O'Brien consortium. None of us that day could have guessed that this decision would dominate the proceedings of a tribunal of inquiry for many years to come.

When the story broke linking Michael Lowry to Ben Dunne, I sought out the Fine Gael minister who had gone to ground without making any public comment. He agreed to meet me in the Green Isle Hotel on the outskirts of Dublin. We recorded a short interview in the hotel car park. 'I won't be knee-jerked out of government,' the embattled politician said. It was an amazing performance which some of his party colleagues said ended any prospect he had of ever overcoming the Dunne revelations.

Lowry was a cute operator as I discovered some years later when I had a story that the Revenue Commissioners had sent his file to the Director of Prosecutions. He faced the prospect of a prison sentence if a trial proceeded and he was found guilty. Somebody close to Lowry gave me the story. I rang Lowry to get a quote and he lied outright to me. 'I know nothing about this,' he said.

I rang my source back. 'He's lying,' the source said. Whatever about not telling me the truth, what really annoyed me was that he followed our private conversations by ringing other journalists to tell them that the Revenue had leaked confidential information to me. Lowry knew that neither the Revenue Commissioners nor the DPP had leaked the information—he should have looked elsewhere.

Chapter 8

MEETING WITH THE IRA

I stood outside Bewley's Café on Westmoreland Street in Dublin. It was a weekday afternoon on a summer's day in 1993. The street was busy with passing people and the usual heavy traffic. I was scanning the faces, trying to see if anyone made eye contact. Inside, I was apprehensive. To be honest, I was frightened, and there was reason to be— my appointment was with the IRA. 'Just stand there. We'll recognise you,' I had been told.

The republican movement was still shooting and bombing in 1993. Almost every other day, when I arrived into work in RTÉ, there was news of another death in Northern Ireland. But there were whispers about the possibility of an end to the violence which had scarred the island since 1969. Unknown to most people at that time, the peace process was being born in the background, through separate contacts between the IRA and the governments in Dublin and London.

Joe Mulholland believed that RTÉ needed to prepare for the possibility of a dramatic decision by the IRA leadership. While many newspaper reporters had contact with republican figures, the continued existence of Section 31 of the Broadcasting Act had limited the scope of RTÉ's dealings with the paramilitary organisation. It was known that other media outlets, including several leading British newspapers and the BBC both in London and in Belfast, already had open lines of communication with the Provisional IRA.

Mulholland, RTÉ's Director of News, first discussed the matter with Ed Mulhall, a senior newsroom executive who, a few years previously, had moved into the world of television news after a successful period as a producer of RTÉ radio programmes. His transfer from radio to television was a surprise to many, but the quiet-spoken County Kildare man has in recent times become one of the most influential figures in

Irish broadcasting. The two men subsequently widened the discussion about possible IRA contacts to include Tommie Gorman who was then RTÉ's Europe Editor but for many years had been the station's North Western Correspondent, based in Sligo. During his years in that region, Gorman had built up an amazing range of contacts, and, throughout his career in RTÉ, has been known for his commitment and passion for the peace process in Northern Ireland. A decision had been taken that RTÉ would try to establish contact with the IRA. I was asked to be the contact person. The initial approach was organised by Tommie Gorman who put me in touch with a leading republican figure. This act of generosity was typical of the Sligo man. A few weeks later, I met my first republican contact in the northwest of the country. I set out the RTÉ position. No commitment was made, only the promise that my request would be passed on to the relevant people.

Not long after that meeting, I found myself outside Bewley's Café on Westmoreland Street. 'How are you?' a man with a Northern accent asked. I swung around to see a tough-looking figure alongside me. My IRA contact had arrived. 'Let's go for a walk,' he said. We seemed to walk forever through a series of back streets in and around the Temple Bar area before crossing over the Ha'penny Bridge to the north side of the city. There was no chat along the way. I simply followed a couple of steps behind. 'This guy is making sure we're not followed,' I thought.

We eventually came to a halt outside the Winding Stair bookshop on Ormond Quay. 'You'll know me from now on as Brendan,' the contact informed me as we sat down at one of the small tables in the café area upstairs in the bookshop. Brendan paid for two cups of coffee. Our conversation lasted for about 15 minutes. 'I am authorised to speak on behalf of the IRA,' he said in a hushed voice. 'Anything I tell you will be correct and accurate.'

I later discovered that Brendan was not this man's real name. His was not a household name but he was a senior member of the IRA. Some of our initial contacts were organised through a Sinn Féin figure. Naturally enough, I didn't have a telephone number for Brendan. I used to ring this Sinn Féin person and ask to meet Brendan. Word would eventually come back—Brendan will meet you at such a place, at such a time. It was real cloak-and-dagger stuff.

Over the following 12 years, I had four different IRA contacts—I will call them Brendan, Patrick, Conor and Thomas. None of my contacts were household names but neither were they junior members of the republican movement. I suspect—but I cannot be certain—that each of these contacts was a member of the IRA's army council.

I never went to meet any of my IRA contacts without telling somebody in RTÉ. I established a routine with Ed Mulhall, my immediate boss, that I would tell him about my movements—where I was going and when I was due back in RTÉ. In the early days, up until the IRA ceasefire was restored in July 1997, there was some apprehension about these contacts, on safety grounds. The IRA was, after all, an illegal organisation with a habit of killing people. I was cautious and, indeed, I was often scared when going to meet the IRA contacts. I suppose the longer the contacts went on, the more secure we all became about personal-safety issues.

I drove the Dublin to Belfast road often in those years. Sometimes I would literally get the latest IRA statement and, when the story was of significance, I would go live on air. On those occasions, it was a race to get the material out. Competition to be first with the news when there was a breaking development in the peace process was always a consideration. 'Have I got this one myself?' I would always ask my contact. I was given the material exclusively on several occasions—never more dramatically than when the first ceasefire ended in early 1996.

There were times when I asked myself whether I was doing the right thing—had RTÉ made the correct decision? There was always a danger of acting as a postman, simply delivering IRA statements. Some people criticised RTÉ for being a 'mouthpiece of the IRA' although it was not the only station broadcasting stories obtained from contacts with the republican movement. The BBC in Northern Ireland and Downtown Radio in Belfast were engaged in a similar news-gathering exercise. As I saw it, RTÉ had decided to authorise these contacts to help improve our understanding about what was going on within the republican movement. Journalists are in the business of communicating to the public what's happening . And that was what we were doing in this case. We had an insight that few politicians or other public figures were able to provide. We were also reporting exclusive stories, which is something else that RTÉ gained from having such informed sources. There was some resentment within the media in the Republic as, time and time again, RTÉ was given access to IRA stories. I know some colleagues outside RTÉ were miffed. There were also some barbed comments from

Sinn Féin figures when I turned up to report on their events. 'Hey, here's the guy who knows what's happening before we do,' they used to remark, half-jokingly.

Over the years, I have had considerable contact with the leadership figures in Sinn Féin. Gerry Adams has an affable manner but keeps his distance. Like any party leader, Adams is well protected by his press office staff. In more recent times, however, as the peace process has become more stable, he has become more approachable and willing to discuss developments. Martin McGuinness, on the other hand, is probably easier to deal with. Over the years, I sometimes met McGuinness to talk about developments in the peace process. It was just an opportunity to have a cup of coffee and to get his insight.

While much praise is given to leaders like Adams and McGuinness for the republican movement's move away from violence, I believe that there is one other person within Sinn Féin who deserves considerable credit. The individual with whom I have had most contact in the Sinn Féin leadership is Rita O'Hare, who is often known as the *Bean Rua* because of her fiery red hair. O'Hare was the party's press officer for many years in Dublin, and more recently has been the Sinn Féin representative in the United States. I have come across Rita O'Hare several times huddled in secret conversations with top Irish government officials, obviously discussing the latest twists and turns in the peace process. On occasion, she asked me not to report what I had seen because of the sensitivity of the contacts at the particular time and the damage exposure would have done to the process. O'Hare's significance can perhaps best be summed up by the response of Bill Clinton when meeting her at a conference in Dublin some years ago. On seeing O'Hare, the former us President moved beyond Gerry Adams to plant a kiss on the cheek of the Sinn Féin official. This extraordinary act was captured on camera.

Despite my contacts with Sinn Féin officials, I was never able to ring the IRA. I would usually get a phone call from a public pay phone with the request to be at some location at a certain time. Sometimes notice of IRA statements or briefing would be quite short. There was usually a rush to drive north out of Dublin in the direction of Belfast. On several occasions, I had to check my speed which was slipping over the limit. I recall one time ringing a Sinn Féin figure with a request to get a message to my IRA contact that I was going to be a few minutes late as my car was stuck in traffic on the way into Belfast. Fortunately, they obliged.

The relationship with the IRA was built on a degree of trust. Not once in all our dealings was I ever misled by any of my IRA contacts. It was never said but I think we all knew that if I had ever been misled, the relationship would have been ended immediately. I never felt compromised in the work I was doing. After our first meeting in the summer of 1993, I dealt with Brendan for several years as the peace process broke into the open and the IRA embarked upon a course of actions which led the organisation to destroy its weapons in the autumn of 2005. But those actions were far away as I sat in the Winding Stair in 1993. I knew Brendan was sussing me out. I suppose I was doing the same with him. I asked a series of questions to glean what was going on within the IRA. 'Is there any truth to the speculation about a ceasefire?' I ventured.

As I discovered over the following years, Brendan had a certain style. He was very disciplined. Small talk was not his forte. He told me only what he had been told to tell me. He was always very precise in what he said. He never offered anything more than a direct answer to any questions I posed. He was not a man to venture off the specific topic. As I pressed for information on issues like decommissioning or the future of the IRA, he would simply sit in front of me, poker faced.

There was a huge irony in the fact that I was sitting talking with this IRA man in 1993, at a time when RTÉ was banned from broadcasting interviews with any members of the republican movement, including Sinn Féin representatives. I could not have recorded an interview with Brendan for inclusion in a television or radio report. To broadcast such material was illegal.

For much of my career in journalism, Section 31 was a source of controversy. From 1 October 1971 until 19 January 1994, the Section 31 broadcasting ban was in place. The legislation prevented broadcasters in the Irish Republic from transmitting interviews with members of certain organisations associated with the Troubles in Northern Ireland. We were precluded from broadcasting on television or radio any material that included IRA or Sinn Féin representatives, regardless of what they were talking about. So, Sinn Féin members who might have been in the news for any reason, even subjects that had nothing to do with politics, were excluded from the airwaves. Section 31, as it was implemented by RTÉ, became, in effect, a blanket ban.

It was a contentious subject which was always on the agenda and a matter of considerable internal and external debate. There were many rows about how journalists in the RTÉ newsroom should deal with the restrictions imposed upon them by the ban. The whole situation was highly divisive. The ban produced all sorts of difficulties. During the 1981 hunger strikes, RTÉ could not interview Sinn Féin representatives and when Gerry Adams defeated Joe Hendron in the 1983 Westminster election, RTÉ was left to discuss the result with the unsuccessful SDLP candidate. Like other RTÉ staff, I frequently took abuse from Sinn Féin representatives who could not be interviewed.

Many people in the RTÉ newsroom took the view that as Section 31 was the law of the land, we had no choice but to work within the restrictions. It was the more moderate viewpoint. Others argued that we should fight the censorship head-on. That was the opinion of the leadership of the National Union of Journalists (NUJ) in Dublin and London. A majority of the members of the Dublin Broadcasting Branch—effectively RTÉ journalists—favoured a less strident approach. Most NUJ members in RTÉ were against taking industrial action to pressurise the government into removing Section 31. This position clashed with official NUJ policy which had been adopted in 1986, promising to support industrial action against the annual renewal of Section 31 and to back any member disciplined for refusing to work within the limits it imposed. The situation was ludicrous as Section 31 affected only RTÉ members yet the other NUJ branches had adopted a policy which they would not have had to implement. We opposed the NUJ stance at the union's annual conference.

The ongoing tension about the ban would every so often escalate into a full-scale row. On one occasion, in August 1985, there was a 24-hour strike in protest at a decision to prevent an interview with Martin Galvin, a representative of Noraid, a republican fundraising group in North America. Neither Galvin nor Noraid was actually banned under Section 31 but a decision was taken to deny him access to the airwaves. Early the following year, there was a two-hour work stoppage over the decision to renew Section 31. The endless debate about the broadcasting ban continued but there was little prospect of a change in attitude in Leinster House, where Section 31 had the support of all the main political parties. As journalists, we simply got on with our jobs. There was no mood for an outright battle with the political establishment.

But then the Jenny McGeever case in March 1988 brought the ban to the top of the news agenda.

McGeever was a new recruit to the newsroom. I did not know her terribly well. She was working as a reporter on *Morning Ireland* at the time of the shooting dead of three IRA members in Gibraltar, by British SAS officers. There was huge controversy over the circumstances in which the three republicans had been shot. Reports emerged that they were unarmed and that no attempt had been made actually to arrest them.

It was against that backdrop that the three bodies were brought back from Gibraltar. McGeever was one of many journalists reporting on the story on 14 March 1988. The coffins were taken off a plane at Dublin Airport in the afternoon. Leading republicans, including Gerry Adams and Martin McGuinness, were there and accompanied the funeral cortège on the journey back to Belfast. There were huge crowds in Dundalk as the three hearses with their coffins draped in tricolors made their way through the town. The flags became a source of conflict at the border where a large security presence was situated. The British wanted the tricolors removed. Angry exchanges followed before a compromise was reached, with wreaths covering the flags. McGeever was there with her microphone.

McGeever's report was broadcast on *Morning Ireland* on 15 March. It opened with a description of the funeral cortège leaving Dublin Airport. There was sound actuality from the first confrontation between republicans and the RUC. McGeever then introduced McGuinness. The voice of the Sinn Féin politician—who was widely believed to be a leading IRA man—was heard explaining to those present that the RUC would not allow the coffins into Northern Ireland because they were draped with tricolors. McGeever had not interviewed McGuinness but she had recorded him telling the gathering what was happening.

The audio clip of McGuinness lasted for 17 seconds. Then the report returned to McGeever who said, 'Two local priests intervened, and Gerry Adams briefed journalists on the problem.' The report was then cut off. In all, McGeever's report lasted about 90 seconds before it was pulled. The section with McGuinness's voice lasted 17 seconds.

McGeever had been up all night covering the story. She was under pressure to prepare her report. Neither of the two editors on *Morning*

Ireland—David Davin-Power and Barbara Fitzgerald—was aware of the controversial material in the report. Davin-Power was also presenting the one-hour morning programme when the report aired. A shortage of staff on the programme was put forward as one reason why the report had got through the normal vetting procedures. Davin-Power and Fitzgerald faced a disciplinary hearing but they were exonerated of any blame.

There was uproar and it started almost immediately after the McGeever report was broadcast. RTÉ was attacked from all sides. Ray Burke of Fianna Fáil—who was the party's communications spokesman—issued a statement condemning the station. A few hours after the controversial broadcast, McGeever was suspended. A week later, her contract was terminated.

At the time of the McGeever case, I was chairman of the Dublin Broadcasting Branch of the NUJ. There were very different views about how we should respond. Meeting followed meeting. The discussions were frequently very heated. There were calls for management resignations. Many people believed that the management response was excessive. It was true that Section 31 had been breached but most people considered it a technical breach. Matters were not helped when it became clear that some in the NUJ viewed the episode as an opportunity to challenge Section 31, using the McGeever case as an issue of press freedom. In the Dublin Broadcasting Branch, we were reluctant to go down that road. There was little appetite for a long and divisive battle with RTÉ management and the government itself. There was a lively debate within the NUJ over our stance. 'Members in RTÉ are governed by union authority. Do Charlie Bird and his members want to defy us?' one NUJ officer asked in a national newspaper. The answer was 'Yes, if required.'

McGeever initially tried to argue her way out of her predicament. She told one emergency NUJ meeting that she was acting on her interpretation of Section 31. Her job was on the line. Quite rightly she had taken legal advice. The situation was complicated by the fact that McGeever had being on contract for only a short period and doubts were raised about whether she qualified for protection under employment law.

Management at RTÉ responded in a less-than-confident manner. A few days after the McGeever incident, Sinn Féin Ard Comhairle member Lydia Comiskey was interviewed on the *Gay Byrne Show*. She spoke about how her husband had had to emigrate in search of work. At first, RTÉ management said Comiskey's appearance as 'a housewife and mother suffering hardship' did not breach Section 31. But they quickly backtracked—no Sinn Féin member was permitted on the airwaves, in any circumstances. So, a second statement was issued. Then a directive was issued, demanding that every person being interviewed on radio should first be asked if they were a member of Sinn Féin. I wasn't shy about putting the boot in. 'Without going into the rights and wrongs of the case, how can Jenny McGeever be expected to know how to operate Section 31 when clearly senior management don't understand it,' the *Irish Press* quoted me as saying.

We eventually decided to hold a ballot on whether or not to take industrial action in support of McGeever. It was a big decision to go down that road. There was little certainty that a strike would actually resolve matters. A blue ballot box was positioned on a table. I turned the key in the lock to ensure that the box was secure. Then the 230 NUJ members in the Broadcasting Branch in RTÉ were invited to cast their votes. But before the day in question was over, the ballot was suspended. McGeever took a judicial review of her case in the High Court.

The decision took the immediate heat out of the controversy. I still wanted to know what way my colleagues were moving. I believed a strike would have split the NUJ and done irreparable damage to the RTÉ newsroom. I took the blue ballot box home to Bray, and, without anyone else ever knowing, I opened it and counted out two piles of votes— in favour of and against strike action. When I had finished the exercise, I returned the papers to the ballot box, secured the lock, and the following day brought the box back into RTÉ where the papers were ultimately destroyed. The talk in the newsroom was about how we would have supported McGeever. Only I knew the truth. Not everyone had cast their ballot when voting was suspended but most people had had their say. And a clear majority was opposed to a strike in support of McGeever who eventually settled her case against RTÉ.

It was one of the low points in my involvement in trade union activities in RTÉ. I still feel even today, after all these years, that I could have provided stronger leadership during the McGeever controversy. Relations were strained within the newsroom over the episode. There were also huge differences in the stance of the NUJ and the view of its

Dublin Broadcasting Branch. Later, in 1988, the NUJ announced that it was to challenge Section 31 at the European Commission of Human Rights in Strasbourg. This decision to challenge the Irish government was taken without consultation with the union's members in RTÉ. I was furious, and duly resigned as chairman of the NUJ's branch in RTÉ. I told one newspaper that the court-case decision was 'knee-jerk'. It is an opinion I still believe to be true. A decision in the case was eventually handed down in April 1991, with the European Human Rights Commission backing the need for Section 31.

In any event, within three years the broadcasting ban was gone, when the then Fianna Fáil–Labour coalition ended the restrictions as a gesture to the developing peace process. Michael D. Higgins was the minister who, in early 1994, ended the controversial ban, which in its time had brought down an RTÉ Authority and had seen the jailing of the broadcaster, Kevin O'Kelly. Interestingly the first post-Section 31 interview with Gerry Adams was conducted by Conor Lenihan, a future Fianna Fáil TD who was then a reporter with the Dublin radio station, 98FM. RTÉ took a deliberate decision that Adams's first RTÉ interview would be broadcast on the *This Week* radio programme some days after the ban was lifted. The political climate was changing. Secret talks with the IRA pointed to a unique possibility for peace. I believe that the decision to remove the broadcasting ban in early 1994 actually helped the peace process as it was then developing.

Contacts between representatives of the government in Dublin and the IRA had been under way since the late 1980s. Those discussions laid the ground work for the Downing Street Declaration in December 1993, which set out the views of the Dublin and London governments on how a post-IRA ceasefire environment would unfold. All during 1994, speculation increased about a ceasefire. My contacts in government buildings were talking positively about the possibility of an end to IRA violence. As usual, getting an interview with the main participant was a journalistic objective. I rang my Sinn Féin contact. 'If there is a ceasefire, do you think the IRA will put forward a spokesperson for an interview?' I asked.

'Charlie, how would I know that?' the reply came back.

'Will you see if Brendan will meet me?' I ventured.

I travelled north of Dublin to County Louth in the middle of August 1994 to meet Brendan, my IRA contact. A Sinn Féin official was sitting in the passenger seat of my car. It was a bright summer's evening. On the road beyond Dundalk, the Cooley Mountains were visible. 'Do you see over there?' my companion said. 'That's the Long Woman's Grave.'

I gave a nervous laugh. 'What the hell have I got myself into?' I thought.

Sometime later, I discovered that the site of the Long Woman's Grave in the Windy Gap in the Cooley Mountains takes its name from a prehistoric tale. A Spanish princess was deceived into marrying an Irishman, who convinced her that he owned everything that could be seen from his home. But when the princess arrived at her new home at the Windy Gap, she fell dead with disappointment. So the legend goes. But on that August evening in 1994, mention of the Long Woman's Grave induced visions of the IRA and other terrible atrocities. We drove for a couple of hours up and down the back roads of the Cooley Mountains, crossing over at one point into Northern Ireland before returning to the south. My passenger was giving the directions which eventually brought us to a small rural pub.

We were sitting inside for a few minutes when Brendan arrived. The Sinn Féin person moved aside from us. 'You're on your own now,' the person said.

I greeted Brendan.

'You wanted to see me,' he replied in his direct way which I had become more familiar with over the previous few months.

I asked about the possibility of an interview if a ceasefire was called. I was doing my best to sell the idea to him. We discussed the logistics of what would be involved and how the identity of the interviewee could be concealed. As ever, Brendan was true to form in offering no indication about how the proposal would be met by the IRA leadership.

'I will take your request back,' he said.

The three of us walked back to my car together.

'Do you mind giving me a lift?' Brendan asked. While we had been inside the pub, the sun had gone down. I was now faced with the prospect of travelling along isolated rural roads with two passengers in my car—a leading Sinn Féin figure and a man with an IRA record. I was terrified but had no choice in the matter.

'Where will I leave you to?' I asked as I turned the key in the ignition.

'Just drive ahead. I'll tell you when to stop,' Brendan said from the back seat.

We drove for some time on the darkened roads along the border. No other cars passed. 'Stop here,' my IRA contact eventually said. We were in the middle of nowhere. There were fields on either side of the road and no lights anywhere nearby to indicate a house or even a waiting car. Brendan bade me farewell.

The Sinn Féin person also got out of the car. 'I'll be back in a few minutes,' this person said.

They walked together about 50 yards down the road in the pitch dark. I could just about make them out in my rear-view mirror. 'What the hell is going on?' I thought.

Having stopped and talked for a few minutes, the two republicans embraced. Brendan then walked on into the dark while the Sinn Féin person returned to the car and got back into the front passenger seat. 'Do you mind me asking,' I ventured, 'what was that about?'

'Charlie, over the next few days, something momentous is going to happen. It will be a really big thing for all of us,' my passenger explained.

There was more contact from Brendan later that week. My request for an interview was turned down. On 30 August, I got another call. 'Charlie, be on O'Connell Street tomorrow morning at ten o'clock,' was the instruction. I was waiting for Brendan at the appointed time when another person, whom I recognised, walked up to me. I was handed an envelope which held a very small piece of paper and a Dictaphone cassette. 'You're not to use that before eleven o'clock and then you're to destroy everything,' the man ordered.

I had already booked a room in Barry's Hotel on nearby Great Denmark Street. A camera crew had set up their equipment. They were ready to go when I burst in the door, having run the whole way up O'Connell Street. The IRA ceasefire statement was typed out on a tiny piece of paper which had been folded in two. I read the opening line:

Recognising the potential of the current situation and in order to enhance the democratic peace process and underline our definite commitment to its success, the leadership of Óglaigh na hÉireann have decided that as of midnight, Wednesday, 31 August, there will be a complete cessation of military operations.

I did a live report just after 11 a.m. on Radio One. The written statement and the tape had also been given to Andrew Hanlon of 98FM in Dublin and the BBC's Dublin correspondent, Shane Harrison. A woman's voice reading the IRA statement had been recorded onto the cassette. There was some hissing in the background, which I was later told was the sound of a hairdryer. The IRA was conscious about not leaving any sounds on the tape for the security forces to identify the location where the message had been recorded.

It seemed as if the whole world wanted to talk with me, including the gardaí, although there was nothing I could tell them. As it turned out, the ceasefire announcement was not the end of the conflict in Northern Ireland. There were many twists and turns in the years that followed. I had more contact with the IRA than I could ever have envisaged when I had first met Brendan in the summer of 1993.

I would often meet my IRA contact for a briefing and to talk about the latest developments in the peace process. Sometimes I would not file any story after these meetings. However, as the peace process stumbled on, the number of IRA statements became more frequent.

I remember, in the summer of 1995, getting a phone call from Brendan, which was unusual in itself as he normally contacted me through a republican intermediary. 'I need to meet you,' he said.

'I'm in Schull in west Cork,' I replied. 'I'm on holidays with my family,' I added. This fact did not put off the IRA man.

'Don't worry. I'll meet you somewhere along the route. How long will it take you to get to Cashel?' he asked.

It was 10 p.m. when I drove into the car park of a hotel in Cashel where we had arranged to meet. We went across the road to a local pub. 'We want to brief you on a speech Gerry Adams will make later this week. It's important that you know the IRA leadership supports everything he will say,' Brendan advised.

Sometimes our meetings were like that one in Cashel. There was no immediate story, just the provision of a background briefing. In the immediate aftermath of the 31 August IRA ceasefire, the absence of the word 'permanent' from the IRA statement was an issue for many unionists and political figures in Britain. But what would happen to IRA weapons soon became the real block to the start of multi-party talks on the future of Northern Ireland, with Sinn Féin as an invited party. There were debates, discussions and rows about when decommissioning would take place—before, during or after the multi-party talks.

One of my final briefings from Brendan—before a new IRA contact arrived on the scene—was in early February 1996. There had been some speculation about the status of the IRA ceasefire, but all pointers indicated that, despite a delay in starting multi-party talks, there was no real danger to the process Adams and his colleagues had embarked upon.

It was Friday, 9 February 1996. I was suffering from a very heavy head cold. It was very unusual for me to go home sick but, as it was a quiet day, I decided my time would be better served at home, clearing my cold. What I didn't realise was that not long after I left for home, all hell broke loose in the RTÉ newsroom. Brendan was looking for me. The battery on my mobile phone had gone down. So he rang my extension at work. It was 5.30 p.m. A colleague took the message. 'Tell Charlie, Brendan needs to talk with him,' the IRA contact said before giving the text of an IRA statement.

The wording was ominous. Eighteen months after the August 1994 statement that had been handed to me in central Dublin, the IRA was back in contact, with confirmation that the organisation was ending its ceasefire 'with great reluctance'. However, in the newsroom, they were not sure whether the statement was true or simply a hoax. Calls were made to Government Buildings but nobody there knew anything about an IRA statement. The newsroom eventually got in contact with me. I had no quick way of contacting Brendan, but I rang a number of Sinn Féin contacts, none of whom was aware of what was going on. I then decided to drive to the home of a senior republican figure whom I trusted and who I suspected might be able to get in touch with Brendan and find out what exactly was going on.

When I got to this person's front door, it was obvious there was panic inside in the house. I could hear this person on the phone. The conversation was with Gerry Adams who I knew was in the United States. The voices were agitated. The front door opened. 'What's going on?' I asked. As we started to speak, my mobile rang. It was Brendan.

'Why didn't you go with the statement?' he asked.

'We needed to be sure it was for real,' I responded.

'It's for real, Charlie. You can go with it,' Brendan advised.

I drove to RTÉ and went live on the main evening television news at about 6.50 p.m. The IRA ceasefire was over. Minutes later, a massive bomb exploded near Canary Wharf in London's Docklands. The statement from Brendan had not mentioned a bomb. But in London another IRA man had called the police with a very different statement. Because of the confusion between Brendan and me, few people knew that the IRA ceasefire was over when the London bomb warning was received. If I had been in the office when Brendan called, the statement would have been broadcast by 6 p.m. As it was, I didn't get into studio until about 6.45 p.m. to deliver the news that the IRA ceasefire was over. At 6.59 p.m., the bomb exploded. Without the delay, there would have been the best part of an hour longer to deal with the bomb threat. The explosion caused huge damage. Police had managed to clear most of the area, but two men were killed in the blast—Inan Bashir and John Jeffries who worked in a newspaper kiosk near Canary Wharf. It was the lowest point in my dealings with the IRA, and I know that was a view shared by others in RTÉ, including Ed Mulhall. If the statement had been reported earlier, those two men would probably still be alive. I felt I had let people down.

It was a frantic evening which didn't ease off until close to midnight. There were extended news programmes on television and radio. There was also a sense of sadness in the newsroom and much head scratching. Everyone was trying to understand what exactly the strategy of the republican leadership was. All through the evening news, stations from across the globe had been calling RTÉ, asking to speak with me. I did interviews with the likes of CNN, explaining the confused political atmosphere that the IRA statement had created. One journalist working for a radio station in the United States had an unusual request. 'Mr Bird, could you please pass on to us a telephone number for your contact in the IRA,' the woman actually asked. I just laughed.

Despite the general pessimism, I knew that the peace process was not over. But there was no certainty about how and when the IRA ceasefire could be restored. From my Sinn Féin contacts, I was aware of the total breakdown in relations between republicans and the governments in Dublin and London. Elections to Westminster and to Dáil Éireann were due during 1997. It seemed that nothing would happen until the results of those two contests were decided.

In the meantime, I readied myself for further contact from the IRA which was now back in the business of shootings and bombings. I had a new IRA contact. No reason was given for the change. I jokingly described the new man, Patrick, as the 'schoolteacher'. I would never have picked him out as a member of the IRA. Sometime later, I was flabbergasted to see this man at a big Sinn Féin event. He wasn't there as a significant figure but the very fact that he was in attendance was remarkable given the link role he was playing between the IRA and RTÉ. Patrick was also from Northern Ireland but, unlike with Brendan, whom I had met mainly in Dublin, I nearly always travelled to meet Patrick, and we nearly always went for a walk before he briefed me on the latest IRA statement.

Patrick was more conversational than Brendan. He was prepared to elaborate and expand on the wording in any given statement, whereas Brendan stuck rigidly to the text of what he was giving me. Once or twice, I recall, Patrick even asked me for my opinion. I remember once responding to something he had said with the line, 'But Sinn Féin has been saying. . .'

He immediately cut across me: 'Look, we're not talking about Sinn Féin. We're the IRA.'

When the IRA contacts rang me, it was usually from a public phone box. Over the phone, there was little small talk. I would usually be asked, 'Have you a pen?' I was abroad on one occasion.

'Where are you?' Patrick asked.

'I'm in South Africa. What's going on?' I said.

He had an IRA statement dealing with the subject of victims of republican violence who had literally 'disappeared'. There was some hesitation when I said I was in South Africa. 'I don't think I have enough coins for this call,' Patrick said. He had to hang up and some-time later he called me again. 'I'm here with ten pounds in coins. That should be enough,' he informed me before we talked about the IRA statement.

Patrick had a habit of catching me at the wrong time. I recall one morning being in the car driving through Milltown in south Dublin. My daughter, Neasa, was actually doing the driving. I was sitting in the passenger seat—I was giving her a driving lesson. I was giving instructions and directions when my mobile rang. It was Patrick. 'Charlie, I don't care where you are—you have to take this statement down now,' he said. I told Neasa to keep driving as I turned my concentration to the IRA statement. I know she was in a state of blind panic as I had stopped giving directions!

The election of Tony Blair in Britain in May 1997, followed a month later by Bertie Ahern's victory in elections to Dáil Éireann, opened the way for a restoration of the IRA ceasefire. I spent much of the general election reporting on the Ahern campaign and so I was very familiar with the speculation about how the republican leadership would respond to a new political environment in both Dublin and London.

In mid-July, Bertie Ahern rang me on my mobile. 'I think you're going to get a call in the morning,' the new Taoiseach said. There was certain choreography at work, although with a secret organisation like the IRA, nothing was ever taken for granted.

Sure enough, at about six o'clock the following morning, Patrick called. 'Can you get to Dundalk by half-past eight?' he asked.

It was a stunning summer's morning as I arrived in the appointed meeting place in the car park of the Fairways Hotel, just outside Dundalk. I had met Patrick there on several occasions. But this time, he was uneasy. 'There's a garda car outside,' he said, discreetly pointing to the main entrance where two gardaí were sitting in a parked garda vehicle. 'We won't stay here,' he added. So we drove in his car down the road to a nearby garage. We parked beside the car wash. Patrick handed me the much-anticipated IRA statement. 'Write it down,' he said. 'It's for the nine o'clock news and nobody else has it,' he added.

As I started to transcribe the statement into my notebook, Patrick pulled open the bonnet of the car and made himself look busy, 'fixing' something inside the engine. When I had finished writing, the IRA man asked me to read back my notes. 'A statement from the IRA,' I started before he interjected, 'No, it's a statement from Óglaigh na hÉireann.'

Many people object to the IRA's use of Óglaigh na hÉireann, the official name of the Irish army, and I found it odd that on that morning Patrick was making such a fuss about the term.

'I don't think I'm going to make nine o'clock,' I said when we eventually got back to my car in the Fairways car park. Having to switch locations had added to an already tight timetable.

Patrick departed and I rang Peter Driscoll on the radio desk in RTÉ. Peter, who died suddenly in October 2005, was a brilliant chief sub-editor. He was thorough and very precise. 'Charlie, at last,' he said. 'The world has been looking for you. I've even had Mo Mowlam's office on.'

I had missed the 9 a.m. bulletin on Radio One where the governments in Dublin and London had been told by their republican contacts that the IRA statement would first be broadcast. But Peter was not going to let the missed bulletin stand in the way of our exclusive, so it was arranged that we would break into the pre-recorded *Playback* programme at about 9.15 a.m.

Sometime later, I was asked to meet Patrick in Belfast. The IRA statement he was giving me was not hugely important but the meeting was also used to introduce a new contact. I had been told to go to the Falls Road. I was sitting in a local community centre, having a coffee, when a man approached me. 'Come this way,' he said. We walked up and down some narrow streets in west Belfast before entering a red-brick terraced house. Patrick said his farewells. It was a strange situation as I had built up a good rapport with this IRA man.

The new contact, Conor, was, as I soon discovered, an entirely different personality. He was very difficult to deal with. Whereas Patrick had enough confidence to go beyond the wording in any given statement, Conor would never stray from the exact text of an IRA statement. He rarely gave me any additional information. The man would hardly confirm what day of the week it was. In that way, he was not much different from Brendan, the first contact. However, in comparison with Brendan, this new man was scattered and far less organised. I found myself nearly pulling my hair out when dealing with Conor whom I generally met in Belfast. Sometime later, I saw him in a newspaper photograph at a republican gathering in Belfast. 'My God,' I thought when I discovered his standing within the IRA.

After the initial series of statements and briefings from the IRA, gardaí often used to pay me a visit in RTÉ. 'Is there anything you can tell us?' they used to ask, more in hope than anything else as my answer was always in the negative. On a number of occasions, at very sensitive times in the peace process, I came across a senior government official meeting with Sinn Féin figures. Twice, I saw this influential civil servant in the company of senior republicans in out-of-the-way locations. Both times, I decided not to report what I had seen. There was no huge news story, but the embarrassment would have been huge for the government. In a way, these decisions paid off for me because, in return, I got more than my fair share of exclusives from both sides.

In the summer of 2005, there was much speculation about when the IRA would issue a statement probably as important as those I had received in August 1994 when the first ceasefire was called. The previous months had been filled with drama—the multi-million-pound robbery of the Northern Bank in Belfast was followed by the brutal murder of

Robert McCartney. Gerry Adams and his supporters were, for the first time, seriously on the back foot. It was time for the IRA to make a significant decision to breathe new life into a floundering peace process. The 1998 Belfast Agreement had pointed to a new future for Northern Ireland but distrust was naturally high between unionists and republicans. There was a general consensus that the IRA had to act on decommissioning before any form of political stability would arrive in the North.

The republican leadership was under huge pressure to make a final and decisive step in the direction of constitutional politics. But when I called my usually reliable republican sources, I quickly discovered that nobody seemed to be clear about what was happening. These were senior people within the republican movement whose judgment and insight I trusted. They had always pointed me in the correct direction. But now these sources were saying nothing about the continuing speculation over IRA decommissioning and the very future of the organisation itself. Then Gerry Adams gave me a good lead.

After a Sinn Féin press conference in Buswells Hotel in Dublin, Adams said that he was not certain when a statement from the IRA would come. Then he remarked that he was not going on holidays until after the August bank holiday weekend. The statement was never going to be issued while the Sinn Féin president was on his summer break. So, if the IRA was to act, it would probably be in July or the situation would not be resolved until September. A republican source rang me to say that talk about September was inaccurate. 'When you hear that Martin McGuinness and Rita O'Hare are travelling to Washington, then you'll know we're on,' one Sinn Féin figure eventually admitted.

I was at home in Ashford when I finally received a phone call about McGuinness and O'Hare's travel plans. I was out at Dublin Airport the following morning, Wednesday, 27 July, for their departure to the United States. It was a crazy day filled with news reports and live interviews. A process was under way but it was not clear what the IRA was intending to deliver. That evening, at about 8.50 p.m., I was standing outside Government Buildings on Merrion Street, running through my thoughts, preparing for a live interview on the nine o'clock news. My mobile rang. 'Can you get to Dundalk tonight?' my IRA contact asked. I was confused. I had been expecting a statement early the following morning. I didn't mention this conversation when I speculated on the news that an IRA statement was imminent.

After the live interview, I got into my car and drove north. There was no time to go home to Ashford. I met a republican figure at the Fairways Hotel outside Dundalk. This person sat into the passenger seat of my car. 'You'll need to be in Belfast from half-past ten tomorrow morning. There'll be enough time to get back to Dublin after that,' he said. I was now totally confused.

'Why the rush to meet me tonight?' I thought. But there was no time to ask as my source was gone. I booked into the Fairways. The restaurant was closed. An egg and chicken sandwich was all that was on offer.

I was at the agreed meeting place at 10.30 the following morning, Thursday 28 July, when, out of nowhere, my latest IRA contact—who I'll call Thomas—appeared. He had replaced Conor sometime before this latest development. He was my fourth and, as it turned out, my final IRA contact. It was clear that Thomas was a significant player in the republican movement. He was always at ease when we met and was highly confident in briefing on developments. 'Lock your car. We're going for a little walk,' Thomas said.

It was now almost 12 years since my first IRA contact had met me outside Bewley's Café on Westmoreland Street in Dublin with a similar instruction. Much had happened over those years. Now it seemed an end to the IRA was in sight. We walked for some time in and around the back streets off the Falls Road in west Belfast. 'You're not to describe the inside of the house,' the IRA man said as we eventually stopped outside a red-brick terrace house.

Inside the house, another man was sitting at a table in the kitchen, reading a newspaper. I followed my contact into the small front living-room. He handed me a large white envelope. The IRA statement was set out over two pages. It was the first time I had been given any material from the IRA on official headed paper. The 1994 ceasefire statement had been typed on a tiny sheet of paper which, when folded, could fit nearly into the palm of my hand. The 28 July 2005 statement was printed on paper with large lettering that proclaimed 'Óglaigh na hÉireann' in a bright green masthead.

The statement was even more dramatic than had been anticipated. As I sat reading this statement for the first time, I thought to myself, 'So the IRA's war really is over.'

The leadership of Oglaigh na hÉireann has formally ordered an end of the armed campaign. This will take effect from 4pm this afternoon. All IRA units have been ordered to dump arms. All volunteers have been instructed to assist the development of purely political and democratic programmes through exclusively peaceful means. Volunteers must not engage in any other activities whatsoever.

Back in 1994, I had been given an audiotape of the IRA statement. Now I was handed a DVD prepared by the republican leadership. 'I want you to watch this before we go,' Thomas said as he put the disc into a DVD machine. A middle-aged man appeared on the television screen, but before he started speaking, the image froze.

'The technology may have improved but you can't get it to work,' I joked as Thomas took the disc out of the machine and gave it a quick wipe. As he was doing this, he started to tell me about Séanna Walsh, the IRA man who had been selected to read the text of the organisation's historic statement. Walsh had spent most of his adult life in prison and was a friend of Bobby Sands, the republican hunger striker. With a deep-rooted family involvement in nationalist politics, Walsh had the necessary pedigree to deliver the historic statement. The formalities concluded when the DVD ended. I had the statement. I had known this IRA man for some time. Thomas had been a good contact. He was always reliable. We both knew this was the end.

'How do you feel yourself,' I asked.

'I've a busy day ahead of me so there'll be no time for thinking. I suppose I'll think about it later but it's emotional,' Thomas responded.

The atmosphere was more relaxed than usual at such a meeting. I pressed a number of issues. 'And what will you be doing after four o'clock today?' I asked, half-joking.

'Just what it says in the statement there,' the IRA man replied, gesturing at the two pages on the seat next to me.

'What happens to the IRA now?'

He looked straight at me. 'That depends on others.'

'Will there be a split?' I ventured.

'There's been a long discussion over a long period of time. Some people will be unhappy but they'll just walk away. There'll be no major split.'

It was almost 11 a.m. It was time to leave if I was to make the 2 p.m. deadline which the IRA had set as an embargo for broadcasting the

The first ceasefire ended in early 1996 but was restored in July 1997. I furiously noted down
the wording of the IRA statement announcing its second ceasefire.
Source: *Derek Speirs*

Albert Reynolds was always available to answer questions from the media during his controversial and dramatic term as Taoiseach between 1992 and 1994.
Source: *Photocall Ireland*

John Bruton became Taoiseach unexpectedly in late 1994 and succeeded in holding together the country's first multi-party government since the 1950s.

Interviewing Brian Cowen in November 1994 on the day Fianna Fáil elected Bertie Ahern as party leader.
Source: *Derek Speirs*

Trying to get a little quiet ahead of an interview with Bertie Ahern. His trusted advisor, Joe Lennon, is watching closely behind me.
Source: *Photocall Ireland*

A few moments of relaxation with Bertie Ahern and Celia Larkin during their official visit to China in 1998.

Recording a piece-to-camera for a television news report, with the Great Wall stretching out behind me.

The red carpet was rolled out in Tiananmen Square in Beijing so we took advantage when recording this news report.
Source: *Photocall Ireland*

BRANCH: CARRICK—ON—SHANNON

REPORT POINT: Interest on Current Accounts

WEAKNESS/POTENTIAL ADVERSE CONSEQUENCE

It was noted that Interest Charges were increased without legitimate reason or customers' knowledge on twenty accounts in November 1989 and thirty—three accounts in February 1990.

The above practice could lead to loss to the Bank through customer dispute, litigation or adverse publicity.

REMEDIAL ACTION REQUIRED

Interest amendments may only be made to correct Branch errors. The practice of "loading" interest in this manner must be discontinued.

RESPONSE BY BRANCH MANAGEMENT

We note that as and from now only branch errors can be corrected using interest amendment sheets.

While we only loaded interest rates for customers who were very demanding, we were certain that we were safe in applying the additional interest charges. No queries ever came back from customers who interest was loaded.

We note and confirm that this practice will be discontinued.

9.

One of the confidential documents that sparked RTÉ's investigation into wrong-doing by National Irish Bank. Representatives of the bank initially tried to rubbish the RTÉ reports but this document clearly shows that NIB was fully aware of its illegal activities.

Neither George Lee nor I had any idea that our NIB investigation would cause us to be involved in the longest-running libel case in the history of the state. There were smiles when the jury decided not to award damages to Beverley Cooper Flynn.
Source: *Photocall Ireland*

The libel action was a huge strain on all involved. My boss in RTÉ, Ed Mulhall, was a tremendous support.
Source: *Collins Photo Agency*

Beverley Cooper Flynn took her libel action all the way to the Supreme Court but ultimately had her case rejected. There was a brief handshake at the conclusion of the case in April 2004. Source: *Courtpix*

As Finance Minister, Charlie McCreevy was initially sceptical of RTÉ's investigation into NIB. In the end, the taxpayer was almost €60 million better off.
Source: *Photocall Ireland*

Liam Lawlor leaving the Flood/Mahon Tribunal in his typically robust style. In recent years, Dublin Castle almost became my second home, after the Leinster House plinth.
Source: *Photocall Ireland*

Reclusive businessman Jim Kennedy was a long-time associate of Liam Lawlor although he refused to co-operate with the Flood/Mahon Tribunal. Tracking him down was a real coup.
Source: *RTÉ*

The scale of the devastation in Sri Lanka after the December 2004 tsunami was hard to describe. I travelled there with cameraman Neilus Dennihy.

Reporting on an aid airlift to the survivors of the catastrophic earthquake in Pakistan in 2005.

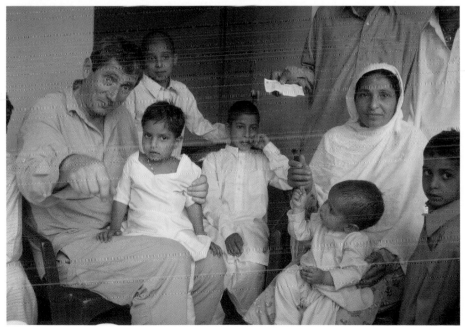

While in Pakistan, I reported on the story of Lubna, a woman who had lost both of her legs in the earthquake. Even before I had arrived back in Dublin, viewers had sent almost €50,000 unsolicited to RTÉ. This money was used to get medical treatment for Lubna, as well as to build a new house for her family.

Dr Bird! UCD awarded me an honorary doctorate in November 2004.

My RTÉ colleagues, Ed Mulhall, Joe O'Brien and George Lee, joined me in celebrating the day.

My daughters, Neasa and Orla.

Another family occasion: Neasa qualifies as a barrister.

From Beijing to the White House, Conor O'Clery of *The Irish Times* was always a helpful colleague.

On Inis Oírr with my friend
Peadar Póil.

And the Bird takes flight! A birthday gift from Orla and Neasa in 2005—a parachute jump.

statement. We shook hands. 'For what it's worth, I believe this is the right thing to do,' I said.

'I think we do, too,' the IRA man responded.

I had enough time to get back to Dublin to meet the 2 p.m. embargo. As I left Belfast, I rang the RTÉ news desk and read out the statement to Ray Burke who typed the wording up for inclusion in the internal newsroom computer file which everyone would to able to read. A former news editor at the *Irish Press*, Ray Burke is one of the most experienced newsmen in the business and was fully aware of the significance of the statement. I then called Joe Lennon in the Department of the Taoiseach. He told me a government official was off getting a copy of the IRA statement somewhere in Dublin.

What happened next contained elements of pure farce. I was driving out of Drogheda when I got a call to say that a local radio station in Dublin, Newstalk 106, had just broadcast part of the IRA statement. I rang a Sinn Féin contact. 'What's going on? I asked. This person didn't know. Other journalists were now ringing me to check if what had been broadcast was accurate.

My IRA contact rang. It seemed that the text had been put out by the printers of the weekly republican newspaper, *An Phoblacht*, the publication of which had been delayed in order to report on the IRA statement. The radio station had a few lines but nothing else.

'I'll have to break the embargo,' I told Thomas. I was on air before 1 p.m. with the full IRA statement, and the DVD was broadcast not long after on special RTÉ radio and television programmes. I was able to describe my meeting in Belfast earlier in the day, the body language of my contact and some of the details of our conversation after Thomas had eventually got the DVD to play.

I was intrigued about the response I got to my question about the IRA's future. 'That depends on others,' Thomas had said. But on the day that was in it, the emphatic sentiment in the IRA statement dominated the headlines. There was continued speculation about when the IRA would decommission its arsenal of weapons. The timing of actual decommissioning was not set down in the statement. On the evening television news, I said it was my impression that decommissioning would happen fairly quickly. It was a guess based on all the conversations I had had over the previous weeks with a variety of republican sources.

A short time later, I got a phone call from a republican figure who would not normally have rung me. 'It won't be that soon, Charlie,' he told me.

I had raised the issue of IRA decommissioning with Thomas earlier that day in Belfast. 'Will I be seeing you again? I had asked as I sat into my car.

The IRA man smiled. 'Probably, but not as soon as you think,' he said as he walked away.

Chapter 9 ⟶

THE COLOMBIA THREE

'Something big is going to happen in the next 24 hours,' my republican contact predicted. It was August 2005. 'You'll need a camera but the cameraman has to be somebody you can trust and he'll need lights,' he added. My adrenalin levels increased. Despite everything the IRA had said, it now seemed that the organisation was going to allow the decommissioning of its weapons and explosives to be filmed. 'You'll get more arrangements later so keep your mobile on,' he said. 'Nobody is to be told for now,' he added. As he walked away, my source turned back towards me, 'Charlie, you'll have this story on your own.'

We both laughed. Our conversation that afternoon had started with a discussion of the previous week's IRA statement and how it had been received. I had teased him about not being able to organise the release of the statement. I had actually been very surprised when he had called me on my mobile phone the previous evening. I had not expected to hear from the IRA so soon after the 28 July statement. When we did meet in early August, the location was a park in Dublin and not the usual coffee shop. The man was being extra vigilant about who was around. He phoned me again later that same afternoon. I was to meet him at the Coachman's Inn out by Dublin Airport at 10 p.m. but I would not be travelling anywhere that night. Even by the standards of my earlier contacts with the IRA, this was bizarre.

My boss, Ed Mulhall, was in the United States on holidays. So I went to see Cillian de Paor, who was head of television news. I now did to him what my IRA contacts had been doing to me for years. 'Cillian, I need you to walk with me,' I said. 'I have a major story but I'm not exactly sure what the story is. I need a cameraman but I'm not sure when I'll need him or where we'll be going.' I half-jokingly admitted to being convinced that decommissioning was the story which meant the cameraman would probably have to film off his shoulder without a tripod stand and would probably have to work quickly. In reality, we were playing a guessing game. De Paor arranged for Michael Lee, one of the most experienced cameramen in the RTÉ newsroom, to be rostered for my story. Michael was told I was working on a special report about immigrants. The news desk was told to keep the story off the diary schedule but already people were asking why I was at work. I was dressed casually and most people knew I had been waiting for the IRA statement before going on annual leave. It was time to get out off the RTÉ campus before somebody took a guess at why I was still around the place.

The cloak-and-dagger approach continued when I got to the Coachman's Inn. My republican contact arrived at 10 p.m. but he had little information to give me. I was to meet another IRA person the following day at 12 noon in Dundalk and I would have to leave my car. I didn't ask about the story—I knew I was not going to be told. But now, more than ever, I was convinced that we were going to film the destruction of IRA weapons. I had heard rumours that the IRA had gathered together all its arms into two big underground bunkers. If that was so, we were going to have some story.

After a day of intrigue, I eventually got back home to Ashford at around midnight. I was up at six o'clock and met Michael Lee in RTÉ shortly after eight. Michael had all his equipment packed and ready to go. He even had a back-up camera. It was now time for a little honesty. I told him that the story was not about immigrants. 'It's got something to do with the IRA. These are people I trust. I think we'll be fine,' I said. I was conscious that this meeting was very different from any previous ones with my IRA contacts. I was not going alone. Michael would have been entitled to walk away. However, he was just as curious as myself and was attracted by the big scoop of filming the IRA decommissioning its weapons.

We drove into the centre of Dublin in Michael's car to get some breakfast. I didn't want any more questions about why I was still at work. I was also conscious of being on time although we had several hours to play with. We took the coastal route out of Dublin, stopping in Malahide where Michael checked and rechecked his equipment and I went for a walk along the beach. I was nervous. I was sure it was decommissioning but none of my previous dealings with the IRA had ever been as bizarre as this one.

We got to Dundalk with about 40 minutes to spare so, to put down the time, we took a drive out to Carlingford Lough. When we arrived back at the meeting place, we sat in the car, watching every movement. 'They're here,' I said as a white van drove into the car park. But it was just some local workmen coming in for an early lunch. Moments later, just after noon, another van swung into the car park. There were two people in the front of the van. I recognised one of them as Thomas, my IRA contact from the previous week.

We were told to leave our mobile phones in the car. 'It's not what you think,' Thomas added. 'We're going to see Jim Monaghan.'

I looked straight at him. I was totally taken aback. 'Jim Monaghan?' I thought. 'What the fuck is this all about?'

I had first heard Monaghan's name four years previously when I was sitting in a motel about 100 miles outside Boston, watching the early-morning news. I was on holidays but my ears pricked up when the news anchor introduced a report about military police in Colombia having arrested three Irishmen at Bogotá Airport. The men had arrived on a flight from the southern part of the South American country which was controlled by left-wing anti-government rebels.

The ingredients of the story, which was big enough to make network news programmes in the United States, were intriguing. The three men were reported to have been travelling on false passports. They were said to have been in Colombia to train anti-government rebels in the urban terror tactics used by the IRA in Northern Ireland. It was reported that forensic evidence pointed to traces of cocaine and explosives on the men's clothes. The Farc guerrilla group was said to have paid substantial money in return for the training the three Irishmen were providing. The fact that this money was derived from the illegal drugs trade added an extra twist to an already bizarre story.

The three men had false passports but the authorities soon established their real names as Niall Connolly, James Monaghan and Martin McCauley. They were all senior republican figures. Monaghan was said to be the IRA's head of engineering; McCauley was an explosives expert; while Connolly was the Sinn Féin representative in Cuba.

When I got home from the United States, I immediately started to make calls to see what was actually going on. Sinn Féin figures, including

Gerry Adams, denied any knowledge of why the men were in Colombia. Adams was forced to make a rare clarification, having originally denied that Connolly was operating on behalf of his party in Cuba. The episode was hugely damaging for the peace process and, particularly, for Sinn Féin's credibility in the Untied States where even the party's most die-hard supporters were uneasy about allegations of republican links to the drugs trade in Colombia.

It was not totally clear who in the republican leadership knew what the men were up to, but I quickly ascertained that there was huge anger within the Sinn Féin leadership at what was being described as a 'free-lance operation'. The Colombian authorities claimed that the men were sharing bomb-making expertise with the Farc guerrillas. The three men claimed that they were observing the peace process in the war-torn country. Some of their supporters later described them as 'eco-tourists'.

However, I knew, from my contacts, that the men's explanation of their presence in South America was not believed by senior republican leaders. Nevertheless, the annoyance and anger that I was picking up in private conversations with senior republican figures were never going to be expressed in public. The three men were never going to be disowned. The so-called Colombia Three were still part of the big republican family and, as such, they had to be looked after.

A few weeks later, I found myself in Bogotá. I arrived on 9 September 2001. It was the first of six trips I would make to Colombia to cover the trial of McCauley, Monaghan and Connolly. The flight always arrived at night-time and I got the same uncomfortable feeling every time I walked through the arrivals area in the airport in Bogotá. There had been immediate consequences of the arrest of three Irishmen. People travelling from Ireland now needed a visa to gain entry to Colombia. The travel visa had to be issued by the Colombian embassy in London. A huge volume of paper work was involved, including bank account details. At passport control in Bogotá, my documents were checked and rechecked. The guards watched me with some suspicion.

I had been warned never to take a local taxi. To do so was to run the risk of being kidnapped. I always arranged to be met at the airport by someone who would drive me to my hotel. I also left my good watch at home. There was no point in attracting the wrong type of attention for the wrong reasons. To be honest, the best part about Colombia was being on the plane when it was taking off from Bogotá Airport.

My initial stop on my first trip to Colombia in early September 2001 was the office of the men's lawyer. Whatever nervousness had been generated by the scene in the airport was now increased dramatically. The lawyer's offices had bulletproof windows, and most of the senior staff members were wearing bulletproof vests. I asked that a note be taken in to the men, in which I asked to meet them with a view to doing an interview. Two days later, the lawyer had a response for me. Niall Connolly sent back a handwritten note. It was dated 11/9/01.

Dear Charlie, Sorry we won't be able to do an interview as the time is not right. We think if things have cooled down next month we could talk to you, we are interested but time is not right. If you get a chance could you send in three jumpers as it's very cold and phone cards. Thanks. Slán. Niall Connolly.

The fact that three members of the republican movement were being held in Colombia on bomb-making charges was problem enough for the Sinn Féin leadership. But the situation got much more complicated as, at the time Connolly was writing that note to me, the Twin Towers of the World Trade Center in New York were collapsing.

I couldn't but respond to the request for clothing. I had brought a good fleece jacket with me from home. I sent it into the prison and, later that day, when I had some free time, I took a taxi down town to the main shopping district where I purchased three heavy jumpers and some phone cards. It was the human thing to do.

Despite making repeated requests to meet the three men, I found that all my requests met the same fate. Over the following five trips to Bogotá to report on the trial, I never got to talk with any of the three men, not to mind interviewing them. So I suppose there was a certain irony in August 2005 when the story about IRA decommissioning turned into an interview with one of the so-called Colombia Three.

The only time I saw the three men in Colombia was when they appeared in court. Caitriona Ruane, the Sinn Féin politician who was fronting the Bring Them Home campaign, was instrumental in ensuring that no journalist ever got near the men. It was a deliberate policy. Several Irish politicians travelled to Bogotá and they were all given access to the prisoners. There were many discussions, mainly involving Ruane on one side and myself and Deaglán de Bréadún of *The Irish*

Times on the other side. 'You'll allow Niall Andrews and Mary White in, so why not us?' we asked.

Ruane usually blamed the men's lawyers for denying a meeting. But I believed that the republican leadership had imposed a blanket ban on the men having any direct dealings with the media. It was very frustrating. Ruane continually claimed that the men were being held in poor conditions. There were even claims that the men feared their food might be poisoned. However, without access to the men, there was no way of getting to the truth of these allegations.

Both Deaglán de Bréadún and I put a considerable amount of time into the story. We travelled to Bogotá on numerous occasions and our employers invested heavily in covering the story. Time and time again, when we asked to meet the men, the response was negative. I suspected that Ruane and the others involved in the Bring Them Home campaign feared the publicity generated from any questions we might ask about the real reasons why the men were in Colombia in the first place. There was a big element of control going on. I resented the way we were being treated.

I was always uncomfortable with the story of the Colombia Three. Senior republican contacts had sown serious doubts about the men's reasons for being in Colombia. But that did not take from the fact that the story was newsworthy and deserved attention. RTÉ took a lot of flak for covering the trial but armchair criticism is easy to write. I have always believed that my job as a reporter is to cover the story, irrespective of my personal opinions or views. In that regard, the Colombia Three was no different from any other story. There was a job to be done.

Several Irish politicians travelled to Bogotá to witness the trial proceedings. One of the oddest aspects of that side-story concerned the Fianna Fáil TD, John Curran. I interviewed Curran outside Leinster House for the main evening news after his announcement that he would be travelling to Colombia. But almost immediately after the report was broadcast, there were criticisms from the Progressive Democrats. The following day, Curran said that he would not be travelling after all. When I contacted him, he declined my requests for an interview to explain his U-turn, which I thought was somewhat unusual.

The Colombia Three story had another intriguing twist in that Niall Connolly was a brother of Frank Connolly, a well-known journalist in

Dublin. At the time the story broke, Frank Connolly worked for the *Sunday Business Post* and he would later be caught up in huge controversy about his own travel arrangements in April. It was alleged that the reporter had travelled to Colombia on a false passport, a claim he long denied but never attempted to kill off by revealing where he was at that time.

I knew Frank Connolly fairly well from covering the various tribunals of inquiry at Dublin Castle. He never said too much about his brother's predicament even though he would have known that I had been asking to meet him when I was in Bogotá. Once the stories concerning his alleged trip to Colombia emerged, Connolly went silent. I don't think I had spoken to him for about a year when, in the middle of 2003, I received a call on my mobile phone. It was Frank Connolly and he was being very friendly. He was working with *Ireland on Sunday* and said that a rival newspaper, *The Sunday Times*, was about to publish a story about my involvement in media training and coaching people on how best to approach interviews. The suggestion was—did I want to come clean in *Ireland on Sunday*?

'I don't know what you're talking about, Frank,' was my honest response. I had never done this type of work and, in fact, there was no story about me in *The Sunday Times* the next day. The experience was an eye-opener.

The charges against Monaghan, McCauley and Connolly were serious. They each faced up to 20 years in jail in Colombia for training illegal armed groups and travelling on false documents. The Colombian authorities seemed intent on getting a guilty verdict. In the months after the men's arrest in August 2001—and before their trial started—the Colombians claimed that long-range mortar bombs made from gas cylinders bore the hallmarks of the IRA. One of those bombs had recently killed 115 people in a church. In a situation very different from what we were used to in Ireland, the Colombian prosecutor general had no difficulty in speaking in public about the case. 'These are techniques we are certain were taught by this group [the IRA],' he said.

Supporters of the three men pointed to serious flaws in the case. They insisted that the forensics had been contaminated, and highlighted the fact that paid informers' evidence had to be withdrawn. One of the points that Caitriona Ruane continued to make was that the men had been unfairly tried in the media before being subjected to a secretive and biased non-jury legal system. The Bring Them Home group was very successful in generating publicity. As well as various Irish politicians travelling to observe the trial, a number of international human rights lawyers were signed up to argue about the unfairness of the charges

Despite my criticisms of Ruane for refusing the media access to the three men, I had a certain admiration for the way she was not afraid to stand outside the main entrance to the courthouse and openly criticise the Colombian authorities, including the country's President. It took a certain kind of guts in an area populated by armed military and court officials wearing bulletproof vests.

There was a huge military presence around the courthouse. Soldiers with machine guns were strategically positioned at every access point to the building which was located at the end of a small cul-de-sac. The courthouse was overshadowed by several modern skyscrapers. One day, a plate of glass from a window on the fifteenth floor of one of these high-rise buildings shattered. The noise led people on the ground to think of one thing—a bomb exploding. They all started to run before it became apparent that the noise had been caused by a breaking window. Bogotá was that type of city. Everyone was on edge. On my third trip there, a bomb exploded in a local disco, killing 60 people. My hotel was said to be owned by the military. It was certainly heavily fortified.

For all the military presence outside the courthouse, the room where the trial was held was quite small. We were all seated close together in the courtroom. It was my first time to see the three Irishmen in the flesh. They looked relaxed but they never even made eye contact. The proceedings were held in Spanish, with a translator on hand to give an English-language version of events. Informality was the order of the day. At times, the local journalists would actually speak up and ask the judge to clarify some points that had just been made.

There can be no doubt that if the trial had been heard in any court in Ireland, the charges would have been dismissed very early in the proceedings. Even allowing for differences between the Colombian and Irish judicial systems, the case was bizarre. The judge seemed to be totally unimpressed by the evidence that was presented against the men. Several witnesses were totally unreliable in what they had to say in court, and there was occasional laughter from the court staff and lawyers at the stories these witnesses were coming out with.

The central plank of the Colombian authorities' 300-page indictment was a claim that traces of explosives had been found on the men's
clothes. There was also the testimony of a Farc defector who was prepared to identify the men as bomb-makers. There was little doubt that
the three men were in Colombia on false passports. Their explanation
for being in the country lacked any credibility. But there was no solid
evidence to substantiate the claim that they had been training anti-
government rebels in make explosives. Neither did the authorities seem
to have any hard evidence to confirm media allegations about the
men's involvement in drug-dealing. As I sat in the courtroom, listening
to the various legal teams making their cases in Spanish, with a delayed
English translation, all I could think was that the truth was missing
from both sides in the case.

I was back in Bogotá for the final time in late April 2004, although
my mind was very much at home in Dublin where the Supreme Court
judgment was due in Beverley Cooper Flynn's appeal in her libel case
against RTÉ. It would actually necessitate a very quick exit from
Colombia, but not before the verdict in the Colombia Three case was
handed down. I was convinced that the men were going to be found
guilty, despite all that had gone on during the trial. My opinion was that
the political pressure for a guilty verdict would win out. But then the
judge showed a real sense of independence by throwing out most of the
charges against the men where, it's fair to say, no real evidence had been
presented during the trial. He did, however, find them guilty on the
false passport charges. The state prosecutor decided to appeal the case.
The three men were freed on bail and they immediately disappeared.
The appeal judge took a very different view from his colleague in the
original trial. The men were convicted in their absence and sentenced
to 17 years in prison. That was in December 2004. Nothing had been
heard of the whereabouts of the so-called Colombia Three until I met
my IRA contact in the car park of the Fairways Hotel in Dundalk in
August 2005.

We had moved as much equipment as possible from our car into the
van belonging to the IRA men. My contact with the IRA, Thomas, could
see my disappointment at the news he had just given me about meeting Jim Monaghan. I really believed all the secrecy over the previous
two days had been a prelude to arriving at some underground bunker
in rural Ireland to witness the destruction of the IRA's stockpile of

weapons and explosives. 'We can talk as we travel,' Thomas said as we sat into the back of the van. 'There's plenty of time. We're in no rush. You'll be back in time to meet your deadlines.'

The back windows of the van were painted black although through a couple of scratches I could just about make out some daylight, but not the route we were travelling. Thomas sat in beside Michael Lee and myself. 'I'm not used to this type of transport,' I joked. Thomas laughed. 'Well, over the years, I've become very used to it,' he responded.

He lit a cigarette. 'This is a thank you,' he said.

I didn't respond immediately. 'What do you mean "a thank you"?' I eventually asked.

'Let's just say, over the years, you've been fair in how you've reported us. That's all.'

I wasn't sure how to respond but decided to let the topic go. Journalism is about building up trust with a contact. I had had my fair share of exclusives. I was doing what any reporter would have done. And now I had another scoop even if it was far from what I had expected. All my focus had been on IRA decommissioning. No subject had been mentioned but the timing made decommissioning the obvious guess. Now I needed to concentrate on Jim Monaghan and what I was going to ask him. The atmosphere in the back of the van was fairly relaxed. I would not have got in the van five years earlier, not to mind have brought a work colleague into such an environment. But the situation had been transformed and, I have to say, I trusted my IRA contact. No matter what this man and his colleagues were responsible for—and I knew from Thomas's CV that he had a hard-man background—I was convinced that I would not have been put in any danger.

'The lads said you did them a good turn in Colombia,' Thomas said. The fleece jacket and purchased jumpers had not helped get me an interview in Bogotá, but now, four years later, I was seeing some return! I was not sure where we were travelling to but I suspected we were on the southern side of the border. From what little I could see through the van windows, it was a bright summer's day outside. Our journey lasted for about an hour. Every so often, to break the silence, I asked in a kid's voice, 'Are we there yet?' Eventually the van stopped. It was just after one o'clock. The driver parked as close as was possible to the front door of a modern house out in the countryside. We went into the kitchen area where four other people were waiting to greet us.

'Hello. How are you?' Jim Monaghan said as we shook hands. He looked an older man than when I had last seen him in the courthouse in Bogotá. He looked drained and tired, and his appearance was not helped by a yellow dye in his previously white hair.

I was surprised to see that one of this welcoming group included another republican figure who I quickly gathered was not too keen to be identified with the location. He handed me a couple of sheets of paper. 'They might help. I know we've caught you by surprise,' he said. It was a chronology of the Colombia Three story from their initial arrest in Bogotá Airport in August 2000 to their skipping bail in 2004.

Michael Lee started to set up his equipment in the living room off the kitchen area. While he was getting ready, I sat down at the kitchen table with Monaghan and the other men. 'Are there ground rules?' I asked.

'No—just don't identify the house or any of the furniture. Ask what you want. Jim will answer what he wants to answer,' Thomas replied.

A big plate of sliced and buttered French bread was in the centre of the table. 'Let's eat first,' somebody said. A pot of chicken curry with rice was placed on the table. It was somewhat strange as we all sat around the table eating lunch.

I guessed that Monaghan had travelled a distance to get to the house. There was a lot of speculation later on about when the Colombia Three had actually arrived back in Ireland. My guess was that Monaghan had returned to the country within only a few days of our meeting. I was more convinced of this from our brief conversation over lunch, when it was clear that he was not totally up-to-speed with the latest twists and turns in the peace process.

He talked about the conditions in the prison in Colombia but he gave no sense of how he had got back to Ireland, although it was clear he was not a man who saw himself as 'on the run' from the authorities. The episode had been hugely embarrassing for the Sinn Féin leadership. Regardless of what the men had been doing in South America and regardless of who knew of their escapade, there was considerable annoyance in Sinn Féin. In particular, the controversy created difficulties for Sinn Féin in the United States. Now, as I sat talking at this kitchen table with a handful of senior republican figures, I realised that the timing of the return of Monaghan and his colleagues had to have been a deliberate move by the IRA leadership. The organisation's 28 July statement had moved republicans onto the cusp of full democratic participation, but the fate of the Colombia Three was one of the embarrassing episodes hanging over their future progress. It was a boil that had to be lanced, and better now than later.

'If I stumble, can we stop and start again?' Monaghan asked as we sat down in the living room. It was a less than ideal set-up for an interview of this type. Had we had more information about what we were filming, we would have brought other equipment. It would also have been preferable to have had two cameras—one to record me on tape as my questions were asked.

I knew that Monaghan was not going to change his well-rehearsed story for me. He had stuck rigidly to his version of events during his imprisonment and trial in Colombia, so there was no reason to expect a confession now. Therefore, I decided to steer clear of questions about the innocence or guilt of the three men. I would get more news from Monaghan with a different approach. I started off by asking him if a deal had been done to allow the men come back to Ireland.

'No, not that I am aware; there hasn't been any deal of any sort. We returned as soon as we were able to return,' he replied.

'How long are you back in Ireland and can you tell me how you got here?' I asked.

'I'm back in Ireland only a few days and, as you can imagine, a lot of people in a lot of countries had to help us, and I can't endanger those people by giving any details about who they were or even where they were.'

'Do you consider yourself on the run here in Ireland today?' I asked.

'No. I wouldn't be giving this interview if I was on the run. I'm back and I would hope that I would be left in peace, and the Irish government was quite good during the time we were away and the Taoiseach asked that we would be sent back while we were waiting on the appeal, so I would hope that they would continue in that vein and that they won't place any unnecessary things. But if it's the case that the guards or someone want to talk to us or want to talk to me, that's all right.'

Monaghan claimed that he had gone to Colombia with his two colleagues to see the peace process in that country at work. I then opted for a somewhat leading question. 'Can I press you just once again: can you put your hand on your heart and say you did not go to Colombia to train the Farc?'

'Yes, with my hand on my heart, I didn't go to train the Farc; I went because of the peace process, because of our own involvement in the peace process. I was delighted to go to Colombia and, as I say, I have no regrets about it.'

He refused to be drawn on the Farc and their tactics and claimed that the American authorities were involved in their case, through the provision of false evidence.

The interview lasted for about twelve minutes without any interruptions. There was a brief handshake and Monaghan left. We returned to Dundalk in the van with the blacked-out windows. 'I'd appreciate it if you didn't use your mobiles for the next hour,' Thomas said as he left us.

I viewed the tape as Michael drove us back to Dublin. When I had the interview transcribed, I called Cillian de Paor in RTÉ. 'It's not what we thought but it's a huge story,' I said. The Monaghan interview was big enough to warrant disturbing Ed Mulhall on his holidays in America. Out of courtesy, I also called Tommie Gorman in Belfast and Deaglán de Bréadún, who had soldiered with me in Colombia. I'm convinced very few people knew at 1.30 p.m. that Monaghan, Connolly and McCauley were back in Ireland. But by four o'clock, the extraordinary news was seeping out. The Bring Them Home people had started to brief their supporters. All eyes were on the *Six One News* on RTÉ television. There was consternation in Government Buildings. The story was world news.

After the fuss of our exclusive interview had died down, I took a walk down Nutley Lane, but I had not gone very far when the news desk called me on my mobile. The gardaí in Harcourt Street were looking for me. I had a live interview to do for the nine o'clock news and was then definitely going on the holidays I had put off until after the release of the IRA statement. I rang the number the gardaí had left and arranged to meet them in RTÉ at about 8.30 p.m.

I had done similar interviews previously. The two senior officers knew that there was no information I could give them. They were as stunned as everybody else to see my exclusive report. 'Where did you record the interview?' I was asked.

'I really don't know,' was my honest reply.

'Were you in the Republic?' one of the officers asked.

I was not prepared to give anything away. I knew I was on the island and I suspected we were south of the border, as Monaghan had spoken about not running from the gardaí. The two Harcourt Street officers were clearly frustrated that the IRA men had surprised them with such a dramatic return. As they were leaving, one of the gardaí turned to me and asked jokingly, 'You wouldn't have a mobile number for Jim Monaghan, would you?'

Chapter 10 ～

TRAGEDY: MAN-MADE AND MOTHER NATURE

'Charlie, you've got to go to New York. Get out of there as soon as you can.'

I couldn't have agreed more with my colleague back in Dublin. It was the morning of 11 September 2001. In the space of a few minutes, the world had suddenly changed. The job of a news reporter is to reflect that change—to tell the story. As the planes were flown into the World Trade Center in New York, news executives from across the world had but one thought—how to get their reporters on the ground to tell the story first-hand.

I was sitting in the breakfast room of my hotel in Bogotá on the morning of 9/11. The BBC's Fergal Keane, my old colleague from RTÉ whom I had last met in South Africa, was also in the Columbian capital. We were both there to report on the case of three Irishmen arrested on suspicion of assisting anti-government rebels. We had booked into the same hotel.

Most people can remember where they were for important news stories like the assassination of President John F. Kennedy, the Omagh bombing or the 9/11 attacks. I was sitting in a hotel in Bogotá, chatting over breakfast with Fergal Keane about the Colombia Three, when the dramatic images started to appear on the television screen in the corner of the room. CNN was on the television, and the international news channel was showing footage of aeroplanes flying into the World Trade Center in New York City.

We left breakfast and went upstairs to Fergal's bedroom where his producer and cameraman were glued to the television screen. Within minutes, I had the RTÉ news desk on the phone. Getting to New York was everyone's priority. The BBC was trying to charter a private plane.

'If we can get this organised, you're welcome to come along,' Fergal said, generous as ever.

Unfortunately it was a plan that never came off. Instead, I made my way to the main airport in Bogotá where there was total chaos. Everyone seemed intent on getting to the United States as rumours spread that the country's international borders were about to be closed. I eventually booked a flight to New York, but as I was handed my ticket, an announcement was made that all flights into the United States had been suspended. It was time for Plan B. There was an afternoon flight to Mexico City, which I decided to take. At least, I was moving in the right direction. I found the staff at the Irish embassy in Mexico City helpful, but ultimately there was no way of getting into the US.

Meanwhile, the calls from Dublin were growing increasingly desperate. RTÉ's correspondent in the US, Carole Coleman, was stuck in Washington. Jim Fahy, the Western Correspondent from Galway, was trying to make his way to Canada. Another reporter, Peter Leonard, who had been on holidays in New York, was providing radio coverage, but the story was so big that a single reporter was never going to be able to cover all bases.

I spent two days in Mexico City, and I booked seats on several flights into the US, all of which were eventually cancelled as the US remained a no-fly zone. I eventually got a flight to Ciudad Juarez, an industrial city in northern Mexico, which borders the United States. I met a Finnish businessman who was similarly keen on getting into the US. He had a plan to walk the short distance from Ciudad Juarez to the border crossing near El Paso. It was the best option available, so I decided to go along and see where it got me.

We actually took a taxi for the 15-minute trip to the border crossing. I was now on the verge of finally getting into the United States but I knew I had another problem. I had my passport but I did not have my US visa which was at home in Ashford in County Wicklow. I still had the return part of an official entry/exit form which had never been collected when I was last leaving the US. 'I may have a problem,' I told my travelling companion as we got to the official desk. The Finnish businessman said that he would wait ten minutes to see if I got out of Mexico and into the US. I was honest with the passport officer about my problem. 'Hey, you're ok,' she said, pointing to the out-of-date entry/exit slip. 'You've got that.' My passport was stamped and I was waved through passport control, probably around the time George W. Bush was talking about the strengthened security at all border crossings into his beleaguered nation.

It was a Friday afternoon and baking hot as I literally walked into the United States. When I got to the airport in El Paso, an announcement was being made that internal flights were restarting. The first internal flight arrived from Texas a short time later. I booked a flight from El Paso to Houston, with a connection onwards to New York. But when the desk assistant was processing my credit-card payment, the machine sent back the message—limit exceeded. With all the flights I had booked over the previous few days, I had used up the credit on my credit card. It had taken a huge effort to get this far. 'Let me pay,' my Finnish friend, who was behind me in the queue, said. It was a problem that had to be resolved, so I put a call through to RTÉ, where another call was made to the credit-card company, and, thanks to the wonders of computer technology, my limit was increased. Within minutes, I had a ticket in my hands. There was no quick departure but, after another three-hour delay, we got onto the aircraft destined for Houston.

I bade farewell to my Finnish travelling companion in Houston where I stayed the night. The following morning, I was on a flight bound for New York and Ground Zero. For the first time, I saw signs of the promised extra security. It was somewhat intimidating on the plane. Armed air marshals were travelling on all internal flights. Random seat numbers were selected and those passengers had to go through additional security checks. It was a lovely sunny day as the aircraft descended over New York and, as we came in over the city, smoke was still rising from the ruins of the twin towers. The pilot made reference to the devastation. Otherwise there was silence in the plane and we all stretched our necks to see the scene of the attacks.

My journey from Colombia had been somewhat dramatic but RTÉ was just like all other foreign news stations covering the 9/11 story. With the suspension of air travel, most television outlets experienced great difficulty in getting reporters to New York, and it took a few days to get on top of what was one of the biggest stories in the history of television news. The images of the planes crashing into the World Trade Center were broadcast across the globe as soon as the attack happened but there was a lag of a few days before on-the-ground reporting was possible.

RTÉ was fortunate in that Peter Leonard, a newsroom reporter, had been in New York on holidays when the attack took place. But it was five days after the event before the station had a full contingent in place to convey the enormity of what had happened. Over a crazy few days, I had travelled from South America. My colleague, Jim Fahy, arrived in New York via Canada. Carole Coleman was covering the story from Washington where the implications of the attack on the Pentagon were still being digested. The RTÉ cameraman in Washington, Harvey Cofske, travelled to New York to work with Jim Fahy and myself.

I had worked for many years with Jim Fahy in RTÉ. Few journalists can match his ability to tell a human-interest story and, for many years, the Galway-based correspondent, with his distinctive white beard, had been chronicling the Irish emigrant community. So there was nobody more suited to tell the powerful personal stories of the Irish who were caught up in the 9/11 attack. We shared the reporting workload and, as I concentrated on the story of the day, Jim Fahy captured the raw emotion of the terrorist atrocity.

After my arrival in New York, my first destination was City Hall to apply for media accreditation. Reporters from all over the world, who were finally able to land in New York, were engaged in a similar task. Accreditation was vital to be able to work and to get access to many of the main locations now out of reach to the general public in a city under siege. I started to queue at about two o'clock in the afternoon. It was shortly after midnight before I got my accreditation. It was a long wait but nobody complained. There was an acceptance that this was a huge story that was going to outlive the next available news bulletin. Patience—not always a characteristic of a news journalist honed to the pressure of deadlines—was on open display. There were reporters from a variety of countries, including Steve Evans of the BBC who, a couple of days previously, I had seen reporting on the dramatic scenes at the Twin Towers. Evans had taken a few hours off to sort out his own accreditation. When people left the queue, their place was held. Pizzas and refreshments were ordered. The absence of jousting was noticeable. When I finally got to the top of the queue, two New York policemen took my details which were processed onto an official form on a manual typewriter.

I had been to New York on many occasions previously. I suppose I felt I knew the city fairly well. Now there was undoubtedly a strange atmosphere about the lower Manhattan area. It was very odd to see armed soldiers on the streets. The smell of burning from Ground Zero was particularly noticeable. The streets, normally filled with people, were eerily empty. Shops were shut. It was hard to comprehend what had happened and to see a city so shocked.

It was still unclear how many people were dead. Families were holding out hope that their loved ones were missing, not dead. The grief was very visible. Photographs of missing people were starting to be put up on street corners. Candles were lit on sidewalks. Down at the scene of the attacks, the authorities had started to take control. I met up with Padraig McCormack, the policeman in charge of securing the site. An Irishman from County Donegal, he had spoken with Conor O'Clery of *The Irish Times* and, true to Conor's generosity, he put me in touch with the Donegal man.

We started work at 5 a.m. Two hours later, we were at the heart of Ground Zero, and the enormity of the tragedy was overwhelming. It was difficult to comprehend the loss of so many lives in such a confined space. As we walked through the site, several fire crews continued to pour water on the smoldering ruins. On a couple of occasions, a shout went out and the emergency services stopped work as the remains of another victim of the attack were pulled from the rubble.

I was overcome by the scale of the destruction. I was also hugely impressed by the Irishman's authority. In his mid-thirties, this man had worked up the career ladder, and, as he brought us around the site, we were never stopped. We had amazing access and delivered really powerful pictures for later news reports. Over the three weeks reporting on 9/11, I visited several fire stations in the city. These men had lost colleagues and friends. I also saw them bury their colleagues. The funerals were hugely emotional occasions as the firemen formed a line as each coffin passed them by. Yet, despite all this grief, it was also amazing to watch the city getting back to some form of normality.

The appetite for coverage was huge and the work was relentless. One of the strangest stories allegedly involved three brothers from County Monaghan who had been caught up in the 9/11 attacks. The well-known Irish-American commentator, Niall O'Dowd, published a story about these men in his newspaper, the *Irish Voice*. The story had originated with the Sinn Féin TD, Caoimghín Ó Caoláin. One of the men was said to be recovering in hospital in New York, although no one had the name of the hospital. So, after speaking with O'Dowd, I spent most of a day calling the hospitals which had taken in those injured in the 9/11 attack. But my search was futile. Nobody had any information to give me. It seemed a rumour back in County Monaghan had worked its away across the Atlantic, and, in the process, had been transformed from talk to fact. It was a hugely frustrating exercise.

I travelled to Washington on my way home. I wanted to see the Pentagon site where the bombers had crashed another plane. What surprised me about Washington was the silence. The city was even more deserted than New York. It was very strange to pass the White House and not see scores of tourists outside the perimeter gates. The absence of the normal hustle and bustle was very strange. I met up with Carole Coleman, with whom I was in a relationship at the time, and we hired a small rowing boat to take out onto the city's main lake. It's a relaxing way to pass a few hours and a big attraction in the city for natives and visitors alike. But eerily on that day, we were the only people out on the lake. Just like New York, Washington had become a ghost city. What was supposed to be the most powerful capital city in the world was still reeling.

The terrorist attacks of 9/11 had huge international consequences. The toppling of the Taliban in Afghanistan and the regime of Saddam Hussein in Iraq can be linked to Ground Zero, as the Bush administration in Washington, aided by the Blair government in London, embarked on the so-called War on Terror. I did not cover the war in Afghanistan and was not due to report on Gulf War II as the build-up to military action commenced in early 2003.

RTÉ had a presence in Baghdad in the lead-up to the start of the war, with Richard Downes, a former BBC correspondent who was familiar with the city. Along with Lara Marlowe of *The Irish Times*, Downes worked in very difficult circumstances and, with the constant danger of military attack, I was not envious of them. Once the American-led bombing began, it was decided to concentrate reporting efforts from Kuwait. It was a good location as, at that time, most military movement into Iraq went through Kuwait City. Brian O'Connell, RTÉ's correspondent in London, had been set to travel to Kuwait at the start of the war. A cameraman from Dublin also got a visa to travel with Brian. But in the days before the attacks started, it was decided that Brian O'Connell was too important to RTÉ's coverage in London, where he was reporting on

Tony Blair at Westminster. O'Connell has been RTÉ's presence in London for many years and is one of the station's most experienced and widely travelled correspondents.

With the change of plans, I was asked to step in, and I was fortunate to get a last-minute travel visa from the Kuwaiti Embassy in London. But just as I was about to travel, the original cameraman had misgivings for family reasons about going to a war zone. He decided to opt out and unfortunately there was no time to get accreditation and a visa for a replacement. So I travelled to Kuwait without my own camera facilities. It was to become a serious handicap in how I could do my job.

There was some newspaper criticism of my work during the Second Gulf War. I resented the comment that I was 'hiding under the bed' by being in Kuwait—this was where my bosses wanted me to be. It was also a good location in the initial phase of the war. There was a serious contingent from the ITN, the BBC and Sky in the city. It was also a crazy place to be as there were real fears that Saddam would launch a chemical or biological missile attack on Kuwait. During the first few days I was in the city, the sirens went off repeatedly—once or twice, it happened while I was on air doing a live interview. Everyone in the hotel would troop down to the basement, put on their gas masks and then wait for the all-clear. That waiting period was very difficult as we were never sure whether the threat of attack was real or not. So we used to sit there, in what looked like a small cinema, waiting. I recall the ITN news anchor, Trevor McDonald, sitting opposite me, wearing his gas mask.

Saddam did succeed in landing one missile in Kuwait City. I heard the explosion from my hotel bedroom. A nearby shopping mall was hit. The war was closer than any of us had ever imagined. While not having camera facilities seriously limited my reporting options, I had no problem doing live reports—for the main television news programmes, I went to a satellite feed-point near my hotel which was being used by most other broadcast outlets. RTÉ also sent out a small portable satellite disk with a small camera, which allowed me to do live interviews for early-morning and late-night news programmes. I could simply set up the camera on the balcony of my hotel, press some buttons on the control panel, point the dish in the right direction, and I was ready for air.

From Kuwait City, the black smoke of the burning oil wells in southern Iraq—torched by fleeing Iraqi troops—was visible. I eventually travelled into Iraq to the port city of Um Quassar, with a contingent of British troops and several other reporters including Fergal Keane from RTÉ Radio. It was a surreal experience, watching as the British sought to impose order. I did a live interview into the television news using the portable equipment and helped by Fergal Keane who, amid much amusement, held the antennae up high to establish a connection with the overhead satellite. I spent the best part of two weeks in Kuwait. It was probably too long but the decisions were made elsewhere. I left there for Doha where the coalition forces had their command centre. The daily press briefings were fascinating to attend as the 'war-by-other-means' was fought over stories and headlines that the Americans and British sought to make a priority.

———

The 9/11 attacks and the war in the Gulf region were tragedies started by man. In late 2004, I reported on the terrible devastation caused by Mother Nature. Over my career, I have covered many natural disasters, including famines in Africa and earthquakes in Turkey and India, but nothing prepared me for the scenes of utter ruin left behind by the Asian tsunami.

I had spent Christmas Day 2004 at home in Ashford with my two daughters. We had a really good day and, as is usual, I did all the cooking—it's one of my favourite pastimes which I don't get enough time to enjoy doing. Orla left early on St Stephen's Day as she was travelling on a skiing holiday. I had the radio in the living room tuned to BBC Four that morning, and I didn't think twice about news reports of an earthquake in Indonesia. Neasa and I had decided to take in a walk before lunch and we were strolling along the beach at Brittas Bay when my phone rang. It was Ray Burke from RTÉ.

We exchanged festive greetings before Ray got to the reason for calling.
'The story in Asia is developing. We should be sending somebody.'
'What?' I responded. 'It's Stephen's Day.'
'Yeah, I know. Can you go?'
Back in Ashford, I quickly got up to speed on the latest developments. A huge earthquake had ripped apart the sea floor off the coast of northwest Sumatra in the Indian Ocean. It was the first act in a

serious of events which, as the world would learn over the following hours and days, impacted on the lives of millions of people. An ocean-wide tsunami was unleashed by the earthquake. Massive tidal waves reaching heights of some 65 feet crashed into Sumatra. The northern Indonesian city of Banda Aceh bore the brunt of the tidal wave as tens of thousands of people were killed in less than 15 minutes. The tsunami maintained its awesome force as it moved across the ocean, crashing into the coast of Thailand and onwards to the southwestern area of Sri Lanka. These initial reports speculated that thousands were dead across the region.

As I tried to work out what flights to take—and how I was going to get them with the world on holidays—I had a choice of three locations. The situation in Thailand at that stage was not as bad as that in Indonesia, which had borne the full brunt of the tsunami, and Sri Lanka which had also been very badly damaged. I soon established that Indonesia was not a realistic option as visa problems would make the country a bureaucratic nightmare to get into quickly. I rang the out-of-hours emergency number used by RTÉ for travel bookings. The call was answered by a woman somewhere in the United States. 'Happy Christmas,' I said as I quickly asked about getting from Dublin to Sri Lanka, and getting there in a hurry.

The following morning, I was at an airline desk at Frankfurt Airport with RTÉ cameraman Neilus Dennihy by my side. We had a serious problem. The woman at the American call centre had booked a Dublin –Frankfurt–Colombo route but it now turned out that the Frankfurt to Colombo flight was cancelled. The woman at the counter in Frankfurt was checking all sorts of combinations of flights out of the German city, any route that would get us to Sri Lanka. 'I've got business class to Dubai. You can get a connecting flight from there to Colombo. You'll be there by tomorrow afternoon,' she said.

The tsunami story was getting bigger with each passing hour. The scale of the destruction was enormous and the numbers dead just kept on rising. In the two days from when I left Dublin to my arrival in Colombo, the estimate of those dead across the region had increased from about 20,000 to 50,000. Even those figures were widely wrong. The final death toll in Sri Lanka alone was put at 30,000. Indonesia suffered most, with the number of deaths there estimated around 180,000. The overall death toll in the region is estimated at over 200,000.

But the scale of the tragedy was only emerging in the first few days after 26 December 2004. Thousands were still missing, and dead bodies were still being located. For most people in this country, the tsunami happened on St Stephen's Day, but for the people of Sri Lanka, as I discovered when I arrived in the city of Colombo on 28 December, the awful natural disaster occurred on Poya Day. That's the name they give to the day each month when a full moon appears in the sky. The majority of Sri Lankans are Buddhists and, as they do not work on Poya Day, the fishing boats were in the harbours when the tidal wave arrived. The coastline was ravaged. I was immediately struck by the sight of boats everywhere as we drove from the airport to the centre of Colombo.

An Irish diplomat in Sri Lanka, whom I had tracked down on the phone, had arranged for a local man, Hinton, to work with us. Over the following ten days, Hinton drove Neilus Dennihy and myself and helped with translation. Hinton wanted only to talk about the 'missing train' as he drove us into the centre of Colombo. The city had few of the trappings of Christmas which we had left behind in Ireland. Instead, in keeping with Buddhist tradition, white bunting was flying from the lampposts as a symbol of mourning.

Local officials had compiled notebooks with family names listed in one column and the numbers dead and missing in a second column. Few families were left untouched. One woman told us that her grandmother had tried to run as they saw the wave approaching but she had stumbled and was simply swept away. One man admitted that he would never recover the bodies of his wife and baby daughter. We interviewed another man who had lost four members of his family. We left him wandering around the ruined remains of his home. We also met an English tourist who told us how he had been forced to bury the bodies of other European tourists who had been staying at the same resort as him. He had taken pictures of these people for identification. There were tears in his eyes and emotion in his voice. There were so many bodies and, with a real threat to public health, mass graves had been opened. And now, several days after the tsunami had hit, the authorities and the local people were still finding bodies. One man brought us to the river side to show us where several bloated bodies were still floating in the water.

Most days, we set off from Colombo around 5 a.m. Fruit and water were packed into the car. Hinton used to listen to the car radio, translating the local news reports as he drove us to yet another scene of destruction, all the while talking about the 'missing train'. The area was like a battle scene: there was debris everywhere; roads had been destroyed; the people were dazed—they had nothing left. On our third day, we arrived at the twisted remains of the 'missing train', the *Queen of the Sea* which normally ran along the coast between Colombo and the city of Galle. The train had been packed with passengers when it left Colombo on its 75-mile journey on the morning of 26 December.

The engine and eight carriages had been swept away like a toy train, such was the force of the tidal wave. The carriages were filled with water as the twisted wreckage settled in what could best be described as a bog. There was debris all around, bits of track and fallen palm trees. Most of those travelling on the train had been killed. The official death toll was put at about 1,700, with only a handful of survivors. Local people told us that there were many more passengers on board, travelling home to celebrate the Buddhist full moon holiday. It took a huge effort to get the bodies out of the carriages. When we arrived on the scene, there were still an estimated 200 bodies unaccounted for in one of the overturned carriages. Many of the bodies were rotting. Local religious leaders decided to bury many of the dead in a freshly dug mass grave nearby. It was the world's worst railway accident.

Each day, we drove as far as was possible along the coast road. There was huge devastation in an area that took the full force of the tsunami. Cars moved slowly and were often diverted off the main route because roads were impassable or bridges simply gone due to the impact of the tidal wave. A few days into reporting from Sri Lanka, and when we were making this now daily journey, my mobile phone rang. Then the other phones in the car started to ring. The messages were all the same—get off the coast road; there's been a warning about another tsunami. I could see the panic in the cars around us as the same news reached other drivers and their passengers. Cars were doing U-turns on the two-lane road. Everyone was driving towards the nearest crossroads, to move inland. Hinton, our driver, almost crashed as he swung the car around. But my priorities were almost recklessly different. 'We can't do this,' I said. 'We have a good story today; we need to go back to Colombo.' There was a brief discussion in the car. Fortunately Neilus and Hinton were in agreement. So, we turned around again and drove back along the coast road, all the time keeping a close eye on the nearby sea. The road was now empty. 'Drive as fast as you can,' I told Hinton. After about an hour or so, we started to relax. It had been a false alarm. Three months later, I returned to Sri Lanka and experienced similar terror over a threatened tidal wave. The local mobile phone company even sent out a text message. 'Please evacuate from Sri Lankan coastal areas as soon as possible,' the message read.

The first tsunami trip was exhausting, with early starts and long days. Normally after a couple of days, the appetite for disaster stories reduces, but this time the story just kept growing. The death toll kept on increasing. The television images were so utterly powerful. There were no New Year's Eve celebrations in Colombo but the white bunting was now everywhere. There were similar sights in the resort city of Galle which was a four-hour drive from Colombo. In what was left of the local cricket stadium—where test matches had once been played—the clock was stopped at just before 9.30 a.m., the time the tidal wave had struck on 26 December. They were still finding bodies in the rubble of the ruined city. The numbers dead in Galle alone were being put at around 10,000. Many of the dead had not been identified. The smell of death in the local morgue was totally overpowering. At the main hospital in the city, a room had been set aside and, on a previously bare wall, almost 1,500 photographs of unidentified dead people were posted. These people had already been buried in mass graves. What remained now was for their loved ones to come and confirm their identity so that the authorities could cross them off the missing list. Many of the photographs were of infants and young children. It really was a room of death and these were walls of the dead. There was hardly a sound from the people walking around looking at the photographs. As we filmed, one family came across a photograph of their 18-year-old brother. They were able to identify him only from his distinctive trousers belt. He had come to Galle only a week previously, to start his first job.

When I returned to Sri Lanka three months after the tsunami, there were some signs of a return to normality. In Galle, the fishermen had retuned to the sea. Along the coast of Sri Lanka, fishing is the main livelihood of many people. Half of the fishing fleet had been wiped out, but these people had shown remarkable spirit. The aid agencies were doing good work with the work-for-money programmes, encouraging the local people to start rebuilding properties and repair their damaged boats. But the scale of the undertaking is so huge that it will take a generation, if not longer, to return to normal. Thousands of people were still homeless, living in tents.

On that trip early in 2005, I also travelled in Indonesia and visited the province of Aceh, which was probably the area worst hit by the tsunami. It was the closest land point to the epicentre of the earthquake which had given birth to the tidal wave. Much of the region had been devastated, including the city of Banda Aceh on the island of Sumatra. Almost 130,000 were dead, while another 100,000 were still listed as missing. There were so many bodies that thousands had been buried in mass graves. Remarkably, even when I was in the region three months on from the 26 December tsunami, they were still finding bodies.

Banda Aceh was a wasteland: roads were gone; bridges had been washed away. Everything was out of place. Ships were lodged inland in the middle of what had once been residential areas. I was amazed to see one 3,500-tonne barge over a mile inland. We were taken by helicopter about 150km up the coast. It was really like the nuclear winter that had been described by so many people. This scene of total destruction was captured on camera by RTÉ's Michael Cassidy. Known to his friends and colleagues as Butch, Michael had been in Banda Aceh three months previously with Mark Little. Now, three months on, it was still difficult to convey in words or pictures the scale of the havoc wreaked by the tidal wave. On one of those days in Sri Lanka, I started to get urgent calls from home. The news services were reporting a new tsunami warning. 'This is it,' I thought. It was not far off midnight local time. Word was spreading fast. It was full moon day, which only added to the sense of fate that many local people accepted. Michael Cassidy and I left our guesthouse and stayed out in the open for several hours. Eventually the sense of panic eased. But just like on that day three months previously in Sri Lanka, when there had been another false alarm, I was introduced to the fear these people must have felt as the tidal wave approached. There was only one word—terrifying.

Chapter 11

THE NATIONAL IRISH BANK ROBBERY

W<sup>e gathered in the O'Reilly Hall at the Belfield campus of University College Dublin in November 2004. It was in one of the university's car parks a few years previously that I had met one of the contacts who had helped RTÉ's investigation into National Irish Bank. It was probably that news story that had led me to this graduation ceremony. The college was marking its 150th anniversary with a ceremony to award honorary doctorates to individuals chosen to represent various strands of Irish life. We were an interesting collection of people, all decked out in our newly acquired academic regalia. Among those seated near me were Kevin Heffernan and Mick O'Dwyer from the world of Gaelic football, as well as Niall O'Dowd and Bruce Morrison who had played important roles in the Irish-American contribution to the Northern Ireland peace process. The dancer Michael Flatley gave our group a touch of genuine celebrity.

I was proud, especially as my two daughters, Neasa and Orla, were watching when I received the honorary title, Doctor of Laws. I had missed this type of ceremony, having gone straight from secondary school to full-time employment. 'Dr Bird' sounded funny when I heard it used by people as they offered their congratulations. The citation that was read at the graduation ceremony was generous in its praise for my work as a journalist. In fact, it was quite flattering, mentioning 'hard work in chasing the story' and an 'ability to ask the questions that the man in the street would like to have the opportunity to ask'. I couldn't have asked for more. There was even a smile as the former Labour Party advisor, Fergus Finlay, was quoted: 'Thank God for whistle-blowers and Charlie Bird.'

My honorary doctorate from UCD came in the aftermath of several of the most eventful years in my reporting career, much of my reporting entangled with tax evasion and customer theft at National Irish Bank. Ed Mulhall was appointed Director of News in 1996, succeeding Joe Mulholland who became overall head of RTÉ's television output. Mulhall wanted to develop the area of investigative reporting in the newsroom. Within the station, this type of journalism was more associated with the current affairs division, as the newsroom generally stuck to reporting daily news. The current affairs division in RTÉ has a proud tradition of strong investigative output, stretching from *Seven Days* in the 1970s through to *Today Tonight* in the 1980s and on to *Prime Time* in more recent years. The *Seven Days* moneylending programme caused great controversy; criminals like Martin Cahill were confronted on *Today Tonight*; while *Prime Time* programmes like 'Cardinal Secrets' exposed clerical abuse in the Dublin diocese, and the Leas Cross revelations highlighted inadequate care of the elderly.

In the early 1990s, there was, however, considerable criticism of the structure and the content of RTÉ's current affairs programmes. Morale in the division was not helped by the praise heaped on British television stations for breaking Irish-related stories, including Susan O'Keeffe's exposé on the beef industry and ITV's investigation into the child-abusing priest, Fr Brendan Smith.

Against this backdrop, there was therefore an opening for Ed Mulhall to give an investigative edge to news reporting. He was also feeding into an area where newspapers had done well in unearthing important stories, going back as far as 1973 and Joe MacAnthony's groundbreaking investigation into the Irish Hospital Sweepstakes. In more recent times, Mark Brennock and Frank McDonald in *The Irish Times* had put the spotlight on planning corruption in the Dublin region, an area which was further explored by Frank Connolly in the *Sunday Business Post*. Over many years, Vincent Browne was one of the few journalists—and I personally witnessed him in action—to question Charlie Haughey persistently about his financial affairs. In the 1990s, with the re-launch of *Magill* magazine, Browne was to the fore in high-lighting political and corporate wrongdoing.

Many of the more recent revelations had their origin in the story of Ben Dunne and his infamous exploits in a Florida hotel. Without the Ben Dunne affair, it might have been much harder to unravel the truth about these important stories. While an *Evening Press* reporter, Des Crowley, had pointed to AIB's role in Haughey's finances, the full truth began to emerge only after Sam Smyth's exclusive story about the generous financial relationship between Dunne and the Fine Gael politician, Michael Lowry. Smyth's story was followed by Cliff Taylor in *The Irish Times*. These stories underpinned a new era in investigative reporting from which RTÉ News benefited, and the work we did certainly helped others, including Liam Collins in the *Sunday Independent* when he revealed details about bogus non-resident accounts. Without doubt, Ed Mulhall made the correct call in giving RTÉ newsroom reporting an investigative edge. One story, however, dominated all the exclusives that were broadcast—the investigation into wrongdoing by National Irish Bank. It was a story that consumed my life for almost six years, starting with a phone call on Monday, 12 January 1998.

I didn't know the caller very well although we had dealt with each other previously, through his involvement in the trade union sector. 'I have a story for you,' he said. 'Will you come and see me in my office?' His story concerned a leading Irish financial institution and the promotion of tax evasion. He had received information almost 12 months previously from a close friend in the banking world. They had decided it was best to wait some time before releasing the material. My source had been so protective of the information that he had even posted it in a sealed envelope to his parents' house, for safekeeping. He had just sent it to the Revenue Commissioners, and now he was providing me with evidence in the form of a document with certain numbered accounts at National Irish Bank, the fourth largest financial institution in the country.

As I listened attentively, he described the scheme as the 'poor man's Ansbacher'—a reference to the Ansbacher deposits, an elaborate multi-million pound/euro offshore tax evasion arrangement which had recently emerged into the public domain. My source said that what NIB had been up to was a 'scam'. I got the gist of what was involved but much of the technical financial detail initially went over my head. My source was explaining very carefully what had been going on at NIB but even he wasn't *au fait* with every aspect of the scheme. When, at one stage, I asked for clarification on a point, he decided it was best to ring his banking friend to ensure that I received a totally accurate answer.

Essentially, as I understood it, funds were invested in insurance bonds sold by an Isle of Man-based company, Clerical Medical

International (CMI), but promoted in Ireland by NIB. The scheme was organised to allow Irish people to invest money offshore, out of the gaze of the Revenue Commissioners, although their money eventually ended up back with NIB. The account holders paid the bank a high commission for the arrangement but they did so in the understanding that the tax authorities had no knowledge about the funds. 'Tax evasion,' I thought. 'This has to be a huge story.'

The document my source provided contained no customer names, only a series of account reference numbers. It was handwritten—eleven eight-digit numbers, two four-digit numbers preceded by the letters PP, a single prefix PA, four monetary amounts ranging from £40,500 to £580,883 and three words, '173 accounts altogether'.

'Those account numbers and accounts were copied down from a computer screen in National Irish Bank over a year ago. They all refer to CMI accounts,' the source explained.

As I left his office, I knew that a considerable amount of work was going to be needed to get to the core of the story. Back at RTÉ, Ed Mulhall suggested bringing George Lee on board. George worked as Economics Editor in the newsroom although, at that time, I actually knew very little about him. 'He has a head for finance,' I thought. 'We're going to need that.'

George Lee and I were thrown together on the NIB story but our skills and personalities complemented each other very well. I quickly discovered that although he had worked in the financial sector, including the Central Bank, and was seen as an economics whiz kid, he had a genuine social conscience. He was likeable, deadpan and enthusiastic.

We developed a close friendship although it later caused him some sleepless nights when, before the 2002 general election, I jokingly mentioned to Niall Ó Muilleoir, Fine Gael's press officer, that they should consider George as a general election candidate. To my surprise, Michael Noonan, the Fine Gael leader at the time, pursued the matter. Fortunately, however, my colleague decided to remain in the world of journalism. I learnt a lesson with that recommendation and it was the last time I would joke about people changing career to move into political activity.

Throughout the NIB investigation, George Lee's financial expertise matched my general news experience. Ed Mulhall had made a good decision. In the days after my 12 January meeting with my source, we worked the phones. We were looking for more information about the offshore scheme. Every time I rang NIB offices, when asking receptionists to connect my call to certain bank officials, I used the name 'Joe McGrath'. I did not want to create any suspicion by using my own name which might have alerted the bank to our investigation. One banker agreed to meet me but opted out at the last moment. In fact, I was sipping my pint of Guinness at our agreed meeting place when my mobile rang. 'Charlie, I'm scared. That CMI thing could cause big trouble for the bank. It's too dangerous,' the bank official said, explaining why he couldn't meet me.

We spoke to a number of people who had invested undeclared income in the CMI scheme. People were nervous and somewhat defensive. 'How did you get my name?' one man asked. The more people we contacted, however, the more certain we were about the story. Eamon Kennedy, RTÉ's in-house legal expert, was brought into the loop as we teased out how the story could be broadcast. He was incredibly positive about the investigation but set the standards we had to reach. 'You need proof: documents, letters, memos. You really can't touch it until you have something in writing to back it all up,' Kennedy concluded.

I rang my original source. His initial documentation had been important in kick-starting the investigation but now I needed something else. One of the account statements with a balance of €106,000 in the offshore CMI account belonged to a businessman from County Mayo. My source provided his name. A quick check of the phone directory gave me the Mayo man's number. He was stunned to get my call. 'Listen, we're not interested in exposing you. We just want to find out about the scheme, the way it was sold.' He promised to call me back but I was impatient to get access to documents that supported the story.

I was given the name of a businessman from the midlands who had invested with NIB. When I rang this man and told him what I knew about the CMI scheme, he readily agreed to help me out. This man had put money—undeclared to the Revenue—into NIB's offshore scheme. 'Sure, aren't they all at it?' was his response. We now had confirmation from a bank customer about the CMI scheme. What we were still missing, however, was what Eamon Kennedy had described as 'proof'—documentation.

The process was frustrating, with no sign of a whistle-blower until one of the bank officials I had contacted in the first few days of the investigation rang me back. This man, who we called 'the duffel-bag man', proved to be invaluable to the investigation into wrongdoing by National Irish Bank. I can still clearly remember the first time we spoke on the phone.

'Is that Charlie Bird?'

'Yes. Who's this?'

'You rang me earlier…'—the man's voice was hesitant—'…about the bank…about the investment scheme.'

'Bingo,' I thought. 'We're in business.'

He was willing to meet me the following day. 'It would have to be very early. I don't want to be seen,' the bank official added.

At eight o'clock the next morning, I arrived at Bewley's Café on Grafton Street in Dublin city centre. I waited outside the building, trying to guess which of the people arriving for their breakfast could be my contact. Then my mobile rang. 'No, not again,' I thought, considering the possibility of being stood up for a second time.

'It's too open there. Somebody is going to see me. Have you got a car?'

'Yeah,' I replied. 'It's parked outside the passport office on Molesworth Street.'

I gave him the registration number of my silver-coloured Opel Vectra. 'Give me twenty minutes,' he said. I made my way to the car and waited. It was Friday, 16 January 1998.

The man simply sat into my car, placed his duffel bag on his lap and said, 'Hello.'

He was incredibly cagey. I was upfront with him, telling all I knew, in the hope that this approach would help to cement a trust, although, to be honest, I was not sure what exactly this man knew about CMI. He worked with NIB but so far nobody remotely connected with the bank had been willing to help our investigation. My hunch was correct, however, as this banker turned out to be a font of information.

In plain language, he explained to me just how the CMI scheme operated. He had the inside track. The Financial Advice and Service Division at NIB contacted all bank branches. They were targeting people with large amounts of cash on deposit; much of this money was known to be 'hot' and undeclared to the Revenue. Meetings were set up between these customers and financial advisors from NIB who then did the 'sell' on the CMI scheme.

The administration fees charged by the bank were high but the benefit of non-disclosure to the Revenue was important to most of these customers. Their money was invested with CMI but the amount involved, less fees, was then lodged back on deposit in a numbered account in the NIB branch from which it had come in the first place. Despite the money being 'offshore', investors had easy access to their accounts. The whole arrangement was structured to keep the eyes of the Revenue away from 'hot' money. It was a classic tax-evasion scam.

This inside information—a blow-by-blow account of how NIB operated the scheme—was crucial in confirming that our story was accurate. However, I still knew that without written material it would be difficult to get the story on air. 'Our lawyers will insist on documents before we can report it,' I said.

The whistle-blower looked at me. 'I have your number,' he said getting out of my car and taking the duffel bag with him.

National Irish Bank was the fourth largest financial institution in the Irish market. It was controlled by National Australia Bank which had ambitions to increase NIB's market share. The bank had gained a reputation as an aggressive player in the banking sector. There had been numerous difficulties, and several scandals in the world of Irish banking, but nothing was comparable to what we were uncovering. NIB was promoting a product that facilitated tax evasion. The consequences of publicly revealing this fact would be huge for NIB. Another way of considering our investigation, however, was that the consequences would be huge for RTÉ if we were wrong.

George Lee and I had generated a considerable amount of information on the CMI scheme. The product was lucrative for NIB. The bank officials promoting the scheme were also well rewarded. First-class trips to Australia for the staff and their partners were on offer for those who achieved certain sales targets. One source in the financial sector in Dublin provided the names of those who had gone to Australia. One particular name on this list attracted our interest. The exact role played by this individual would ultimately be determined by the highest court in the land. Yet, at that time in early January 1998, for all the information we had accumulated, there was still need for conclusive documentation to back up the allegations we were hearing. I decided to ring the duffel-bag man once more.

A few days later, I was parked as arranged opposite Heuston Station in Dublin. Shortly after 8 p.m., the bank official sat into the front passenger seat. 'We meet again,' I said.

'Yeah, but at least it's dark this time. And, it's a quiet location too.'

I brought him up-to-date with what George Lee and I had been working on. As I spoke, he opened his duffel bag.

'I might be able to help,' he ventured. He had several files with him. One set of records concerned a businessman from County Cork who had put £0.5 million in undeclared income into the CMI scheme. Five months later, however, having changed his mind, the businessman was hit with a £45,000 penalty fee for withdrawing his money. A row developed between the bank and its disgruntled customer. I was now reading internal bank correspondence about the case. Confirmation of NIB's role in selling the CMI scheme was now in my hands.

There was silence in the car as I read the material the duffel-bag man had handed me. Then I hit a key paragraph in a letter between two senior NIB managers about the County Cork case: 'I know we have a sum of the order of thirty million pounds in investments in CMI and I can foresee similar difficulties as this one in the years ahead.'

'Thirty million pounds,' I repeated the amount in my head. 'We've got these guys now.'

The duffel-bag man was intent on making my evening. 'I have something else here which you might find useful,' he said, handing me another bundle of papers that he had just taken from his bag. They were copies of withdrawals and lodgment slips related to the CMI investments in the other documents. We now had all the 'proof' necessary to say that NIB had operated an offshore tax-evasion scheme.

The key break in the investigation was making contact with this NIB employee who was willing to talk about practices at the bank. Without the help of this individual, I am not sure that our investigation would have developed sufficiently to broadcast the reports that we eventually did. We knew that the bank operated an offshore scheme and, crucially, the documentation showed that the bank was targeting customers who it knew had 'hot' money. What's more, NIB targeted these individuals after the announcement of the 1993 tax amnesty which was supposed to have been used by people with tax problems to regularise their affairs. We could now confirm NIB's guilt.

The day after my meeting with the duffel-bag man down by Heuston Station, we were ready to contact NIB formally. We had the 'proof' that RTÉ's legal advisors had requested. I signed my name to the letter which was sent by courier to NIB and addressed to Philip Halpin, the bank's Chief Operations Officer.

> RTÉ is working on a story for transmission during tomorrow night's bulletins, Wednesday 21 January [1998], on National Irish Bank's involvement with Clerical Medical Insurance based in the Isle of Man, London and New York.

Nineteen separate questions were posed. Having read those questions, the management at the bank would have known straightaway that we had access to confidential information. I can only speculate as to the reaction at NIB's Wilton Terrace headquarters as they pored over the letter. I suspect they were really shocked to be faced with the questions we posed.

> RTÉ has learned that in 1996 there were somewhere in excess of £150 million in these Clerical Medical Insurance Company Limited personal portfolio accounts being held at Wilton Terrace. Is this correct?

Included on the list was a crucial question which got to the very core of who had authorised the offshore scam.

> RTÉ understands that the initiative for the arrangement with Clerical Medical Insurance Company Limited came from the Financial Advice and Services division of National Irish Bank and was approved at Chief Executive level with the bank. Is this correct?

It is amazing to write this even now but—as later events ultimately showed—NIB lied. RTÉ received a letter from NIB's legal representatives in response to my questions. 'The Bank does not condone tax evasion and our investigation in the very brief time available has found no evidence to sustain the very serious allegation Mr. Bird makes,' they observed.

The bank also tried to pass responsibility to CMI, a responsibility the company quickly denied when we rang a CMI representative at their offices in England. There was even the threat of legal action against RTÉ.

They used every possible reason to knock back our story, including at one stage claiming that the documents we had were stolen. We were told that there was no story in our investigation and that we were on the wrong tack totally. I suspect that in other times RTÉ would have walked away from the story at that juncture, accepting what on the surface appeared to be fairly rational explanations by NIB. However, the approach to this investigation was different, and that is to the credit of Ed Mulhall and Eamon Kennedy. Their attitude was very much—what do we have to do to get this story to air? It was refreshing, and fully supported by Kevin Feeney and John Traynor, the barristers employed by RTÉ to review the material we planned to broadcast. As we put the final touches to the report, it emerged that the Revenue Commissioners would be investigating NIB's CMI scheme.

The first NIB story was broadcast on 23 January 1998. The introduction to the report laid out the facts of our investigation:

> RTÉ News has learned exclusively that the Revenue Commissioners have been provided with details of an offshore investment scheme operated by National Irish Bank. RTÉ has learnt that some account holders have used the scheme to avoid or evade tax. It is believed that the Revenue Commissioners will be examining the information which has been passed on to them. This report from our Special Correspondent, Charlie Bird, and our Economics Editor, George Lee.

As the pictures were broadcast, I told the story.

> Prior to 1994, representatives of National Irish Bank gathered information in relation to about 180 of its customers throughout the country. These included people who held non-resident accounts, accounts in false names, and accounts with funds which have not been disclosed to the Revenue Commissioners.... The money was handed over by bank draft to Clerical Medical International in the Isle of Man. Within days, this money, minus the set-up charges, came back to the National Irish Bank.... The bank was able to retain on its balance sheet most of the funds belonging to the holders of the accounts involved and also earned sizeable commissions from

Clerical Medical International for selling the bonds ... [the bank] was paid close on £20,000 in commission for persuading a customer to invest half a million pounds... in excess of 150 National Irish Bank customers accepted the bank's invitation to invest in the CMI bonds... in August 1994 the total amount still invested through the scheme was of the order of £30 million....

There was a huge response to the story. The level of tax fraud in the Irish economy was emerging as a burning public and political issue. A series of revelations in a short space of time had shown a pattern of tax evasion by high-income earners. We had just added a very significant scam to the list. The money involved was considerable—some £30 million had been invested in CMI for the purposes of evading tax. The government appointed official inspectors to investigate all the offshore insurance products sold by NIB. Naturally enough, the Revenue Commissioners were very interested in the content of our report. As was their legal right, the Revenue ordered the bank to supply a list of names of CMI investors.

Interestingly NIB changed its attitude from the hard-line denials, and a few hours after our first broadcast, it issued a statement confirming that it was carrying out an internal investigation. 'The allegations [in the RTÉ report] are of a most serious nature and [are] in contravention of the bank's policies,' the NIB statement declared.

Our investigation was, however, far from being over. NIB was concerned about what we would broadcast next. The bank hit back, obtaining a temporary court injunction on 30 January, which prevented us from using any information contained in internal bank documents, pending a decision of the Supreme Court. In correspondence NIB prepared for the case, it was stated that the bank 'pride themselves in keeping the business affairs of their customers confidential'. It was an almost humorous line given their efforts to keep their customers' affairs confidential from the Revenue Commissioners.

A team of public relations experts headed by Joe Murray of Murray Consultants was drafted in by NIB. With the injunction in place, we were constrained in what we could broadcast. The bank made good use of that time as its advisors worked to undermine our investigation.

Waiting for the court case to be held to decide on the NIB injunction was hugely frustrating. There was an endless round of meetings with

RTÉ's legal team, preparing our case. There were, however, a few loopholes in the court order. While we were prevented from using confidential NIB documents, we could still contact current and past NIB employees, and we could report on any stories unearthed by print journalists.

It was assumed by the bank and others that by seeking to continue our investigations into NIB, we were intent on reporting further revelations about the CMI scheme. The scope of our investigation had, however, changed totally.

As the original NIB news report was having a huge impact, the duffel-bag man called me again. We arranged to meet near UCD. It was raining heavily as I sat into the car he was driving. We parked in a quiet spot in one of the UCD car parks. 'I have some important documents to show you,' he said. The black folder was bulging with files.

'There's enough material in here to wipe out the bank,' he warned. 'I have to be careful with this material. I can't let you use it for a while.'

My curiosity levels were now sky-high but I was not about to land this man in trouble. He had been totally reliable and up-front with the information he had given me about the CMI scheme. 'Don't worry,' I said. 'I promise I won't do anything without your agreement.'

The banker then started to go through some of the documents. They were internal audit reports from National Irish Bank, showing deliberate overcharging of fees and interest charges on customer accounts. The whole exercise was summarised in a single paragraph in a report from the NIB branch at Carrick-on-Shannon in County Leitrim: 'Interest charges were increased without legitimate reason or customers' knowledge on twenty accounts in November 1989 and thirty-three accounts in February 1990.' As my source talked about the significance of the reports, I was formulating an explanation in my head in plain English—NIB had stolen money from its customers. It was unbelievable. As serious as the CMI story was, this new information was stunning.

'This can't be for real,' I said. 'It has to be a hoax.'

'Oh, it's for real, all right,' my source responded. 'It went on all the time.'

He took another file from his duffel bag. It was an internal audit report from the NIB branch at Carndonagh in County Donegal, which showed the same activity as the Carrick-on-Shannon report. 'There are plenty more where they came from,' the banker said.

We talked for a few more minutes. It seemed that little had been done by NIB when the internal auditors discovered the illegal over-loading on customer accounts. No money was ever returned and no member of the bank's staff was ever disciplined. The story was bigger than the CMI tax-evasion scandal. It took a little persuading but I departed from my source with the original NIB documents in my possession. I also left him with a request—to do an interview about the CMI scheme. He would be presented on camera as an NIB insider, but his face would not be shown and his voice would be distorted. 'I'll give it some thought,' he said.

I went back to RTÉ, knowing that I had just been told about a hugely significant story. I met up with Ed Mulhall and George Lee. 'It's bigger than CMI and no judge will stop us this time,' I predicted as I watched their stunned expressions as they read the internal audit reports.

We agreed that every fact would have to be checked and rechecked before this story could be broadcast. As with the CMI story, we had to be 100 per cent certain, especially as this time we were going to accuse the fourth largest bank in the country of theft.

It was a relatively simple story. Every few months, bank officials at NIB reviewed computer print-outs of quarterly account statements. These staff members, acting with the approval of some senior manage-ment at NIB, determined the interest and additional fees to be charged to these accounts and then selected certain accounts for loading. It was an act of theft. The bank was stealing from its customers. Having reviewed the computer printouts, the bank official noted the 'loaded' amount on a debit slip. A new statement was duly prepared, with the 'loaded' amount deducted from the account balance. It would have required a very diligent account holder—with a very good understand-ing of interest rates and bank charges, and how they were applied—to spot the wrongdoing. Overcharging increased branch performances and added to overall bank profits. The practice was known to senior NIB executives for many years but, despite some internal expressions of concern, nobody had called a halt.

As we digested the implications of the latest story about NIB, the duffel-bag man rang me about the CMI interview request. He agreed to an interview which was recorded the next day. He spoke slowly and in a measured way but his answers damned his employers.

Customers were informed that the bank was concerned that the Revenue Commissioners may have access to bank records at a future date, and that the bank could not guarantee the customer total anonymity from the Revenue Commissioners. They were told that this scheme would remove their names completely from the account, replace the name with a number, and on that basis it would guarantee them protection from Revenue inspection of bank records should that arise at a future date.

The whistle-blower said that the bank was fully aware of the type of customers they were targeting and that it would have been highly unusual for senior management at NIB not to know what was going on. It was powerful stuff. I prepared a report for the main evening news while George Lee edited a longer package for the *Prime Time* programme. The impact of a bank insider talking was to put the spotlight very firmly on how NIB operated the CMI scheme. NIB insisted that there was no evidence that it had knowingly helped its customers to evade tax. Now we had a bank official saying otherwise, and documentation to support this version of events, including an internal NIB letter directing one bank manager to check into the 'hot money potential' of a farmer who happened to own 250 cows.

The interview with the banker generated considerable public and political reaction, and it added to the pressure on NIB.

In the days leading up to the High Court decision on the NIB injunction, the duffel-bag man called again. He was pleased with the TV interview, but he wanted to meet. There was speculation inside the bank that private investigators had been brought in to weed out the whistle-blower. My source was now concerned about having a duffel bag stuffed with NIB files. He wanted to give me all the necessary documents to back up the fee and interest-overcharging allegations.

We arranged to meet in a hotel in Galway. I booked a room where we could talk without fear of interruption. The documents certainly told the story. I was looking for the first time at detailed files from several NIB branches, including internal bank debit slips from branches in Cork, Dublin and Carrick-on-Shannon in County Leitrim. It was simply amazing that an apparently reputable financial institution had been ripping off its own customers in the way these documents confirmed.

The debit slips recorded the amounts to be taken from customer statements. Computer-generated bank statements were changed so that bank customers did not get to see the additional withdrawals from their accounts. Instead, the original statements were destroyed and new ones were typed up. 'The calculation of interest on overdrafts is far too difficult for most people to follow. That's why it was so easy for the bank to get away with it,' the duffel-bag man explained.

The top brass in NIB knew that this illegal activity was boosting bank profits, while branch managers were rewarded with generous annual bonus payments.

It took about an hour for the banker to work his way through all the documents, explaining the significance of the material as he took even more files from a white plastic bag. When he had finished, and had answered all the questions thrown at him, I asked the inevitable: 'We need an interview. It would be the same as before. We'd hide your face and get an actor for your voice.'

The duffel-bag man was silent. He had come this far. The interview would be the final act. A few moments passed as he considered the request. 'Okay, I'll do it. I might as well get it all over with,' he eventually said.

We recorded the interview the following morning in the bedroom of the hotel in Galway. It was a sensitive arrangement with cameraman Robin Boyd recruited for the task. In all, we spoke on camera for a few minutes short of an hour. This man explained the background to how overcharging had become a regular feature of how NIB did its business. 'There was extreme pressure on branch managers to increase their fee income and their interest income. League tables were presented by senior management in the bank, highlighting the top achievers in this area. People at the bottom of the ladder felt pressurised,' he said. The man admitted to having loaded fees on accounts during his own career with the bank. He was not the only bank official to have acted in this way—National Irish Bank had earned millions in the late 1980s and early 1990s from loading interest and fees onto the accounts of its unsuspecting customers.

A few days after we recorded the interview with the duffel-bag man, another NIB official agreed to talk on camera under the now-familiar terms of blacked-out face and distorted voice. 'I'd be surprised if it didn't happen in every branch in the country,' the NIB employee said.

We had the goods but before we could broadcast the story, there was first the matter of the NIB injunction against RTÉ. There was no legal barrier to prevent us from transmitting the fee and interest-loading story but the advice from the RTÉ lawyers was to be patient. So we waited. The case had, in fact, been heard on 26 February in the High Court. The judgment went our way. 'I am satisfied that in such circumstances I should allow the publication of the confidential information pre-ferring, as I do, the public interest in the disclosure of such information as against the interest in preserving its confidence,' Mr Justice Peter Shanley declared.

NIB appealed the decision to the Supreme Court, which meant that the injunction remained in place. There were more meetings with RTÉ's legal team ahead of the Supreme Court appeal as every aspect of the work George Lee and I had undertaken since early January was combed through. Nothing was left unexplored as our lawyers worked on their strategy to ensure we won the case.

Five judges of the Supreme Court delivered their verdicts on the arguments they had heard from the two sides. NIB focused on the breach of confidence and the potential damage if RTÉ broadcast the names of its customers. RTÉ stressed the need for information to reach the public domain when to do so was in the public interest. There was a huge sense of relief when it became clear that the judges had come down in our favour. Three judges—Lynch, O'Flaherty and Barrington—found for us, while two—Keane and Hamilton—sided with NIB's arguments. The essence of the majority court decision was that the public's right to know about a serious wrongdoing outweighed a bank's duty to protect the confidentiality of its customers' transactions.

Mr Justice Lynch concluded that there is 'a public interest in defeating wrong doing and where the publication of confidential information may be of assistance in defeating wrong doing then the public interest in such publication may outweigh the public interest in the maintenance of con-fidentiality.' He was very clear about the seriousness of our investigation:

The allegation which they make is of serious tax evasion and this is a matter of genuine interest and importance to the general public and especially to the vast majority who are law abiding taxpayers and I am satisfied that it is in the public interest that the general public should be given this information.

Legal experts immediately described it as a landmark judgment which significantly advanced the cause of media freedom. There was, however, also a warning for RTÉ in the judgment—innocent bank customers could sue the station if they were defamed. We had to be careful. Ironically, my daughter Neasa would a couple of years later study the judgment as part of her studies to qualify as a barrister.

It was widely assumed that we intended to name customers identified in the NIB documents we had obtained about the offshore CMI scheme, although we had never asserted that our stories about the bank were dependent on any names. Nobody could have guessed, however, that our NIB investigation had gone well beyond the offshore tax-evasion scheme.

The Supreme Court judgment in RTÉ's favour was issued on Friday, 20 March 1998. In a bizarre attempt to twist the facts of the majority court judgment, NIB actually released a media statement expressing pleasure at the outcome. This brazen attempt to deny reality was repeated over the following week as NIB adopted a media relations strategy which attempted to damage the reputations of RTÉ, George Lee and myself. In the end, the strategy proved to be ill-conceived and it backfired very badly.

We went to work on the overcharging report immediately after the Supreme Court found in our favour. I met with the duffel-bag man for several hours over that weekend. I was excited about the material we had gathered but I was equally very nervous. 'This has to be 100 per cent correct,' I kept telling myself. We had a series of legal meetings as every line of the report was examined to ensure that there was nothing which NIB could subsequently exploit to undermine our investigation. Nothing was included in the report unless we had documentary evidence to support what was being said.

We sent NIB a series of detailed and specific questions on the Monday morning after the Supreme Court judgment. They had been expecting to hear from us in the aftermath of the case about more CMI-related material. They could not, however, have expected to receive a list of questions about a whole new area of unethical behaviour in their business. Upon receipt of our questions, NIB was made aware for the first time that we had access to confidential internal documents about deliberate fee and interest overcharging on customer accounts. As with the letter the previous January about the CMI scheme, the correspondence was addressed to Philip Halpin, the Chief Operating Officer at NIB. The questions we were asking were remarkable. Even now, several years later, I am still taken aback over what the bank was up to and what our investigation uncovered.

Dear Mr Halpin,

RTÉ is working on a story for transmission on Wednesday 25th March ... concerning National Irish Bank's retail banking operation. In order to assist us to present a fair and accurate report on this issue we would be obliged if you could provide answers to the following questions.

1. RTÉ understands that internal Audit Reports in 1990 for the Carndonagh and Carrick-on-Shannon branches of NIB revealed that interest charges were increased without legitimate reason and without customer knowledge.
   - Is this true?
   - If it is true what action did the bank take?
   - Were the customers so affected notified and re-imbursed?

2. We also understand that interest loading occurred in Walkinstown in 1989 and in Cork in 1988, 1989 and 1990.
   - Is this true?
   - If it is true what action did the bank take?
   - Were the customers so affected notified and re-imbursed?

3. In how many other branches of the bank did this interest loading take place?
   - Did the bank inform the customers in each case?
   - Were customers re-imbursed and if not why not?

4. When alerted to these practices what action did senior management take to stop practices, to inform customers and to re-imburse them?

5. Were any managers disciplined for engaging in this practice?

6. How much did this interest loading practice contribute to the bank's profits?

7. When did the interest loading practice stop completely in all branches?

8. RTÉ has information that NIB imposed extra bank charges on customers without their consent or knowledge. We have documentation which itemises original net fees, the net fee adjusted, and

the net fee applied. Our information suggests that in many cases the adjusted fees were not made known to the customers.
- Is this true?
- How widespread was it?
- If the bank was aware of this practice what steps did it take to eradicate it?
- Were customers informed or re-imbursed?
- When did the practice cease in all branches of the bank?
- Were any staff who engaged in this practice disciplined?
- How much did this practice contribute to the bank's profits?

9. RTÉ has evidence of interest loading on ordinary term loans. This involved altering the agreed interest on such loans without the customers' knowledge.
- Is this true?
- In how many branches did it occur?
- When alerted what action did NIB take to ensure it could not happen in the future?
- When did it stop?
- Were any officials who engaged in this action disciplined?
- Were customers informed and re-imbursed?
- How much did the practice contribute to the bank's profits?

10. What effect did the Consumer Credit Act have on any of the practices outlined above?

11. What procedures have NIB put in place to ensure that these practices no longer operate?

12. What did NIB do to re-imburse customers who have been over-charged as a result of these practices?

The very fact that the questions in the letter signed by George Lee and myself were asked in the first place was stunning. One of the best-known companies in Ireland, a financial institution of considerable repute and authority, was in huge trouble.

Ed Mulhall insisted that the bank be given sufficient time to consider the import of the material we intended to broadcast. The bank declined to answer any of our 12 questions. It actually refused to make any comment about the overcharging claim for the initial news reports. Bizarrely NIB also seemed intent on fighting a public relations battle right up to transmission time. The bank's PR advisors accused RTÉ of making 'sweeping allegations' against the bank only two days before they knew we were going to reveal that they had stolen money from their own customers. A media statement was issued with the heading, 'NIB challenges RTÉ to produce evidence.' It was one of the best examples I have ever seen of sheer brass-neck arrogance. Then, to cap that, just hours before the damning report was broadcast, Philip Halpin, the NIB Chief Operating Officer, issued a statement seeking an apology from RTÉ because, he claimed, George Lee and a camera crew had trespassed on bank property. 'Maybe they are in denial,' I thought.

Later that day—Wednesday, 25 March 1998—we broadcast our report. A normal television news report runs to about 90 seconds. On big occasions, the duration may be stretched to two minutes; anything beyond that is a rarity for a television news bulletin. On that particular night, however, all the usual rules were dispensed with. The NIB story was totally different. At just under eight minutes, the report was by far the longest single news item I—or anyone else in the newsroom—had ever compiled. I watched the report in the RTÉ newsroom. Few colleagues had known what George Lee and I had been investigating but as transmission time neared, word started to spread about a 'big story'. Now people were gathered around various television screens in the newsroom, all watching in silence as the signature music for the main evening news played.

'Revealed, how National Irish Bank secretly overcharged some of its customers,' the programme presenter, Bryan Dobson, said as he introduced our exclusive story.

> RTÉ's continuing investigation into National Irish Bank has un-covered further irregularities. The pressure to make profits for the bank created a culture where at certain NIB branches money was taken without any legitimate reason from customer accounts and kept for the bank's own profits.

The television screen moved from Dobson and the news studio to the prepared report which included nine different interview clips with the two whistle-blower bank officials.

> Customers were not alerted and no money was repaid and the pro-ceeds went to the bank itself... Our investigations show at least two

separate practices… The first was increasing or loading the interest on customer overdrafts… The second was the charging of extra fees on customer accounts without their knowledge or agreement…

There were cheers in the RTÉ newsroom when the item concluded. Rarely has any news story generated such public and political reaction. The cabinet held a special meeting to discuss the revelations. There was universal praise for RTÉ for putting the resources into the investigation. Having refused to answer any questions—and having engaged in a pathetic mud-throwing exercise just prior to transmission—NIB eventually responded, but it took more than one statement for the bank to realise that it was in very deep trouble. High Court inspectors were ultimately appointed to investigate just how Ireland's fourth largest bank went about its business.

It was one of my best days in journalism. George Lee and I had covered a tremendous amount of ground in almost two months. The end result of our efforts was the naming and shaming of a financial institution engaged first in tax evasion through its offshore CMI scheme, and second in sticking its hands into the pockets of its own customers. George and I were named Journalists of the Year for our work. We were not the only winners. By the time the Revenue Commissioners had reviewed the tax affairs of some 300 investors in the CMI scheme, the Exchequer was better off to the tune of over €57 million. The largest single CMI settlement was for €1.65 million.

Along with the Revenue Commissioners, the High Court inspectors went to work at NIB. They had the authority to comb through the bank, examining all records and files, as well as interviewing staff, past and present. A huge volume of work was undertaken and the report, running to over 400 pages—which was published on 30 July 2004—was a damning indictment of National Irish Bank.

The conclusions reached by the High Court inspectors offered particular satisfaction to George Lee and myself, as well as colleagues like Ed Mulhall and Eamon Kennedy who had supported our work. The report confirmed the issues raised in January 1998 in our investigation about the CMI scheme, and our reports in March 1998 on the loading of fees and interest.

The inspectors found that money had been hidden from the Revenue, including funds held in bogus non-resident accounts and fictitious and incorrectly named accounts. This money was, as claimed by our whistle-blower, targeted by NIB staff for investment in CMI policies. Despite everything the bank had said in early 1998, the High Court inspectors concluded that NIB staff had, in fact, promoted the CMI scheme as a secure investment out of the reach of the Revenue and that this was 'a practice which served to facilitate the evasion of Revenue obligations' by bank customers. There were, in particular, four specific conclusions in the report in relation to the evasion of tax obligations that damned NIB:

1. Fictitious and incorrectly named accounts were opened and maintained by the Bank and existed throughout the branch network during the period of the investigation up until the end of 1996.
2. The opening and maintenance of such accounts by the Bank served to encourage the evasion of tax as it concealed the true ownership of the funds in the accounts.
3. Bank personnel were aware or ought to have been aware of the reason for the opening of such accounts.
4. In 1995 and 1996, when branch managers were directed that all fictitious and incorrectly named accounts must be regularised and/or closed, even where there was a possibility that the business might be lost, managers sought to retain for the Bank the funds on deposit in such accounts by proposing to the customers that they invest in CMI, or by suggesting that they deposit the funds in another branch of the Bank in their correct names.

The evidence was such that the two High Court inspectors—Tom Grace and John Blayney—concluded that it was their view that 'these "solutions" were improper because they served to encourage customers to continue to evade tax.' I was very pleased to read the conclusion reached in the report that staff in NIB branches did target customers who would be interested in the secrecy offered by the CMI scheme and that they provided assurances about confidentiality from the Revenue even after the investor's death. The duffel-bag man was vindicated on every count.

There was a similar bill of health from the High Court inspectors for our work on exposing interests and fee overcharging. The inspectors concluded that the interest was charged to some customer accounts on a quarterly basis which was 'not in fact interest', a practice which was described as 'improper'. They also said that, 'The manner in which branch managers purported to charge fees for administration and management time…[was]…improper, resulting in some customers being overcharged, across the branch network.' There was adverse comment in the report about many individuals who had held senior management positions at NIB, including the company's former Chief Executive, Jim Lacey, and Philip Halpin, the Chief Operating Officer to whom I had sent all those letters in early 1998, asking for answers for our investigation.

The High Court inspectors' report did not just vindicate the decision of the duffel-bag man to turn whistle-blower. The report also acknowledged the work undertaken by RTÉ News. It was a complete contrast to the attitude adopted by the Minister for Finance, Charlie McCreevy, back in 1998, when the first RTÉ report on NIB had been broadcast. Both George Lee and I had been annoyed at some of McCreevy's comments. While describing tax evasion as a form of stealing, McCreevy came down light on NIB. 'All I'm saying for people to do,' he said, 'is to keep a sense of proportion about this, and I think it is important to do that in the light of some of the extraordinary scaremongering that has gone on about tax evasion matters.' He also talked about, bringing 'some reality to the situation with some of the outlandish accusations that have been made all round'.

These were remarkable comments from the Minister for Finance only a week after the first CMI report had been broadcast. While various official institutions had been called in to examine what NIB was up to, McCreevy gave the bank a sympathetic hearing. 'National Irish Bank have pointed out themselves that the sums of money involved represent nought point one percent (0.1%) of their own total resources and that has put something in context.'

In the context of over €57 million paid in outstanding taxes, interest and penalties from the Revenue's CMI investigation, McCreevy's stance now appears even more bizarre. And there was a lot more tax evasion going on at that time. RTÉ's work on highlighting the wrongdoing at NIB led directly to the exposure of the DIRT tax-evasion scam. During the NIB investigation, I received a call from a former AIB employee. This retired bank official wanted to meet me about what he called 'bogus non-resident accounts'. We met in a midlands town. This man had a computer print-out of all the AIB customers in this town who held bogus non-resident accounts. There were hundreds of names on the list. I persuaded the man to do an interview with his identity concealed. It looked as if we had another banking exclusive. A few weeks later, however, as we were about to broadcast the revelations about AIB, the retired bank official withdrew permission for use of the interview. We were bitterly disappointed but, fortunately for the taxpayer, some time later, Liam Collins in the *Sunday Independent* broke a similar story. It emerged that hundreds of thousands of bogus non-resident accounts had been opened in all the leading Irish financial institutions in a deliberate scheme to defraud the Exchequer of legitimate tax payments. The investigation cost NIB €64 million, a figure which included just over €12 million which was reimbursed to bank customers.

The NIB investigations dominated my life in the early months of 1998. That should have been the end of my involvement with the NIB until the High Court inspectors issued their final report; I had done my job as a reporter. I very much wish that had been the case. Bizarrely, however, the wrongdoing at NIB would remain an integral part of my life for a further six years, although not because of anything mentioned in the initial television and radio reports.

Chapter 12 ᨆ

BEVERLEY AND THE
LIBEL CASE

few times in my life, I have been asked to fill in questionnaires for newspapers and magazines. These Question and Answer (Q&A) pieces can be amusing, and I suppose they offer readers an off-beat insight into the lives of well-known people. The questions posed tend to be fairly standard—they ask for your favourite book, film and musician, as well as things like favourite saying and most embarrassing moment. I think one of the first of these questionnaires that I completed was for *Hot Press* magazine in the late 1980s. The music publication has a regular Q&A feature known as 'The Mad Hatter's Box'. I suspect they asked me as I was on the television news quite a bit at that time, chasing around after politicians like Charlie Haughey.

Looking back now at the responses I gave, I think that many would still be the same all these years later. For the record, my answers for *Hot Press* included *An Ice Cream War* by William Boyd (book); *The Ballroom of Romance* directed by my old colleague, Pat O'Connor (film) and Van Morrison (musician). I took my favourite saying from *At Swim-Two-Birds* by Flann O'Brien: 'When things go wrong and will not come right, when life looks black as the hour of night, a pint of plain is your only man.' As for my moment of embarrassment, I recalled covering a Michael Jackson concert in Cork for the main evening news when, near the encore, I realised I was dancing along with the people around me.

Interestingly, almost 20 years ago, my biggest fear was 'losing my script in the RTÉ newsroom computer just minutes before bulletin time.' That's an answer I would seriously change now in light of the period in my life when I seemed to have taken up residence in the Four

Courts. The RTÉ investigation into National Irish Bank had been a huge success but one individual took exception to what we broadcast. The Fianna Fáil politician, Beverley Cooper Flynn, had worked as a financial advisor with the bank. She went first to the High Court and subsequently to the Supreme Court in challenging the accuracy of what RTÉ said about her activities while she was employed at NIB.

The legal case was a harrowing experience. They were among the bleakest days of my life. Walking through the doors of the Four Courts can be a very lonely feeling. I shudder now even thinking about the place. A feeling of physical illness comes over me at the thought of ever again having to go back into the building.

Beverley Cooper Flynn was not on the radar when the inquiries into National Irish Bank first started. Her name was not mentioned in the original report on 23 January 1998. Cooper Flynn, a daughter of former Fianna Fáil minister and EU Commissioner, Pádraig Flynn, had been elected to Dáil Éireann at the 1997 general election. An ambitious politician who was tipped for high office in Fianna Fáil, she had been mentioned in passing during a conversation with one of my initial contacts. One source said that she had sold the offshore CMI product during her career as a financial advisor with NIB between 1989 and 1997. This source also mentioned the fact that Cooper Flynn had won a trip to Australia which had been a bonus for reaching certain sales targets. She was a high-flyer.

I rang the Fianna Fáil TD for the first time on 20 January. She said that she couldn't talk about her career as a financial advisor because of bank confidentiality. Her role was also referred to in passing in a letter sent to NIB just before the first report was broadcast. I recall one of the bank's PR advisors remarking, 'What are you up to—is this a conspiracy against Fianna Fáil?' The reality was that the investigation was far removed from the world of politics and, without supporting evidence, the Cooper Flynn allegations could not be broadcast.

Enough people had, however, mentioned her name, and several sources were aware of the Australian trip. I rang the politician again on 24 January. We spoke for over 10 minutes but she stuck by her position that she was bound by bank confidentiality. She would 'neither confirm nor deny' the trip to Australia but was insistent that everything about the CMI scheme was above board.

George Lee was preparing a follow-up report to the first NIB story.

We decided to include a brief mention of Cooper Flynn's links to the bank. When I rang the Mayo TD, she was at a constituency clinic. We spoke for about 10 minutes but, as previously, Cooper Flynn was unwilling to discuss her previous career with NIB. Later that day, it was decided that George Lee's report would include a passing mention of the politician. In all, the reference lasted less than 20 seconds, in a report of almost three minutes' duration. 'Beverley Cooper Flynn has referred all questions to the bank,' George Lee's script noted. We did not have enough evidence to go any further with a story linking the Fianna Fáil politician directly with the CMI scheme. In any event, she was not significant to our story which moved very quickly into the investigation of interest and fee overcharging.

The reaction to our second NIB exclusive in March 1998 was huge. Everybody had a story to tell. I have never received so many calls and letters from people, all seeking to highlight their own experience with a bank or building society. Early in May, I was contacted by a man from Virginia in County Cavan who wanted me to meet some people who had had dealings with NIB. I travelled to County Cavan and met an elderly couple who had invested in the CMI scheme, as had one of their neighbours, a retired farmer. I listened to these people tell their stories. All three identified Beverley Cooper Flynn as the NIB executive who had sold them the offshore investment product. The couple recalled how she had said that the taxman would never know. Unfortunately they ultimately decided not to record an interview on camera about how they had come to invest. I now knew, however, that there was real substance to the Cooper Flynn allegations.

I needed something more to go on so I placed an advert in the *Anglo-Celt* newspaper in the first week of June 1998. The newspaper covered a population base not far from that assigned to Cooper Flynn when she was a financial advisor with NIB. It was a trawling exercise to seek out sources, but worth the try. I included my name and mobile number in the advert and, a few days after the newspaper was published, I received a number of interesting calls.

A woman from County Monaghan said that Beverley Cooper Flynn had called to her house to make the sale. On 8 June, we recorded an interview in which her identity was concealed. Part of the interview was broadcast a few days later in a story about the ongoing official investigation into the CMI scheme. The next day, as I was driving from Bray to

Dublin, I was contacted by James Howard, a retired farmer and cattle dealer from County Meath. He said that Cooper Flynn was the NIB official who had brought him into the CMI scheme. We met for the first time in the car park of a pub near Gormanstown. He had seen the earlier report—with concealed identities—and was willing to do an interview on the same terms. I arranged for a camera crew and, later that same day, we recorded a lengthy interview. The plan was to do the interview at the beach near Gormanstown but, as it was raining heavily, we ended up recording in the car. He was nervous so I actually asked about the weather and the hay crop at the start of the interview, just to ease him in.

James Howard said he had met Cooper Flynn at the NIB branch in Balbriggan in May 1993. He had undeclared income. She pushed him to invest in the CMI scheme. Howard had an additional piece of information—he alleged that Cooper Flynn advised him not to avail of the 1993 tax amnesty, a controversial measure which gave taxpayers an opportunity to regularise their financial affairs. The allegations by Howard were very serious and had to be put to Cooper Flynn to allow her to respond. I rang her early the next day, outlining the gist of my story and the allegations that various CMI investors had made against her. I wanted her to have a letter with a number of questions based on the information in those interviews. It was important that she understood the seriousness of the story we planned to broadcast.

When I rang her, she was about to travel to a meeting of the Fianna Fáil parliamentary party at the Slieve Russell Hotel in County Cavan. She said she would call me later with a fax number. I rang her again about two-and-a-half hours later, looking for the fax number to get the letter to her. 'Charlie, I have made up my mind. You can do whatever you have to do and I will do what I have to do,' she responded. I had the letter on my computer screen in front of me and, as we spoke over the phone, I quoted sections of the correspondence to Cooper Flynn. It was important that she be given every opportunity to reply to the people we had interviewed. Without identifying any of the individuals involved, I told her about the two people in County Cavan who said that she had advised them that the Revenue would never know about their CMI funds. I also told her that another person, a County Meath farmer, had alleged that she had said to him, 'Why avail of the tax amnesty? Why give the government 15 per cent?'

'Beverley, look, if you are not going to take the letter from me, then I will have no alternative but to go up to Cavan and try to give it to you,' I said just before our conversation ended.

A little over an hour later, I was in my car on my way to Ballyconnell in County Cavan. The allegations were too serious to allow any chance that she might not receive the letter. When I got to the Slieve Russell Hotel, Cooper Flynn was at the Fianna Fáil meeting. I asked the hotel receptionist to track her down for me. I also told a Fianna Fáil press officer that I needed to speak with Cooper Flynn. I spent almost two hours in the reception area of the hotel without any sign of the Mayo TD. Eventually I asked the hotel's duty manager to ensure that the letter was delivered to her. When I later checked with the hotel, I was told that the envelope had been slipped under her bedroom door. Cooper Flynn knew that I was in the hotel. I had done my best to give her an opportunity to respond to the claims my sources were making.

The report which accused Cooper Flynn of encouraging people to evade tax was broadcast on Friday, 19 June. At the time, it never dawned on me the trouble and anxiety the story would bring. 'A farmer who was brought into the National Irish Bank controversial offshore scheme by Beverley Cooper Flynn, now a Fianna Fáil TD…' The report contained anonymous NIB customers, telling of their dealings with Cooper Flynn. All recounted how she had called to their homes and persuaded them to invest in the CMI scheme.

James Howard was not identified in the report but the substance of his comments was damning for the Mayo woman. His story was straightforward. He recalled that a woman named Beverley Flynn (she was not married at that time) had rung him and said, 'I believe you have some money that you're not using.' He guessed that she had her information from working with NIB. The bank financial advisor later told him not to avail of the 1993 tax amnesty. She was insistent that he should ignore the amnesty: 'There's no need to do that. We won't do that. That's final.'

Cooper Flynn had declined to comment on the allegations before the report was transmitted, despite my best efforts. A little over an hour after the first broadcast on the *Six One News*, she issued a statement. The Fianna Fáil TD said, 'I wish to categorically state that at no time in my seven years working with NIB did I ever encourage anyone to invest in a financial product as a means of evading his or her obligations to pay tax.' She also challenged RTÉ to name the man who alleged that she had brought him into the CMI scheme. I was confident in our story. I had done all the correct things a reporter should do in pursuing a story as serious as this one. I also genuinely believed that James Howard was telling the truth.

A few days after the first broadcast, on 25 June, Jody Corcoran, a journalist with the *Sunday Independent*, called me. Corcoran had been tipped off about James Howard's identity and was going to name him in that weekend's edition of his newspaper. I laughed when he asked me whether I would confirm or deny that the farmer was, in fact, James Howard. The idea of one journalist revealing a source to another journalist was, to say the least, odd. 'Jody, I'm not going down that road,' I said.

A short while later, I had a phone call from an annoyed James Howard who seemed to think that I had given his name to the newspaper, which I clearly had not. He was so upset that I actually decided to drive to his home to reassure him that I had not breached our agreement. I met his wife and it was clear that they were upset about the possibility of being 'outed'.

The newspaper put the story on its front page the following Sunday and quoted sources who claimed that 'another female employee in NIB' and not Cooper Flynn had sold the CMI product to Howard. The report said that Cooper Flynn had never met or spoken with Howard and that his story was a 'tissue of lies'. The Mayo TD issued a statement later that day, calling 'on RTÉ and Charlie Bird to confirm that Mr Howard appeared on the broadcast and to withdraw the allegations about me with the same prominence as their original report.'

I again went to see James Howard at his home. 'Do you have any doubts?' I asked. 'If you have even the smallest doubt that it wasn't Cooper Flynn, please tell me now.'

The reply offered me considerable reassurance. 'Charlie, I have no doubt whatsoever.' Howard was angry at what Cooper Flynn had said. He readily agreed to another interview but this time he was prepared to be identified. He said he was '100 per cent certain' that Cooper Flynn had sold him the CMI product in 1993.

I also met his daughter, Marina, who had been present at the family home when the NIB financial advisor had first called to see her father in 1990. Marina Howard also agreed to be interviewed for the camera. 'I remember my father saying she was Pádraig Flynn's daughter and saw her on the TV a couple of times after that and thought, "That's her who came to see Daddy"." Marina Howard's recollection of meeting Cooper Flynn would prove crucial later.

Seeing the Howards now identified on RTÉ provoked Cooper Flynn into issuing another media statement claiming that the allegations in my report were lies:

> The records at NIB show that, in 1993, Mr Howard purchased a CMI product. Those records also show that another employee of NIB sold the product to Mr Howard and was paid commission for doing so. I have received confirmation from NIB today that Mr Howard's file within NIB contains no reference whatsoever to me.

It was a *tour de force* for the Mayo TD. 'I have been shamefully treated by RTÉ,' she alleged. She demanded that RTÉ withdraw the allegations, and she wanted me to read an apology on the television news. When I read about the threat of litigation, I couldn't help feeling sick. The next day, 2 July 1998, the first legal letter was received from Cooper Flynn. The name of this 'other NIB employee' was subsequently reported in the media. Patricia Roche was said to have worked closely with Cooper Flynn who now alleged that the Howards had mixed up the two women. Roche, however, declined to be interviewed, which left us all wondering what she had to say about the claims. RTÉ responded to Cooper Flynn's legal correspondence on 6 July 1998. The matter would conclude in the Supreme Court only on 28 April 2004.

I lost count of the number of meetings I attended with RTÉ's legal representatives in the aftermath of Cooper Flynn's decision to issue libel proceedings. She sued RTÉ, James Howard and me, claiming that the various broadcasts in the summer of 1998 implied that she had instigated a scheme intended to facilitate tax evasion. RTÉ's legal team did not deny the broadcasts were damaging but argued that they were true and justified. There was little movement in the case for a couple of years. Did I think it would go away? Yes, is the honest answer. It was really only when I brought our lawyers to meet some of my NIB sources that it finally dawned on me that the libel case was actually going to proceed.

The court case started on Tuesday, 6 February 2001. The trial period is still a bit of a daze. For 29 days, over a six-week period, my life was turned upside down. It was a terrible ordeal. The RTÉ legal team had warned that the court proceedings would be somewhat like a football match. 'This will be a game of two halves,' was how one lawyer put it. After the opening statements, Cooper Flynn gave her evidence. The cumulative effect of this was that by day four the case against us looked really very strong.

Cooper Flynn was represented by leading barrister, Garrett Cooney, and Hugh Mohan. I had seen Cooney in action at the planning tribunal in Dublin Castle. He was a heavy hitter at the Law Library. His opening statement covered the ground from when I had first contacted his client in January 1998 about her role as a National Irish Bank financial advisor through to the contentious television reports six months later in which several bank customers alleged that she had encouraged them to invest in the CMI scheme.

I did not, however, recognise the way in which the time sequence and my dealings with Cooper Flynn were presented by the lawyer. I was accused of putting words in James Howard's mouth—something which I strongly rejected when it came to my turn to give evidence. Cooney also accused RTÉ of engaging in 'trial by television' and alleged that we had built a 'house of lies' against the Mayo politician.

'This is not in the real world,' I thought as I sat in the courtroom listening to this respected lawyer. Over the following days, I found it very hard to sit and hear terrible things said about me and about how I did my job. Cooper Flynn's evidence told a different story from the one I remembered. I knew that what she was saying was untrue and, fortunately, the RTÉ legal team did a good job in exposing the problems with her version of events.

I established a routine of going into RTÉ every morning for a coffee with colleagues like Seán O'Rourke and Joe O'Brien; we used to talk through the previous day's proceeding and catch up on other news. Those chats kept me sane. Ed Mulhall, George Lee and I would usually drive into town together, parking the car near Dublin Castle, and then walk down to the Four Courts. 'This is the executioner's walk,' we decided one morning early in the case.

We all had our own routine in the courtroom. Ed Mulhall sat upstairs in the public gallery, in the same spot most days. I took a seat alongside George Lee across from the lawyers. I would frequently look over at the 12 members of the jury—eight men and four women—and try to work out how they were reacting to the evidence they were hearing. It was a pointless exercise but I needed any reassurance I could give myself that the case was going well for our side. One juror was always taking notes. In gossip around the environs of the courts, I was told that another juror was an accountant, while another had links to Fianna Fáil and the PDS. There was absolutely no way of knowing how much of this was true but I latched onto every scrap of information.

Early in the trial, I had a fit of the wobbles when several important witnesses were not allowed to give evidence. In the pre-trial period, RTÉ had won discovery of NIB documents which contained the names of other customers whose financial affairs had been handled by Cooper Flynn. They were subpoenaed to give evidence while other people actually came forward voluntarily. It looked as if we had a line of people, all of whom were ready to give damaging evidence against Cooper Flynn. Their involvement in the case was, however, contested. The trial judge ruled that the only people allowed give evidence were those who had purchased the same CMI product as James Howard, which had been referred to in the original NIB story of June 1998. It was a depressing decision. 'Christ, we're fecked,' I thought. There was some good news, however, when it was decided that a number of other NIB customers could take the witness stand. 'We're doing okay,' I now tried to convince myself. My assessment of how the case was progressing shifted by the hour.

Four NIB customers gave evidence—Patrick Duff, Joy Howe, Seán Roe and Joan Quigley. Duff told the court that in 1993, when he was thinking about availing of the tax amnesty, Cooper Flynn had advised him not to do so. She had recommended investing in the CMI scheme and had said no one would know about it. Howe recalled Cooper Flynn telling her that her money would be put into a numbered account on which her name would not appear and to which the Revenue would not have access. Roe said that Cooper Flynn advised him to put his money into an offshore account as that would mean it was tax-free. Quigley said that her husband had money in a bank in Newry in Northern Ireland which had not been declared to the Revenue Commissioners. Cooper Flynn advised her husband not to come clean under the tax amnesty but to invest in the CMI scheme instead.

Two former NIB employees were subpoenaed to give evidence. Nigel Darcy admitted that the CMI products were primarily intended for non-residents. It was an interesting admission as NIB targeted the CMI scheme at residents. The head of the NIB unit which sold the CMI product, Patrick Cooney, had to jump through hoops in explaining what he meant by 'hot money' in a letter to his staff. 'We all know what hot money means,' I thought. 'I just hope the jury does too.'

The courtroom was full every day. I knew many of the faces—journalists from other media outlets who were assigned to report on the high-profile case. Members of the public took their seats every morning. This was the best show in town—and it had no entry fee. My mood used to improve when I saw a colleague, many of whom just dropped in to offer their support. A few kind words went a long way. Joe O'Brien came and sat in the courtroom. It meant a lot. RTÉ's Joe Duffy was there one day and left me a card. I didn't expect such gestures but they were really important in keeping my spirits up.

On a few occasions, I simply had to get up and leave the courtroom. Things were being said that I found upsetting; the stress was too much. My mood would improve somewhat after a brisk walk and a little fresh air outside the Four Courts. A couple of times when I walked out, Garrett Cooney was on the steps of the court building, having a quick cigarette. It was hard going for all involved.

I doubt if James Howard ever thought he would end up in the High Court when he first decided to ring my mobile number. The 69-year-old had retired a few years earlier from his dairy farm at Ardcath in County Meath. Howard was represented in court by another colourful legal expert, Paul O'Higgins.

He did well in the witness box. He told the court how, over the years, he had put aside some money from cattle sales and other farm business—money which he had kept hidden from his accountant and the Revenue. The funds were lodged in an account which was opened in 1987 at the NIB branch in Balbriggan in north County Dublin. Three years later, Howard received a payment of over £70,000 arising out of the sale of shares in a dairy company. Almost £40,000 of this money was lodged to his NIB account and, a few days later, Beverley Cooper Flynn, or Beverley Flynn as she was then known, rang to offer advice on investing the windfall.

Not long after that phone conversation, Marina Howard called her father from the farm yard where he was working. He had a visitor. 'I went up to the house and washed my Wellingtons and took them off

and went in. I met Ms Flynn,' Howard told the court. Having spoken
with the NIB financial advisor for about 20 minutes, Marina Howard
left the room when her father arrived. The farmer, however, was not
interested in putting his money into NIB investment products as he was
about to purchase two apartment properties in Dublin city. Three years
later, however, after a conversation with the Balbriggan branch manager,
James Howard indicated that he would like to discuss investment
options for his undeclared money. In May 1993, he met Cooper Flynn
for a second time. Their meeting was held at the Balbriggan branch
office. 'We have to make this snappy. I am going up the country. I'm late
as it is,' Howard recalled Cooper Flynn saying. The meeting lasted
about ten minutes. 'So she says, "I'm putting this money into a trust for
yourself and your family." And she produced this page of paper and she
said just sign there and that will be that.'

A few weeks after that meeting, details of a government tax amnesty
were announced. Howard was interested in coming clean with the tax
authorities. 'I said now here's my chance. I will take back the money,
pay the tax and, says I, I will ring Beverley Cooper Flynn.' The NIB
financial advisor was having none of it, as Howard recollected. 'No,
there is no need to give the government 15%, I am minding this money.
I am not doing that and we do not do that.'

Garrett Cooney challenged him all the way, even raising my blood
levels by suggesting that 'a deliberate strategy agreed by you [Howard]
and RTÉ and your legal advisors…' was at work. There was one weakness
in James Howard's case. The NIB documents relating to his CMI policy
did not contain Cooper Flynn's name. The name on some of the documents in the file was that of Patricia Roche, the other NIB financial
advisor. In a way, Patricia Roche's shadow was cast long over the entire
court proceedings. She was mentioned on numerous occasions.

James Howard told the court that he had first met Roche when she
contacted him about a month after he had invested in the CMI scheme
in 1993. She was promoting an insurance policy. Right from the first
approach to Roche to talk about NIB and CMI, she opted for silence.
RTÉ's legal team had, therefore, no idea what she might say in evidence,
so the decision was taken not to call her as a witness. We were not sure
what the other side would do. A constant topic of conversation was
whether or not they knew what she might say about James Howard and
Beverley Cooper Flynn. In the end, neither side called Roche to give

evidence, and her recollection of selling the CMI product for NIB emerged later in the subsequent report of the High Court inspectors, which was published well after the libel case had ended. The inspectors' report contained extracts of an interview they undertook with Roche in which she admitted that the NIB sales staff 'would all have understood that hot money was in respect of moncys that people had not declared or that they were concerned about the Revenue becoming aware of.' In many ways, it was a pity Roche was not called to give evidence at the libel trial, especially when it later emerged that she admitted to the High Court inspectors that she 'recognised from the beginning that it [the CMI product] wasn't kosher'. In any event, the libel trial continued without Patricia Roche.

The RTÉ group used to congregate most mornings in the small basement café in the Four Courts. The strategy planned by our external legal advisor, Simon McCormack of Eugene F. Collins and Sons, Solicitors, was for George Lee to give his evidence before me. I was going to be the last witness called by our side. However, the pressure was getting to me. I lost it totally one morning after about 20 days of hearing evidence before the jury and listening to lengthy legal arguments in the absence of the jury. As I sat at the coffee table with Ed Mulhall and several of RTÉ's lawyers, tears welled up in my eyes. 'The sooner I give my evidence, the better,' I sobbed. The plans were revised. Little was going to be gained by putting George Lee in the witness stand. I was going on.

I started giving evidence at 11.05 a.m. on Tuesday, 13 March 2001. It was Day 22 of the case. 'Mr Bird, if you could keep your answers up so that the person in the furthest corner of the jury box might hear it,' Kevin Feeney requested. It was a gentle introduction by Feeney who was RTÉ's lead barrister. I was terrified. I had no idea what was going to happen. Several times in the previous weeks, Ed Mulhall had warned me, 'It's going to be tough. Just be clear about everything you say.'

Kevin Feeney took me through a series of questions about my early career in *The Irish Times* and in RTÉ. He was attempting to give the jury an impression of the work I had done. There were some smiles when he asked if I had ever been sued previously. 'No, never,' I replied. 'The last time somebody told me they would see me in the High Court, I saw the person in the High Court all right but it was the other way round.'

The RTÉ lawyer also asked me about conducting interviews with the NIB sources. I mentioned that sometimes people who are not used to television can be nervous at the idea of sitting down in front of a camera. It applied to experienced politicians—'even lawyers,' I added. Kevin Feeney was quick to respond: 'Does it apply to journalists when they come to court?' There was laughter in the courtroom. 'Yes, very much so. You can take it, very much so,' I replied. I was full of nervous energy although I think I relaxed somewhat as the first day went on.

We had a difficult time going through my handwritten notes from my first meeting with James Howard in June 1998. There were words I could not decipher. I was asked to review the notes, and I was relaxed enough to joke about my inability to read my own handwriting. The unedited version of my first television interview with James Howard was then shown on a monitor in the courtroom, as were several other television news reports.

Twenty-four hours later, on Wednesday, 14 March 2001—Day 23—I was back in the witness stand. Garrett Cooney rose to ask me questions on behalf of his client, Beverley Cooper Flynn. He got off to a confusing start when in his first question he referred to my career as a 'newspaper reporter with RTÉ'. It was, however, merely a slip of the tongue as Cooney quickly moved on to question me about the events of 1998, but from the perspective of Cooper Flynn.

There were several tetchy exchanges, especially when the barrister wanted me to respond to his repeated statement that I knew the original reports on Cooper Flynn would cause 'huge and perhaps irreparable damage' to her reputation. I replied that I knew the allegations would have a serious impact but that we had done our 'damndest to communicate' with the Mayo TD to allow her a right of reply. Cooney was hoping for a different answer which I was not willing to provide. At one stage, the judge interjected, 'Mr Bird, I do not want to interfere but it is not an argument between you and Mr Cooney. He is asking you questions and he wants answers.'

The exchanges were a bit of a sparring match. I was being honest and answered everything I was asked. Cooney, however, was a master of the adversarial nature of courtroom proceedings.

Cooney: Do you consider the impact of this programme upon Ms Cooper Flynn's reputation and good name was most damaging?
Bird: Yes.

Cooney: And would have profound and perhaps permanent effect upon her reputation and her career as a politician?

Bird: No, I don't accept that. [...] I don't think it has happened.

Cooney: We have not had an election yet since the publication.

Bird: I am sure Beverley Cooper Flynn will do all right in Mayo, Mr Cooney.

Cooney: I am sure she is very consoled by that piece of encouragement from you, Mr Bird.

The lawyer's remarks provoked laughter in the packed courtroom. The atmosphere heated up once more when Cooney suggested very strongly that Cooper Flynn had been singled out in RTÉ's investigation of NIB, something which I believed to be untrue.

Cooney: I have to put it to you, Mr Bird, that from January 1998 you went out of your way, not all the time but you went out of your way to target Ms Cooper Flynn and you selected her from all the employees of NIB because she as a TD would be a big scalp on your belt if you happened to bring her down?

Bird: I reject that. [...] No, I fundamentally disagree with you, Mr Cooney.

I spent part of Thursday, 15 March 1998, giving evidence. It was Day 24 of the libel case and my third day in the witness stand. Garrett Cooney questioned me in detail about my attempts to contact his client before the first report about her role in NIB was broadcast. There had been little eye contact with Cooper Flynn over the two previous days. She sat in front of me, occasionally taking notes. On this occasion, however, I noticed her smiling when I was asked about my attempts to deliver a letter to her at the Fianna Fáil parliamentary party meeting in County Cavan.

Kevin Feeney was on his feet on several occasions, once complaining that Garrett Cooney was bullying me. There was, however, time for some gentle laughter before my time in the witness stand finally came to a conclusion. When talking about James Howard, Cooney was momentarily confused and made reference to James Gogarty. Cooney had been involved in 1999 in a very lengthy cross-examination of Gogarty, the man who had revealed details of planning corruption at the Flood Tribunal in Dublin Castle. 'We are all here too long,' I joked, but I meant it.

Marina Howard took the stand after me. She was the last witness in what was now the longest-running libel case in the history of the state. Without doubt, in James Howard's daughter, Garrett Cooney found his match. Asked by the senior counsel about the remark she had made at the end of an interview with me back in 1998—'Charlie, can she come back at me?'—Marina Howard said she feared being sued. 'Surely, you cannot believe you can be sued successfully for telling the truth?' Cooney enquired. There was hardly a pause before Marina quipped back, 'Well, Daddy has.' There was loud laughter from the packed public gallery along with prolonged applause. These were scenes not normally witnessed in the highest courts of the land. The public was impressed but not the trial judge, Frederick Morris, as he reminded those present that such behaviour was unacceptable in a court of law. 'Kindly do not clap,' he added. Garrett Cooney sat down. There were no more questions. It was the final act in the libel case.

During her evidence, Marina Howard had recounted meeting Beverley Cooper Flynn for about 20 minutes in her father's house in 1990. She knew the Mayo woman had come to see her father about a financial matter but was not privy to the details. Both women were around the same age but what struck Marina Howard was the contrast in their positions in life. She had recently returned from England and was unemployed, while Cooper Flynn had a high-flying career. 'I thought, my God, here I am home from England, penniless, with no job prospects,' she recalled. The NIB financial advisor 'had everything' while, as Marina Howard saw it, 'Here I am, a down and out.'

'I remember thinking gosh, even her name is nice. I actually liked the name Beverley,' she told the court. I joined in the laughter in the courtroom and I think even Cooper Flynn smiled. There was one important aspect to Marina Howard's only conversation with Cooper Flynn. She recalled congratulating the NIB employee on her recent engagement. She told the court that her attention had been drawn to the single-stone solitaire engagement ring which was 'more on the generous size than on the small size'. Nobody was contesting that Cooper Flynn wore a generous solitaire engagement ring. If Marina Howard were believed on this fact—I thought—surely the jury would accept all her other recollections.

Throughout the case, the President of the High Court, Frederick Morris, sat upright in his seat each day and had a clipped but measured tone when he interrupted the lawyers and even some witnesses. The judge spent some of a Thursday afternoon and a few hours the following morning giving his closing remarks to the jury. Kevin Feeney took issue with the interpretation that the judge placed on certain evidence during his comments on Thursday. A submission was made at the start of the proceedings on Friday morning. RTÉ's team was unhappy about how our case was summarised by the judge. Morris opted to remind the jury members of what they had heard. I was hugely impressed by the firm but unflashy way Feeney challenged the judge and questioned his interpretation of legal matters.

The jury was given a series of questions to help in reaching a decision:

1. Have the defendants proved that the plaintiff induced the third named defendant to evade his lawful obligation to pay tax by not availing of the tax amnesty? If the answer is 'No' proceed to question two. If the answer is 'Yes' proceed no further.
2. Have the defendants proved that the plaintiff advised or encouraged other persons—being those referred to in the evidence—to evade tax? If the answer is 'No' proceed to question four to assess damages. If the answer is 'Yes' proceed to question three.
3. In view of the finding to question 2, has the plaintiff's reputation suffered material injury by reason of the matters published relating to the third named defendant?
4. If the answer to questions one and two is 'No' assess the damages.
5. If the answer to question one is 'No' and questions two and three 'Yes' assess damages to the material injury to the plaintiff's reputation.

The jury retired at 11.44 a.m. on Friday, 23 March. They took an hour for lunch and, having restarted their deliberations at 2.00 p.m., were allowed to view once more several of the news reports about which Cooper Flynn had complained. Then we waited some more. The entire case had been a huge ordeal. I had lost weight. I wasn't sleeping; I was exhausted. The stakes involved were enormous. Careers were on the line. I am sure it was exactly the same for Beverley Cooper Flynn. Waiting for the jury to decide was a terrible experience. I drank coffee and I paced. I went through every option. 'We're going to win,' I thought one minute; the next, 'It's over, we'll lose.'

The jury came back in at 3.59 p.m., seeking guidance in dealing with the questions. The foreman handed a note to the trial judge. 'Am I understanding you correctly, you want to know the circumstances in which a majority decision can be accepted?' Freddie Morris asked.

After some explanation about the voting procedures on the questions, the jury retired once more. The two legal teams went into little huddles. 'What's going on?' I wanted to know. One of RTÉ's lawyers turned to me. 'Charlie, we're going to win,' he said. I was stunned. At 4.42 p.m., the jury came back in for the final time. The foreman informed the judge that they had reached a verdict. A page—on which the foreman had written the answers to the five questions—was handed to the judge.

We lost the first question. The jury decided that we had not proven that Cooper Flynn had induced James Howard to evade his lawful obligation to pay tax by not availing of the tax amnesty. I was momentarily thrown off balance. Everyone's attention turned to the second question. Now the jury decided that we had proven that Cooper Flynn had advised or encouraged other people to evade tax. On the third question, the jury decided that Cooper Flynn's reputation had not suffered material damage because of RTÉ's investigation. Damages were assessed by the jury. Their decision—'nothing'.

'We've done it,' I said quietly. We could not cheer in the courtroom. That was for later, but I still hugged George Lee. I am not sure he knew what was happening but an enormous weight had just been lifted from my entire being. It was a defining moment in my career in journalism. The trial had lasted for 28 days—surpassing the previous longest libel case by 13 days. Sixteen witnesses had been called; there were three legal teams and over 10,000 pages of documents, not to mention a few VHS copies of our contentious television reports on NIB.

There was pandemonium outside the court. Everyone wanted a comment. 'I'm a working journalist and I want to go back to work on Monday and back to the job that I know best,' I said honestly. As we were leaving the Four Courts, I spotted Cooper Flynn. We shook hands. It was the right thing to do. We had both been thrown into the legal case together but there was only one winner and one loser. I went for a Chinese meal with George Lee later that evening. I hadn't known him before January 1998, but since then we had been through so much together: the highs of breaking some important stories and the lows of the libel case, although the jury decision was the ultimate high.

The legal bills on both sides were considerable. The question of costs was decided in April 2001. The ruling on costs was handed down by Mr Justice Freddie Morris and it went against Cooper Flynn. She was faced with the legal costs for RTÉ's legal team and James Howard's legal team, as well as the costs of her own lawyers. Political pressure increased significantly on the Fianna Fáil TD. Her party colleagues were openly pressing for her to resign or be expelled from the parliamentary party. These were, however, the concerns of other people. I was just relieved that it was all over. Cooper Flynn had the option of an appeal to the Supreme Court, but nobody seemed to think that she would travel that route. The jury verdict had left little wriggle room.

There was, therefore, some surprise when Cooper Flynn announced that she was, in fact, going to appeal. Her legal team put forward a number of grounds for the appeal, concentrating mainly on the original judge's summing up of evidence to the jury and also how he had allowed them answer the key questions posed at the end of the trial. There was no mention of the main thrust of the tax-evasion claims, rather the complaints appeared to be technical and related to the handling of the original case. They were seeking an order overturning the High Court decision and the award of costs so that we would all return to the beginning and hear the case all over again. 'No chance of that,' I told myself, somewhat naïvely.

There were now more legal meetings in RTÉ over the appeal. 'This could be difficult. She has a good chance of winning,' one of our lawyers said. I was shocked. This was back to the worst days of the High Court case. 'How could this be?' I asked. 'That has nothing to do with the main issue of encouraging tax evasion,' I kept saying.

The Supreme Court case was a more straightforward affair with far less of the drama of the original trial. There were no witnesses and there was no jury, just five judges listening to the arguments of legal teams for the two sides. The first morning was taken up with Eoin McCullagh putting the arguments for Cooper Flynn. Having listened to him for several hours, I was completely depressed. The barrister highlighted all the apparent difficulties with the High Court case, and the legal technicalities he mentioned seemed to me to make sense. By lunchtime, I thought we were in serious trouble. Then Kevin Feeney for RTÉ delivered an amazing performance, challenging the judges on every point and undermining the arguments of his colleagues working for Cooper Flynn. I was hugely impressed by Kevin Feeney and understood exactly why some years later he was elevated to the High Court, but on that day in 2004, I was still suffering badly. A loss in the Supreme Court could have had very serious consequences for RTÉ. The station could have been open to cross-party political attack, and there was no knowing what would have happened to Ed Mulhall, Eamon Kennedy and Bob Collins who had been Director-General when the original reports were broadcast. Everybody is supportive when you're winning but a loss, especially with legal costs of over €4 million, was a nightmare situation for everybody involved. Mulhall and Kennedy, in particular, had put their reputations on the line. Kennedy, from County Leitrim, was RTÉ's Director of Legal Affairs. He had shown tremendous courage with the NIB investigations. The prospect of losing and having to go back to the start was eating away at me. I would not have been able to go through another trial. I have no idea what I would have done, but my mental state would not have held up to a re-run of the original case.

On 28 April 2004, the ordeal finally came to an end. In his judgment, the Chief Justice, Ronan Keane, quoted from a famous British libel case involving the former Liverpool goalkeeper Bruce Grobbelaar, where a newspaper had alleged that the footballer 'had accepted bribes, had let in, or attempted to let in, goals during the course of games'. The lessons from the Grobbelaar judgment were damning for Cooper Flynn.

> The verdict of the jury was interpreted in both the Court of Appeal and the House of Lords as treating the 'sting' of the libel as not being justified. It was also interpreted, however, as meaning that the appellant had made a corrupt agreement with and corruptly accepted money from the person in question. In the course of his speech, Lord Bingham of Cornhill said, 'The tort of defamation protects those whose reputations have been unlawfully injured. It affords little or no protection to those who have, or deserve to have, no reputation deserving of legal protection.' I am satisfied that the same considerations apply in this case.

The most powerful judge in the land was effectively saying that the Mayo TD had no reputation deserving of protection. 'I would dismiss the appeal and affirm the order of the High Court,' Ronan Keane concluded. It was all over as the other four judges all agreed with his decision. I saw the devastation on the face of Beverley Cooper Flynn. Despite everything, I felt sorry for her. There should really be a better way of reconciling arguments like the one at the heart of our libel trial. The money involved was huge.

The NIB libel case did not come to end without one final bizarre moment. One morning, while I was walking through central Dublin on my way down to the Supreme Court, a face I recognised came towards me on the street. The man smiled. 'Hello,' he said, somewhat awkwardly.

'I suppose this was always going to happen,' I replied. He had been one of the jurors in the High Court case. I had watched him, as I had watched the other jurors, every day for 28 days back in 2001. 'Would you like to go for coffee?' I asked, as much to say something as anything else.

We had a general chat over a quick cup of coffee. He did tell me, however, that right at the start of the proceedings, another juror had wanted to give Cooper Flynn €1 million in damages. As I thought, Garrett Cooney's opening statement had swayed people, but as the case proceeded, this juror had come around to a different conclusion. 'Thank goodness for that,' I said with a sigh.

Chapter 13 ~

WHERE A LITTLE
INFORMATION LEADS

'Y ou should follow showjumping. There's a good story there,'
the man said. I didn't know who this person was. He had just
called my number in RTÉ. I was curious about the story he had
to tell; he seemed to have plenty of information about what was going
on in the showjumping world. 'There's speculation that a horse
belonging to Cian O'Connor has failed a drug test. O'Connor is on the
Olympic team,' he informed me. I had never heard of Cian O'Connor
before this conversation in July 2004. I was, however, to discover a
whole lot more about O'Connor and the world of showjumping over
the following few months.

People often ask me how journalists get their stories. In my experience, news stories originate in a whole variety of ways. Reliable sources
with whom I have built up a working relationship are often the source
of good tip-offs. People often ring me with information that points in
the direction of a news story, and then I start digging. Sometimes I am
given documents which are the basis for a story. On other occasions, a
story develops from a small piece of information that pushes me to ask
questions, and, when I have asked enough questions of enough people,
a story may emerge. Sometimes all the tip-offs and all the legwork
in the world won't progress a story beyond a mere allegation. The
best stories are often those that start with a whistle-blower—somebody
within an organisation who, for whatever reason, decides that confidential information should be made public. The National Irish Bank
investigation started with a whistle-blower, as did the investigation into
Cian O'Connor, Ireland's gold-winning showjumping champion at the
2004 Olympics in Greece.

The man who rang me with a tip-off about O'Connor sounded a

reasonable person. He was cautious and deliberate in explaining the facts that he wanted to convey. I scribbled notes into my notebook as he spoke. I was quickly being introduced to a world about which I had previously known absolutely nothing.

The whistle-blower gave me a few names to contact. When we concluded our conversation, my first task was to find out who exactly Cian O'Connor was. The Olympics in Athens were only weeks away. After a quick search on the internet, I soon discovered that O'Connor was a leading member of the Irish showjumping team. He was young, highly successful and had the support of Independent News & Media and Waterford Crystal, two leading companies associated with his god-father, Sir Anthony O'Reilly. His main horse was called Waterford Crystal and was owned by the two companies. O'Connor had set down his objective for 2004 on his website—'Both sponsors have given me full support to try and achieve my long-term goal with this one, i.e., to be on a medal-winning Irish team at the Olympic Games at Athens in 2004.' I spoke to people in Ireland, in Holland and in Britain. I also rang O'Connor. I was upfront with him. 'People are saying your horse has failed a drugs test,' I said. He denied any knowledge of the story. To be fair to him, at that point in time he may genuinely have been unaware of the rumours that were circulating in the wider showjumping world.

I was hearing all sorts of allegations but, without supporting documentation, my inquiries were going nowhere and, as I set off on my summer holidays in late July, I put my notes on the showjumping investigation into a folder, not believing they would be used again. Like most other people in the country, I watched as Cian O'Connor on Waterford Crystal won a gold medal at the Olympics. I was more curi-ous than ever but not sure whether there was anything in the stories I had been told.

When I got back to RTÉ in early September, the whistle-blower called again. 'Have you not followed up on that story?' he asked. There was a touch of annoyance in his voice.

'I tried but I couldn't get any firm evidence. I can't afford to give it any more time,' I replied. The whole exercise was deeply frustrating. I had a tip-off on what potentially was a cracker of a story—and even more so now that O'Connor was an Olympic champion—but I had no evidence to support the allegation.

A few days later, Ed Mulhall, my boss in RTÉ, called me into his office. He had been contacted by a reliable source from the political world. 'Charlie Bird was working on a story about Cian O'Connor earlier in the year. What does he know?' Ed was asked. Ed explained the background to the investigation which had yielded no story, only a series of allegations. 'That's interesting,' the contact responded. 'Because I've heard that O'Connor is going to lose his gold medal.'

It seemed that Waterford Crystal had failed a drugs test at the Olympic Games. The story, if true, was going to be huge. I started to work the phones, calling people I had spoken to previously to see if I could add a second source and more detail to what Ed Mulhall had been told. It was just after 1 p.m. 'We're in the middle of a meeting. Things are too sensitive to talk now,' one man said. I quickly outlined what we had been told about the failed drugs test. 'You're doing well,' was the response.

I was certain the story about the drugs test was true but I was un-certain what developments would emerge from this startling news. 'Let's go with it,' Ed said. So, at about 1.30 p.m., I was in the *News at One* radio studio, speaking with Seán O'Rourke. My information was straightforward—the Olympic-gold-winning horse, Waterford Crystal, had failed a drugs test and the stakes were very high for his rider, Cian O'Connor. I did not mention the earlier drugs test that I had been investigating before the Olympic Games.

After the radio interview, I had lunch with Ed Mulhall in the RTÉ canteen. The story was going to develop over the course of the after-noon and would most probably lead the news for the remainder of the day. Several senior managers in RTÉ were also in the canteen, including the Director-General, Cathal Goan, and Bride Rosney, who had previ-ously worked with Mary Robinson but who was now Director of Corporate Affairs. News of the O'Connor story led someone in this group to utter, 'Jaysus. What are we going to do? Cian O'Connor is getting an award at the People of the Year ceremony tomorrow night.' The event was due to be broadcast on RTÉ television. O'Connor saved everyone's embarrassment by deciding not to attend.

In the aftermath of my reports that day, O'Connor denied delib-erately doping his horse before his Olympic victory. A short time later, his advisors contacted Colm Murray, a sports presenter in RTÉ, with the offer of an interview for the *Six One News*. There was one stipulation: 'Cian won't do an interview with Charlie Bird.' It was the only time in

my career in journalism that somebody had singled me out by saying—
we'll do an interview with RTÉ but only so long as Charlie Bird is not
asking the questions.

It was a bizarre request which would not normally have been agreed
to, but it did not preclude Colm and myself from tick-tacking before
he spoke with O'Connor. I briefed him on my investigation and
we agreed a number of key questions to be put. During the interview,
the controversial showjumper confirmed that another one of his
horses, ABC Landliebe, had failed a drugs test before the Olympic
Games. This was the story on which I had been working. This horse
had been entered in a competition in Rome in May 2004. O'Connor
blamed medication administered to the horse during the journey
from Ireland to Italy. The horse was, it was said, suffering from colic. It
appeared that the International Equestrian Federation had accepted
the explanation, as O'Connor had escaped without a ban or serious
financial penalty.

However, now O'Connor was admitting that a mild sedative had
been given to both horses—in ABC Landliebe's case to help with a back
injury, and in Waterford Crystal's to treat an injury to his leg. The world
was told that the 'same medication' was administered to both horses.
The name of the medication was, however, not provided. O'Connor's
strategy seemed to be based on the logic that if the International
Equestrian Federation had accepted his explanation in the ABC
Landliebe case—and as this case was applicable to the Waterford
Crystal case—there was nothing to worry about in relation to the failed
Olympic drugs test.

An already strange story was, however, about to get even more
bizarre. O'Connor had requested the testing of the B urine sample
taken from Waterford Crystal during the Olympic Games in late
August. The A sample had already tested positive for certain banned
substances. The stakes for O'Connor were enormous—a positive test
on the B sample and he faced a suspension from competitive
showjumping, as well as the loss of his gold medal. In late October
2004, a DHL courier left Paris for Newmarket in England, unaware of
the contents of the package he was delivering. As he approached the
Newmarket lab where the B sample was to be tested, the courier was
contacted and told that there had been a change of plan. He queried the
request but the caller knew the security number of the package. Then,

as the courier approached the main entrance to the Newmarket lab—but out of the view of CCTV—he was approached by another man. The package was signed for and handed over. The sample was never seen again.

It was, without doubt, a professionally organised theft. It left open the possibility that the case against Ireland's Olympic champion would never proceed. This theft was followed by a break-in at the headquarters of the Irish Equestrian Federation, during which it seemed that files relating to O'Connor's horses were stolen. I received a phone call telling me to go to the main fax machine in the RTÉ newsroom. A fax duly arrived but without any accompanying number to identify the sender. The information had to have come from files at the Irish Equestrian Federation.

The fax named the drugs that had been administered to ABC Landliebe earlier in the year in Rome. They were drugs usually used to treat anxiety in humans and my sources confirmed that one of these drugs had been given to Waterford Crystal. There were plenty of people in the showjumping world who had spoken to me in private about the use of sedatives to make 'hot' horses more manageable before a jumping competition. The International Equestrian Federation had warned riders before the Olympics about the use of these drugs. A sedative given to cool down a nervy animal in competition was, in effect, a performance-enhancing drug.

Tests of blood samples taken from Waterford Crystal ultimately confirmed the results of the first urine sample. Banned drugs had been given to the horse. A few months later, Cian O'Connor was stripped of his gold medal and Ireland lost its Olympic Champion from the 2004 Games in Athens. I never spoke to Cian O'Connor except for that one phone conversation before the Olympic Games when he had denied that one of his horses had tested positive for a banned drug.

While the drugs story involving O'Connor's horses proved correct, I had less success standing up a separate story that the whistle-blower had also brought to my attention about another Irish rider. 'Wrapping is a big issue. An Irish showjumper was seen wrapping his horse,' the whistle-blower said as he explained that wrapping was a form of abuse. Sometimes nails were placed under cloth wrapped around the legs of a horse. The animal was then forced to jump higher over fences to avoid the pain of the nail sticking into his legs if he hit a fence. It was a cruel exercise.

One contact gave me the name of a groom who had witnessed a well-known rider abusing a horse. I tracked down the groom. He had already told his boss about the incident and was reluctant to talk without permission. I spoke with the man's boss, another leading rider, who it turned out was in a bind. 'Look, I can't help you,' the boss said. He had been having an affair about which his wife knew nothing. 'I've been warned that if either my groom or myself ever go public about this matter, then my wife will be told about the affair,' he admitted.

I was getting a little paranoid myself. In the middle of the showjumping investigation, I awoke in the small hours of the morning to hear horses outside my bedroom window. I initially thought I had been dreaming but the next morning, my garden was dug up and the imprints of horse hoofs were visible in the grass. 'Christ,' I thought, 'Is somebody sending me a message?' I was looking over my shoulder for a couple of days. I even went down to my local pub in Ashford to see if anybody had been in, asking where I lived. When I posed a similar question to a neighbour, she sensed my anxiety. 'You think the horses the other night have something to do with what we see you on the television about at the moment?' she asked jokingly. I shrugged my shoulders but a load lifted when I heard that some horses from a local stable had broken out and, during the dark of the night, had found their way into a number of gardens where I lived in Ashford.

The whistle-blower in the Cian O'Connor case was well informed. Some years later, I found myself sitting in front of an equally well-informed individual but he was a whistle-blower of a totally different type. Denis Donaldson was a senior member of Sinn Féin. A former IRA prisoner, he was a background figure who, since the late 1990s, had been running the Sinn Féin offices at Stormont.

In the middle of December 2005, reporters including myself were contacted about a Sinn Féin press conference that was to be held in a Dublin hotel. It was all very last minute, which was not really the way Sinn Féin operated. The story that Gerry Adams was about to tell, however, was truly remarkable. A few days previously, Denis Donaldson had admitted to two senior Sinn Féin figures that he had been a paid British spy for almost two decades. Donaldson had been duly expelled from the party. It was a huge embarrassment for Adams and Sinn Féin.

In October 2002, police officers had raided the Sinn Féin offices at Stormont outside Belfast, amid allegations that republicans were operating a 'spy-ring' in the assembly building. The dramatic raid was captured on television cameras and threatened the already-fragile relations between Sinn Féin and unionist politicians. Not long afterwards, devolution was suspended in Northern Ireland and Denis Donaldson was one of those arrested and charged with involvement in what became known as the Stormont-gate affair. Donaldson denied the charges. Then, in late 2005, the case was dropped. The British said that a prosecution was 'no longer in the public interest'. The whole episode was bizarre. It seemed, however, that Donaldson's cover was about to be blown. He 'outed' himself to his party, having been warned by police sources in Belfast that his life was in danger. Adams told the press conference that the now-expelled Donaldson was with his solicitor.

I reported on the afternoon's events for the *Six One News* and then received a phone call from Peter Madden, who was Donaldson's solicitor. They had booked a room at the up-market Radisson Hotel near RTÉ. I was given the impression that I was going to interview the former Sinn Féin official. The situation turned out to be very different. A visibly nervous Donaldson walked into the room where the camera was set up. He was going to make a statement but there would be no questions, Madden stated. A row developed as I was not happy with this arrangement. In the end, we let Donaldson have his say; he read a brief statement, expressing his 'deep regret' for his activities which had started at a 'vulnerable time' in his life.

When he had finished talking, Madden interjected, 'And that ends this press briefing.' We kept the camera recording as I attempted to ask a question but Madden was insistent on no questions. It was totally unsatisfactory so I decided that we would broadcast the material after Donaldson had finished speaking, to allow the viewers to see how the briefing had been conducted. My last sighting of Denis Donaldson was on the Stillorgan dual carriageway, getting out of his solicitor's jeep and into a small banger of car. I wondered then about his ability to survive, given the hostility his revelations had generated among his former colleagues. I was not all that surprised therefore when, four months later, I received a brief phone call with the message, 'Denis Donaldson's been shot dead.' His death in County Donegal was brutal but not unexpected.

———

Donaldson was not a real whistle-blower. He was an IRA man who operated as a spy. Nobody will ever know what information he passed on. I had an exclusive in December 2005 in getting access to this spy, but on terms with which I was not totally happy. Stories, however—as explained previously—come in different ways. During 2004, I had a series of exclusive stories about AIB, the largest bank in Ireland. The source for these stories was a classic whistle-blower. The person, who contacted me out of the blue, was employed by AIB. He first rang me in RTÉ in May 2004 and explained the background to how the bank had been overcharging its customers on certain currency dealings. I was intrigued but I was also very wary. The libel case with National Irish Bank had taught me several lessons about reporting on financial institutions. Most importantly, a paper trail was vital to any investigation of financial impropriety. I had been through enough traumas over the NIB investigation and I was in no hurry to revisit the area.

'Look, this is all very interesting,' I eventually said. 'But it could take me months to prove what you are saying. I need some documentation.' I was not foolish enough to think a story damning of AIB could be broadcast without watertight supporting documents. From his response, I realised that the man was not put off by my position. 'Leave it with me,' he replied.

We ended our conversation, and I didn't know if that was the last I would hear from him. In fairness to the man, he did seem to have a great deal of information about AIB but sometimes what are pushed as good stories never develop beyond a single conversation, usually because the person who contacts me never follows through with sufficient evidence to support their allegations. I am well used to this situation which can be disappointing, especially after my appetite has been whetted for a news scoop. For every story I actually broadcast, dozens fall by the wayside, not to mind those that never develop beyond an initial conversation with a potential whistle-blower.

The AIB whistle-blower was, however, intent on following up on our first phone conversation. A few hours later, a package was left for me at the security hut at the main entrance to the RTÉ campus. I wasn't expecting anything important so I didn't rush out of the office to collect the envelope, nor when I got the envelope did I tear it open with any great sense of excitement.

A quick scan of this material, however, revealed that the information I had been sent was truly amazing. The private AIB document confirmed that the software system used by the bank to charge customers on foreign-exchange transactions was known as Castlemain. For almost a decade, there had been a problem with the Castlemain system. The result of this problem was that customers of the bank were overcharged on foreign-exchange transactions. AIB was profiting at the expense of its customers. The confidential document in my possession confirmed that the overcharging was finally being addressed internally, but without the bank admitting to any wrongdoing or repaying the money it had knowingly taken from its customers.

I rang AIB with a query about overcharging but I didn't say I had any documentary evidence to support my questions. The response was very polite. I then put a series of questions to AIB, advising the bank that RTÉ intended to broadcast a story about systematic overcharging in foreign-exchange transactions. In the fax, I asked if the board of the bank was aware of the overcharging and also if AIB was making any arrangements to compensate customers who had been overcharged. I had the answers to many of my questions but I needed the response of the bank to what were very serious matters. An AIB spokesperson said they would get back to me later that same day.

The matter, however, ran into the following day, which led me to speculate about the reasons for the delay in answering my questions. I was worried that AIB might try to scoop me by releasing a general news statement. I decided to ring the Financial Regulator. In hindsight, I can see that this was a mistake as the Financial Regulator most likely knew as much as I did. I was surprised to be told that the Financial Regulator would have a statement for me later in the day. I immediately called the AIB press office again. They promised a statement within an hour. Any concerns that I had about being scooped with a general statement released to media were allayed. It was my story, so I was getting the AIB response first. Only when RTÉ broadcast its story would the information be released to everyone else. I was relieved. One of the remarkable aspects of the AIB overcharging investigation was the straight-up way the financial institution dealt with me despite the embarrassing revelations that were reported. It seemed the bank which had been in trouble previously had learnt a valuable public relations lesson about co-operating with the media.

Not long before the AIB statement arrived, the whistle-blower called me. 'You have your story,' he said, basing his confidence on first-hand knowledge of what was happening within AIB on that particular afternoon. According to AIB's version of events, it had overcharged its customers by around €14 million. I believed this figure to be too low and indeed it increased as files at the bank were fully investigated. The bank blamed human error which had been identified two years previously but which had gone uncorrected. It claimed that senior management and board members were unaware of the problem, but from my sources I knew otherwise.

If the overcharging revelations were an embarrassment for AIB, neither did the story show the Financial Regulator in a good light. The Financial Regulator confirmed that two weeks previously an anonymous phone call had been received about foreign-exchange charges at AIB. The matter was raised with AIB and a report sought from the bank. In fact, the whistle-blower had contacted me only after failing to see any response from the Financial Regulator to his initial call. Now with the story about to go public, it emerged that nobody in the Financial Regulator's office had a way of contacting the whistle-blower. I actually put them back in contact with him.

In another bizarre twist, I also arranged for the whistle-blower to speak with the top executive in AIB. He wanted to talk with Dermot Gleeson, the chairman of the bank. An internal inquiry was under way within AIB into the foreign-exchange overcharging. In an interview I had done with Gleeson, he had said that there would be no scapegoats, and anyone with information should not feel afraid to come forward.

I rang the AIB press office. It was a strange request. 'I need to talk directly to the bank chairman,' I said. About 10 minutes later, Gleeson, a leading lawyer, rang me.

'I hear you're looking for me,' he said.

'This is odd,' I explained—and it was a very strange situation for me, putting my source in contact with his boss. 'The whistle-blower feels he should talk with you.'

Gleeson was taken aback. 'You're not setting me up here, are you?' was his initial response.

For a couple of months in 2004, as the story unfolded, I did many live reports from outside AIB headquarters in Ballsbridge in Dublin. Staff from the bank passed in and out. 'We can't be seen near you,' some jokingly said as they hurried past. For all I know, the whistle-blower was among those who passed me. I never met the AIB whistle-blower. I don't even know what this man looks like although I would probably recognise his voice if we spoke again. As far as I know, he has continued to work at AIB.

A computer error was blamed for the foreign-exchange overcharging. But I was informed by the whistle-blower that some senior managers at AIB had been aware of the problem for several years and that they had started to correct their error only in early 2004. They also wanted the problem to be resolved without the Financial Regulator becoming aware of the overcharging issue.

The Financial Regulator published the report of its investigation at AIB in December 2004. The report could hardly have been more damning of the bank. In relation to the foreign-exchange overcharging, the report concluded that between 1998 and 2004, at least seven opportunities arose for certain AIB managers and staff to disclose the breach of the regulations. But this was not done. In addition, the report revealed that, in 2002, the matter was analysed in an internal bank memo which drew attention to the potential cost of dealing with the issues and the need to inform the Regulator. However, nothing was done, and a cover-up was engaged in by the bank.

Interestingly, the amounts involved had also changed from what had been mentioned when I had first broken the story. Initially the bank referred to a figure of about €14 million. The amount eventually increased to €35 million, all of which had to be repaid to AIB customers. Some €25.6 million related to overcharging on an estimated three million foreign-exchange transactions. Another 24 areas of overcharging had emerged in the investigation, leading the bank to repay a further €8.1 million to its customers. Other information about AIB came into my possession over the following weeks. In response to a series of questions, the bank confirmed that it had repaid €3.4 million to 43 customers over fees which it had not been entitled to levy for the administration of trusts. All in all, it was not a good period for AIB.

———

When reporters get an exclusive story, people always try to guess the source of the story. Sometimes that guessing process leads to a conclusion that is very far wide of the mark. In the AIB case, I never met the source of my exclusive report. The story behind the resignation of Ivor Callely as a minister of state in late 2005 is another good example of how stories arrive in the most unexpected of ways. When Callely resigned, the source of my story, which caused the Fianna Fáil TD so much trouble, was strongly suspected of having come from the world of politics. Indeed, on radio and in the Dáil, Tom Parlon of the Progressive Democrats said that the source was politically motivated. The truth was very different. In fact, few stories have come my way as easily as did the Callely story.

Callely was good at generating publicity but, in the latter half of 2005, he was in the news for all the wrong reasons in his job as junior minister at the Department of Transport. There were a number of media stories about poor working relations between the minister and staff in his ministerial office. On a Monday morning towards the end of November, I was talking with my colleague, Seán O'Rourke, about what direction the Callely story would take. Our conversation was ultimately to determine the course of events.

Seán had been playing golf the previous weekend, and a golf partner had told him a story he had heard several years previously. Ivor Callely was said to have had his house painted for free by a leading building company, John Paul Construction. If this were true, the implications for the Fianna Fáil politician were enormous. Seán O'Rourke's golf partner was the first source of information for my story on Ivor Callely. He had received this information second-hand; it went back several years and he was not even sure that it was true. In addition, he had no involvement in politics. He remembered being told about the Callely painting job only because the Fianna Fáil TD had been in the news over the previous couple of weeks.

I rang Seán's friend. He knew someone who had been getting their house decorated. This person's painter had said that his previous job had been in Ivor Callely's house and that the bill had been paid by a large building company, John Paul Construction. Taking a freebie from any leading building firm was risky but it later emerged that this one was working for the Eastern Health Board at a time when Callely was a leading local councillor involved with the health board. 'Can you get the painter's name?' I asked my source. Half an hour later, this man rang me back. I had the name of Ivor Callely's painter.

I decided to call John Paul Construction directly. I spoke with a senior manager who was most unhelpful. I then had a spot of good luck—the painter was listed in the *Golden Pages*. I had a phone number. I wasn't sure where the story was going when the painter's wife answered the phone.

'I was hoping to speak with your husband.'

'What do you want? My husband's not here.'

'I was hoping to talk to your husband about Ivor Callely.'

'What do you want to know about Ivor Callely? What do you know?'

'I just heard that your husband may have painted Ivor Callely's house.'

There was a short pause in our brief conversation. The woman then said something bizarre: 'How did you find out?'

In the following 60 seconds, this woman gave me enough information to confirm the story. Yes, her husband had done the painting job on Ivor Callely's house and, yes, the bill had been paid by John Paul Construction. After she had finished telling me these brief facts, she again wanted to know who had told me about the painting job. 'Who have you been talking to?'

'Nobody.'

'We were talking about this the other night in the pub. Who was listening to us?'

It took me several minutes to reassure this woman that her conversations in the pub were not the source of my information. A golf partner of a work colleague—who remembered a brief nugget of information received several years previously—was my original source. Now the spouse of Ivor Callely's painter had, without any probing, confirmed the information from the first source. A few phone calls in a few hours—if only all stories could be that easy.

Later that same day, I spoke directly with the painter who also confirmed the story. He told me how a senior manager at John Paul Construction had brought him around Callely's house to discuss the painting job. He had worked on the house for the best part of a week with a couple of other colleagues. I had the guts of the story but decided to contact the construction company once more. They were even more unhelpful than earlier in the day. 'There is no truth in the story,' I was informed.

I left numerous messages at a variety of different numbers for Ivor Callely. He eventually called me on my mobile. The line, however, was very crackly so I said I would ring straight back from the phone at my desk. Unfortunately when I dialled his number, the call went straight to his message service. The day ended without any further contact with Callely. The Fianna Fáil politician was due the following morning to attend a function in his constituency. Having approached him, I outlined the information that I had obtained. 'That was a long time ago,' he said. 'I'll have to check my records.'

By this stage, John Paul Construction had been sent a series of questions. I also got the name of the person at the company who had dealt with the painter and had brought him around Callely's house. I rang this man. 'I can't talk to you,' was his immediate response. 'We're preparing something for you and we'll have it to you before the evening is out.'

The hours passed but there was still no statement from John Paul Construction. The story looked as if it was going to go into another day. I was prepared to wait for the company's version of events. I eventually had a frosty conversation with Callely that evening as I drove home to Ashford.

'This is very upsetting,' he said. 'You've been making allegations about me and my family.' I appreciated that the politician was under great pressure but his assertion that I was 'making allegations' was out of order, and, in no uncertain terms, I let him know it. After a few minutes, an apology was offered and then he confirmed the story. 'Look, it was difficult moving into a new house and then our original painter let us down. John Paul senior knew about this, and he sent over a few lads to sort us out.'

I was at home a short time later when my mobile phone bleeped. A text message had been sent to me. It was 11.17 p.m. 'Hi Charlie. Give me a ring if you can or text me. I have been called in by JP Construction. Jim.' I didn't recognise the number and I had no idea who 'Jim' was. In any event, I dialled the number to discover that the caller was Jim Milton, a public relations consultant.

John Paul Construction was going to issue a statement, confirming my story. The company had paid for the painting work on Ivor Callely's house. I rang a government contact to assess the political fallout of the story that I was going to break a few hours later on the *Morning Ireland* radio programme. 'He's finished,' came the response as I learnt that the Taoiseach, Bertie Ahern, had been unable to contact his junior minister. I arrived in RTÉ shortly before 6 a.m. to prepare my story. Callely resigned a few hours later. I know his supporters blamed constituency rivals and political enemies for the information that I had obtained. In fact, a chance conversation between an RTÉ colleague and a golfing partner, coupled with a lucky chat with the painter's wife, had put me on the right track. Few exclusive stories have fallen into my lap so easily.

Chapter 14 ∿

HIDE AND SEEK

I was sitting in the passenger seat of a car owned by RTÉ cameraman John Curtis, known to his colleagues as 'Rocky'. We were on our way to a gaming arcade in Tallaght in west Dublin. The journey is still lodged in my mind. We were about to use a concealed camera which would allow me to film inside the arcade as part of an investigation into the legality of payouts from one-armed bandits and other gambling machines. Secret filming is never undertaken lightly in RTÉ and the station's Director-General has to authorise its use.

Indeed, I can count on one hand the number of times in my career in RTÉ when I have sought and have been given permission to research a story using a hidden camera. One of those occasions was in County Donegal in relation to gaming arcades in Bundoran. I had worked with Rocky on the Bundoran story and now we were on our way to Tallaght for a similar investigation. But the car journey that day in late 2004 is memorable for more than the fact that we were using hidden cameras. Rather, we had a conversation that shocked me to the core.

'You should be careful. You're being watched,' Rocky said, almost casually, as we drove towards our destination. I thought he was joking but then the seriousness on his face made me think again.

'What the hell are you talking about?' I nervously asked.

After a pause, he explained. 'I shouldn't be telling you this but one of the photographers down at the courts told me he's been sniffing around your house in Ashford. He's been told to get a photo of Carole Coleman and you.'

It took a few minutes to take on board what had just been said. I was totally stunned. 'What is going on?' I shouted. The irony of the situation was also not lost on me. We were headed for Tallaght where I would strap a hidden camera under my shirt to try to expose illegality in a gaming arcade while a photographer was sneaking around after me, looking for an image for some gossip-type story.

My marriage to Mary O'Connor had ended in 1998. It was a difficult time for all concerned. Fortunately, our children were well into their teens and were, therefore, able to understand the situation in which their parents found themselves. We had married in 1974 and we had had many happy years together as a couple and as a family. So, despite the pain of our parting, there were good times to remember. I owed Mary a huge debt. Shortly after our marriage, she had encouraged me to leave my pensionable *Irish Times* position to take a contract job with RTÉ. Indeed, as I had built my reporting career in the station—and travelled the world—Mary had provided the invaluable backup and support at home.

One of our proudest achievements as parents was playing a part in setting up the Bray School Project, which was at the time only the second multi-denominational national school in the country. Both of our daughters, Orla and Neasa, attended the school in Bray, before moving on to Newtown Park Comprehensive School in Blackrock. I suppose I should be thankful that neither of my children received their academic ability from me. Both went to university, with Orla developing a successful career in public relations and Neasa succeeding as a barrister at the Four Courts in Dublin. Indeed, it has been a standing joke with Neasa that, as an investigative reporter, I might one day need her services. They say it is always good to have a lawyer in the family!

While I had always admitted that my marriage had ended, I had never discussed the details publicly. There were a few references in the newspapers. I have long been wary of that section of the media which profits from salacious gossip—and appears not to care whether what gets written is true or not. Nothing, however, could have prepared me for what John Curtis told me in 2004. As an RTÉ cameraman, he spends a lot of time working on legal stories at the Four Courts. A photographer on a job at the courts had told Rocky that *Ireland on Sunday* was looking to get a certain picture of me. I just couldn't work out the motivation behind the newspaper's interest. It was no secret that I'd had a long-term relationship with Carole Coleman. It had been referred to a number of times in a few newspapers and magazines. Our relationship had lasted for several years, even after Carole moved to the United States as RTÉ's Washington Correspondent. We remained good friends but we were no longer going out together. Why then, at this stage, would a Sunday newspaper want a photograph of us? Surely this was old news.

Over the following couple of days, I did not repeat my conversation with Rocky to anyone. I was, however, in a blind panic. When I awoke in the morning, I would look out the windows of my home in Ashford to see if anyone was hiding in the bushes. I would repeat the exercise at night-time, even walking down the cul-de-sac where I lived to check if any strange cars were around. I even asked the staff at my local pub, the Chester Beatty in Ashford, if anyone had called in, asking questions about me. What made the situation even more bizarre was that I actually knew the photographer who had been employed to follow me. I had worked on numerous stories at which he was present as a free-lance photographer.

Eventually, after a few days of looking over my shoulder, I confided in a number of colleagues, although I suspected that they did not actu-ally believe my story. To be honest, I wasn't really sure I believed it myself. During the investigation into National Irish Bank in 1998, I had had occasion to watch my back to ensure that I was not being followed. I had been told by a reliable security source that a team of undercover surveillance experts had been contracted to follow George Lee and myself. We had both changed our mobile phones. It had not been a nice feeling then, and neither was it now.

The situation became much clearer, however, the weekend after my first conversation with John Curtis. I had been asked onto a panel discussion on RTÉ radio to review a new book about the station's news and current affairs department. The book had been written by Professor John Horgan from Dublin City University. When I arrived in the hospitality area before the start of the radio programme, the university lecturer was reading the Sunday newspapers. He looked up at me and made some remark about my 'government press officer friend'. I had no idea what he was talking about. 'Haven't you seen the story in *Ireland on Sunday*?' he enquired.

I had a knot in my stomach as I quickly flicked through the news-paper, stopping eventually at its gossip column. My old relationship with Carole Coleman was news once more. We had failed the trans-atlantic test, according to the article, and Carole was in a new relation-ship in Washington. If the piece had stopped there, I would have shrugged my shoulders and wondered why on earth the lives of two RTÉ journalists were of such interest. Unfortunately, the gossip piece did not stop there. It went on to claim that I was 'close to a government press officer'. I read the sentence over and over again. This relationship was news to me. Actually, I wasn't seeing anybody at that time in 2004. Then everything started to fall into place. The photographer, employed by *Ireland on Sunday* to follow me, was not looking for a picture of Carole Coleman and myself. The newspaper obviously believed that I was seeing someone who worked for the government. They thought they had a great story; you can imagine the headline: RTÉ's chief news correspondent dates government spin doctor. How wrong they were.

I was now fed up with having my every move followed, as a Sunday newspaper satisfied its appetite for gossip, especially as there was no truth in their tittle-tattle. I spoke with my boss, Ed Mulhall, who raised legitimate concerns about my ability to do my job as an investigative journalist if a photographer was snooping around my life. The possibility of seeking a court injunction against the newspaper was discussed with RTÉ's legal representatives. In the meantime, we agreed that I would contact Paul Drury, the editor of *Ireland on Sunday*.

Drury and his counterparts in the *Sunday Independent* had been engaged for some time in a bitter circulation battle. The British-owned *Ireland on Sunday* had increased sales on the back of a huge promotional budget, free CDs and a voyeuristic approach to news. I was just the latest target as the newspaper sought out stories on the private lives of relatively well-known people, and some people who were not well known at all.

I was totally upfront with Drury, telling him that I knew the newspaper had paid a photographer to stalk me and that the previous Sunday they had written a story about me that was totally untrue. I think he quickly realised that I was very upset on both counts. I felt my privacy had been totally invaded for no valid reason. Drury said that he would have to call me back as he was unaware that I had been followed. He also promised to look into the 'story' about the government press officer.

A few days later, Drury rang me. 'We did put a photographer on you for a couple of days,' he confirmed, adding, 'We were trying to sniff out who you were seeing.' So John Curtis had been correct. I was surprised that Drury was so upfront but I was flabbergasted by what was to come.

The editor of *Ireland on Sunday* also accepted that the paper's facts about my private life were incorrect.

'We picked that gossip up on the street. It was wrong. There was no basis for it,' he admitted.

'I'm only a journalist,' I said. 'I don't see how I merit such attention.'

'Charlie,' he replied, 'you're a personality and who you are going out with is news.'

I thought this attitude was very unfair and, in no uncertain terms, I let Drury know my feelings on the matter. 'Does that mean if I go for a cup of coffee with a female colleague, we could find ourselves splashed all over the pages of *Ireland on Sunday*?' I asked. The answer seemed to be 'yes', if newspapers interested in that type of 'news' decided so.

'Paul, I need a guarantee that I won't be followed again,' I said. His response left me as shocked as anything that had happened over the previous week.

'I'm sorry. I can't give you that,' Drury replied. 'I don't think we'll be following you again in the near future as there appears to be no story. But, Charlie, you're a personality, and if you're going out with someone we believe is newsworthy, then we might do it again.'

I was totally taken aback by Drury's candour and also by his news values. The phone conversation did result in a clarification in the following weekend's newspaper about my being close to a government press officer—or not being close, as the truth actually was. I was still throwing a few glances over my shoulder but there I thought the matter had ended.

When my marriage ended in 1998, I moved out of the family home in Bray in County Wicklow, moving first to a rented cottage in Ballsbridge before buying a house in Ashford. I found it hard to accept that a section of the media was interested in these matters. As a high-profile correspondent for RTÉ, I get attention. There is criticism from some newspapers—that is something that goes with the territory. There is no doubt but that over the years in some interviews I have given hostages to fortune.

Both Mary and I were open about the end of our marriage. Despite everything, we have remained good friends. We did, after all, share many good times together. Even today, if I'm in the wars, Mary will phone me with a few words of encouragement. I am also fortunate in having a good relationship with my two daughters. We usually meet for lunch on a Saturday afternoon. It has developed into a little family tradition. To be honest, Orla and Neasa are my closest friends, although they are also my harshest critics. They never let me away with anything. Both now have jobs with close links to my profession. As a public relations executive, Orla has contact with many of my own journalistic colleagues, especially in the business world, while Neasa, as a barrister, knows many legal people who have come across me in one guise or another. Indeed, both Orla and Neasa have received that same quizzical look when they say their surname. 'Are you related to the fella who works on the television?' is a frequent question.

In late January 2005, I met Neasa for Saturday lunch. We were strolling along Baggot Street in Dublin when her mobile phone started to bleep. She had a text message. It was from Orla. 'She says there's a story about you in the *Evening Herald*,' Neasa said. 'I suppose we'd better get a copy.'

I couldn't believe the front-page headline: 'Shock at Bird's Love Nest Probe'. My stomach churned. The secondary headline only added to my shock: 'RTÉ outrage as their star reporter is stalked by paparazzi'.

The story had little to do with concern for my sensitivities at *Ireland on Sunday*'s decision to target my private life. Rather, I was suddenly the meat in the sandwich between the British owners of *Ireland on Sunday* and Independent Newspapers which is controlled by Sir Anthony O'Reilly. I was caught up in the unseemly war of words between the two rival outlets over sales and advertising revenue. By supposedly expressing outrage at how I had been treated, the *Evening Herald*—which is owned by O'Reilly's group—was really attacking the Sunday title of the rival publisher.

The *Evening Herald* story was written by a woman called Sarah Glynn. I had never spoken to her. However, earlier that same week, I had taken a call from John Laurence who reports on entertainment news and has plenty of RTÉ contacts. 'Charlie, I've heard that *Ireland on Sunday* have been following you and are going to write a story about your personal life,' Laurence said, adding, 'Would you like to talk to the *Evening Herald* about this?'

It is one of the oldest ploys in the tabloid journalist's book to get someone to talk about any issue they might be reluctant to discuss. In other words—Those people at *Ireland on Sunday* are awful, so why don't you tell us everything first; we're on your side.

Many weeks had passed since my conversation with Paul Drury. I suspected that the *Evening Herald* reporter had come upon some stale gossip about the *Ireland on Sunday* photographer and was simply chancing his arm with me. I played down the significance of the story. 'Nothing would surprise me any more about the lengths that some newspapers would go to to get stories,' I remarked.

I thought I had done enough to kill off the *Evening Herald*'s interest in the story, and it seemed that I had succeeded as nothing appeared in that day's edition of the newspaper. Unfortunately this conclusion was premature, as I discovered a few days later, standing outside a newsagent on Baggot Street with one of my daughters holding a copy of the *Evening Herald*. The comment I had made to John Laurence earlier in the week made its way into Sarah Glynn's article. Quotes were attributed to several unnamed RTÉ colleagues, expressing outrage at the behaviour of *Ireland on Sunday*. 'It's nothing short of stalking Charlie. This is a new low. We are all 100 per cent behind Charlie on this. We think it is a gross intrusion,' one unidentified workmate said.

I had no idea who this person was or if he or she really existed. The article was a classic stitch-up job; while purporting to come to my defence, it was really an excuse to attack *Ireland on Sunday*. The original article about my 'relationship' with the government press officer was rehashed even though it had already been accepted as incorrect and a clarification had been printed. If the *Ireland on Sunday* article had upset me—and the thought of a photographer snooping around my life had left me very annoyed—I was now really angry. What the *Evening Herald* did, in putting me on its front page, was a complete invasion of my privacy.

Over the years, I have got used to a certain degree of media attention. Sam Smyth, who now writes for the *Irish Independent*, wrote the first profile of me for *In Dublin* magazine in 1987. The magazine dubbed me 'RTÉ's legendary news reporter' which was somewhat amusing given that I was really only making my way as a journalist at that time.

I am not really sure how I have become so well known. The fact that I have been in the business for so long means that the public is well accustomed to seeing me on the main evening news. Maybe it's the uniqueness of my name or my particular reporting style but I have always had a fairly high profile for an RTÉ news reporter. The trial of Fr Niall O'Brien in 1984 certainly gave me a huge public profile as a young journalist. I have slogged for most of my reporting career, doing a job I love and trying my best to do it well. I have been fortunate to cover some really important stories in Ireland and abroad. There was plenty of media interest in me around the time of the first IRA ceasefire in August 1994. In subsequent years, I had several high-profile exclusives, all of which combined to give me a recognition factor not normally associated with news reporters.

Some of the media interest in me has been amusing. In May 1995, I shared the front page of the *Sun* newspaper with Pamela Anderson of *Baywatch* fame. One of my few hobbies outside my job is hill walking. I will often head off on my own around County Wicklow, taking the fresh air and enjoying the silence. On this occasion, I lost my bearings when walking near Lugnaquilla in County Wicklow, and ended up in the middle of the army firing range at the Glen of Imaal.

I was terrified when I heard several loud explosions which appeared to be getting nearer to me. I could see a few ammunition shells on the ground, and this only added to my sense of panic. I decided to ring the RTÉ newsroom on my mobile phone to see if they could get in contact with the army to tell its officers at the practice range at the Glen of Imaal to stop shooting. It took a few minutes to convince the person who answered in RTÉ that I was serious about being shot at by the army. Fortunately, the shooting stopped and I was able to walk away safely.

'Proper Charlie—Shell Shocks for RTÉ Reporter on army firing range,' the *Sun* declared on its front page, alongside 'Pam's Love Palace', a story which promised the inside take on 'the world's hottest marriage'. I know the story most people would have read first!

It was a funny incident. I have, however, never wanted to be the subject of the news. I am a serious journalist. Nevertheless, I would be telling a lie if I did not admit that the attention can be flattering—it is nice to receive this interest, especially as it generally reflects positively on how I am doing my job as a news reporter in RTÉ. I don't think this is unique as it applies to other broadcast and print journalists. I accept that I am well known but I don't think I'm well known as a celebrity. I don't consider myself a celebrity. I don't think appearing as a guest on a handful of light-entertainment programmes has propelled me into the category of 'personality' which might justify *Ireland on Sunday*'s decision to target my private life.

Over the years, I have given a few hostages to fortune in a handful of interviews where, in a very general way, I have mentioned my private life. But I have never attempted to attract profile or sought to further my career on the back of my private life. Now, however, my private life was splashed across the front page of a national newspaper and was the fodder in the commercial battle between two media organisations. I had a miserable weekend trying to work out how to bring this situation to an end.

The following Monday morning—after the *Evening Herald* story—one of the first people I spoke to was Seán O'Rourke, the presenter of the *News at One*. Seán is a good colleague who helped me through the NIB libel case and is someone whose opinion I value. 'Charlie, you've got to do something about this,' were his first words before we even discussed the weekend newspaper coverage. We talked about the possible options available to me. We both agreed that I had to speak up. 'It won't be without a risk. You have to be prepared for that,' Seán warned.

I had decided that I would go public before a researcher called from RTÉ Radio One's *Liveline* programme. They hardly had to ask about my availability which I suspect left them very surprised. There was still, however, one hurdle to cross before I could talk with Joe Duffy on his radio programme. I sought out Ed Mulhall. Like Seán O'Rourke, he cautioned about exposing myself to the ire of the *Evening Herald* and also giving other tabloid publications the opening to put an even greater spotlight on my private life. But he was fully aware of the pressure caused by the original *Ireland on Sunday* story.

Joe Duffy gave me plenty of time to explain my situation. A number of other people who had been the subject of tabloid intrusion into their private lives, including Kilkenny hurler D.J. Carey, were also interviewed. Whether it was bravery or folly, I was very critical of the *Evening Herald* for the way the newspaper had invaded my privacy. After the programme, several colleagues predicted that the newspaper would exact its revenge with even more vicious coverage of my professional and private life. The overall response to *Liveline* was positive, although some people who contacted the programme felt that, as a journalist who had doorstepped others in the past, I should now take my own medicine.

I was simply happy that I had given vent to my annoyance and put some life to a necessary debate about media intrusion. There was a genuine debate over the following week, with even the Tánaiste and Progressive Democrats leader, Mary Harney, arguing that public figures were entitled to a private life, provided that that private life did not impact negatively on their public life. Most of the newspaper titles under the control of Independent Newspapers were critical of me, although the academic, Colm Kenny, provided important support in an article in the *Sunday Independent*. Not surprisingly, I received the full lash of the *Evening Herald* in the days after the *Liveline* appearance. In a touching piece of irony, one writer described me as a 'minor celebrity', which made me wonder why then my private life was worthy of the front page of that newspaper, and why it had given such extensive coverage to my comments on *Liveline*.

One of the most interesting phone calls came from a journalist working with Independent Newspapers. This person tipped me off about a piece of information that I had not known about when I had spoken on *Liveline*.

'You know who wrote the *Evening Herald* article?' the man asked.

'Yes,' I replied. 'A woman called Sarah Glynn.'

'Sarah Glynn doesn't exist,' was the amazing response. 'There is no such person working with the *Evening Herald*. The name is just made up.'

I was stunned by this information. I had spoken to John Laurence, who had extracted a comment from me which had made its way into the front-page article. That article regurgitated the *Ireland on Sunday* story and contained quotes from unnamed RTÉ colleagues. Sarah Glynn was the reporter byline on the story. Now I was being told that this woman was a fiction. She didn't exist. This fact made me even angrier at how I had been treated.

Some weeks later, the editor of the *Evening Herald*, Gerry O'Regan, was asked about the use of a false name on the story. His explanation was that the story had been written by 'five or six people' so it was easier to use a made-up name. I was amazed that it had taken the efforts of half a dozen reporters with the *Evening Herald* to write a story about me. It was cowardly that none of them had put their name to the article. Interestingly, a few months before the fake byline was used on the story about my private life, an instruction forbidding the use of fake bylines had been issued by no less a person than Sir Anthony O'Reilly himself. The order had come after a story in September 2004 in the *Sunday Independent* about the family of British Prime Minister Tony Blair.

The story was headlined 'Blair's "Family Crisis" As Talks on North Fail'. It was reported that Blair's 16-year-old daughter had been hospitalised five months previously, following what the newspaper described as an 'incident' before her Easter school exams. The Blairs were said to have spent much of the previous week attempting to stop—and they had succeeded, it seemed—British newspapers and broadcasters from reporting the 'incident'.

The *Sunday Independent*, however, ran with the story which appeared under the byline Henry Cummins and was marked 'exclusive'. The article brought an immediate response when, within a couple of hours of the newspaper's first edition becoming available, a shocked night reporter at the *Sunday Independent* received a phone call from Downing Street about Henry Cummins's story.

Within the hour, the reporter received a second phone call. 'This is your chairman,' the voice on the line is reported to have said by way of introduction. O'Reilly—the chairman—remarked that he had been trying to get through to the news desk for some time. The night reporter explained that there was only a skeleton staff in the office at that hour on a Saturday evening, to which O'Reilly is said to have interjected, 'And which part of the skeleton am I talking to now.'

O'Reilly wanted details about the Blair article and the name of the journalist who had written the story. He was duly informed that the reporter byline on the story was made up. I am reliably informed that, a few days later, O'Reilly issued an instruction that the practice of using fake names on stories was to be discontinued. It was a great pity that word of O'Reilly's order had not reached the *Evening Herald* before the non-existent Sarah Glynn played a starring role in the article about my private life. I would have preferred to have known the names of the five or six reporters who wrote the article which caused me so much hurt and upset. I wonder how those responsible would respond if their faces were splashed across newspaper front pages with details about their private lives speculated upon in accompanying articles written by non-existent reporters.

We all make mistakes. In some ways, it's inevitable in the media business where there is such a quick turnaround to get material on air or into print. Decisions are made under pressure, and sometimes editors and reporters make the wrong call; I have been in that position. I remember covering the end of a kidnapping of a bank manager and his family early in my reporting career.

In my eagerness to get a story, I attempted to doorstep a member of the family involved in the kidnap ordeal. When the report was broadcast on the lunchtime television news, however, I watched in horror, knowing that I had overstepped a line of what is acceptable. I would not have been happy to see my own family treated in that way. Nobody said anything to me but I re-edited my report for the main evening news with the offending clip cut out. My action was warranted by proper decency, something several newspapers in recent times have not afforded me. Looking back now on my decision to talk on *Liveline*, I am less sure I made the correct decision. Maybe I did bring greater attention onto my private life although I still feel as strongly about the perverse news values that made me a story in the first place.

I accept that I am well known because of my work. It is a good feeling when people stop you in the street to say 'well done' about a recent report or investigation. The vast majority of people are kind and friendly. This recognition factor has, however, led me into some scary areas where I realised that I was dealing with someone on the verge of doing something terrible without my help.

In the weeks after the NIB story was first broadcast in 1998, I got a call on my mobile phone from a man who said he had a story for me. This was not unusual. This man said that his story was so sensitive that he could not discuss it with me over the phone. Somewhat reluctantly— as it was one of my first free weekends in a long while—I agreed to a meeting in Buswells Hotel in central Dublin.

I was wary about the bone fides of this man. A few weeks earlier, I had been led on a wild goose chase over a potential story. A caller had promised an important story and arranged to meet me in the car park of a public house in Chapelizod in Dublin. There is always a bit of a buzz about getting a scoop. I wasn't long at the appointed location when my mobile phone rang. 'Hi Charlie,' my contact said, adding with a laugh, 'We have a big story for you.' With a laugh, the contact hung up. There was no story. I had been set up.

It was a very different situation with the man I met in Buswells Hotel. It's a place I am in and out of regularly. When the Dáil is sitting, the hotel is a sort of focal point for politicians, journalists and lobbyists, mainly because of its close proximity to Leinster House. It's a quieter location at the weekends. I located my source as the young man who waved at me as I walked into the hotel's bar. We sat in a quiet corner as my contact, whom I will call John, set about telling me his story.

He was insistent that I give a guarantee not to reveal him as the source for the story he was about to tell me. Very quickly I formed the impression that something was amiss. John was moving from telling me about a friend and his involvement in the IRA to discussing his girlfriend and how he had bought flowers for his mother a few days previously. There was no news story. I was sitting with an individual who was clearly going through a difficult time in his own life. Somehow, he had obtained my mobile phone number. As we left the hotel, I asked John where he was going next. I was relieved to hear that he was planning to go back to his family home in the west of Ireland.

However, after he left me, I could not shake off the feeling that John had sought me out as a sort of cry for help. He was troubled and I was now concerned that he was about to take his own life. I had given him a guarantee that our conversation was in confidence but I decided I had to contact his family. John had told me where his family was from in the west. I suspected that this had been deliberate to prompt me to seek help for him. I got a telephone number for the family business from directory inquiries. I asked to speak with John's father.

'Hello. This is Charlie Bird from RTÉ. Your son John was with me earlier today and I'm somewhat worried about him.' It was a very strange phone call to make. I was not surprised at the reply I received: 'Who the hell is this? You're not Charlie Bird. Why are you making prank calls?'

The phone went dead. I was now in a dilemma. I had two options— to walk away irrespective of the consequences I feared might ensue or I could make another attempt to convince John's family to intervene.

I rang the number once more, this time speaking to John's sister, but once more I met the same hostile response. I then changed tack by calling the RTÉ correspondent in the region and asking this colleague for the name of a local garda inspector. The man accepted the seriousness of what I had to say. He knew John's family and agreed to contact them to reassure them that I was not a prank caller. The strategy worked. At a third time of asking, I got a positive reaction from John's sister, who said the family would make sure he was okay. A few days later, John's mother rang me to say 'thank you'. Sometime later, I received a letter from John.

Dear Charlie,

You probably don't remember me, but a couple of years ago I had arranged to meet you…. You were worried about me, you rang my dad at the family business … well to cut a long story, things have only been better for me since. I've been meaning to write to you every since…. So anyway I made this CD of the one thing I'm good at, playing music. I decided to make just a few copies and send them to people who at sometime in my life did something nice for me or helped me out in someway. Thank you for taking the time out to meet someone you had never met, listening to me and taking such a weight off my shoulders….

John

As I played the CD, I knew that I had made the correct decision in breaking the original confidence placed in me. Sitting and listening to John's story was important, despite my initial disappointment that he had no exclusive story to offer. It's not something journalists are good at accepting, but what my experience with John taught me was that there are occasions when the circumstances of the story have to take precedence over the natural desire for a scoop.

Chapter 15

AN ORANGE BASTARD AND ABDUL THE DRIVER

'Hey, Charlie Bird!' I turned around to see who had called my name. 'Charlie Bird, you're an Orange Bastard.' I hardly had time to take the insult on board. A man was thumping me. He connected with my cheek bone. Another man was aiming a punch at me. I turned and ran. It was pure instinct. I can't be sure but I think another man had joined the first two. These men were chasing me. I tripped and fell to the ground. My keys and mobile phone went flying across the street. As I attempted to stand up, a punch landed. A pain shot through my entire body. I was trying to protect my face. 'Somebody help me,' I screamed. Another punch. I could see people watching. Nobody was responding. Yet another punch. Now I was being dragged. Two more men were involved. 'Come with us,' one of them shouted. I looked suspiciously at this man. He produced a garda identification badge. They were two Special Branch officers. I stumbled into the entrance way of a shop. One of the men who had attacked me was now being held by gardaí. The others had run away. I sat down. I was dazed. I now knew what it was like to be mugged.

It was Saturday, 18 February 2006. I had come into Dublin city centre to meet a couple of people about a potential story on the health services. A group of Orangemen from Northern Ireland had chosen that Saturday to travel to Dublin. They had planned to march from the top end of O'Connell Street on the city's north side, across the River Liffey and on towards Leinster House. It was billed as a Love Ulster parade, and the organisers said they wanted to remember the victims of IRA violence, although they also stressed that the event would allow those involved to give vent to their opposition to the Good Friday Agreement and what they described as 'the Irish Government's interference in the internal affairs of Northern Ireland'. Gerry Adams and his Sinn Féin colleagues had adopted a low-key stance on the parade, which had left most people south of the border somewhat bemused.

Ahead of the start of the parade, there were some low-level skirmishes, apparently involving hardline republicans opposed to the peace process in Northern Ireland. Pat Brennan, a TV editor in RTÉ, called to know where I was. 'Can you go to O'Connell Street?' she asked. I was curious to see the spectacle and also to see what the public's response was. Orangeism has been a highly divisive feature of life in Northern Ireland. I had seen it at first-hand at Drumcree, as well as in places in Belfast. As I arrived on O'Connell Street shortly after 1 p.m., the atmosphere was tense. Buses carrying the Orangemen had arrived at Parnell Square about half an hour earlier. They were preparing to set off on their march when the trouble started. About 500 demonstrators had gathered at the top of O'Connell Street. Missiles and other objects were thrown at gardaí. It didn't help matters that building material from the improvement works on the street was easily accessible. A riot was under way. The Orange march was effectively called off as a pitched battle ensued on O'Connell Street, between the gardaí and the rioters.

I was watching all this unfold as I stood outside the GPO on O'Connell Street, and I rang the RTÉ news desk to check where the camera crew was located. I was talking to a colleague on my mobile phone, describing the crazy scenes in front of me, when the first punch landed. About half an hour later, I was in the Mater Hospital. I was sore and shocked. My jacket had been torn and I had a cut on my hand. It was only over the following few weeks that the extent of the damage to my back became obvious. Several months of physiotherapy lay ahead of me to ease the back pain.

Why did these people attack me? I suspect that the protestors were venting their spleen on all-comers and, as a fairly recognisable face, I suited their purposes. It was speculated that the 'Orange Bastard' remark had somehow something to do with my Protestant family heritage—something which I think fits a nice argument but which doesn't really stand up to proper scrutiny. I doubt if the men who attacked me knew anything about my family background. Some people talked about my being linked with the IRA in the minds of these dissident republicans, because of my reporting contacts with that organisation for almost 13 years. And as Adams's Sinn Féin was seen by the dissidents as a sellout, anyone even remotely connected with the republican movement was part of that sellout grouping. The next day, one newspaper 'had a go' at me for being on O'Connell Street, claiming that I was trying to become part of the story. It was a nasty piece of journalism.

In a quarter of a century as a reporter, I have experienced fear on more than one occasion and I have been frightened while working in a variety of different locations. Yet, before the incident on O'Connell Street, I had never been physically attacked. It was a terrifying and an unprovoked attack, whatever the reasoning, and it may very well be as simple as that I was a face they recognised in the crowd. Maybe these people were intent on trouble, irrespective of the causes for, and the consequences of, their actions.

It had been a strange twelve months. The tsunami and the earthquake in Pakistan had left a deep emotional impression on me. The assault on O'Connell Street left me reeling and wondering about the public profile I have acquired as a long-standing news reporter. I love doing my job but increasingly I have been attacked by certain print journalists just because of who I am, and now the recognition factor had got me beaten up. It was a bizarre position to have arrived at. The attitude of these people was in complete contrast to that which I had experienced only a few months earlier in another part of the world. It clearly brought home to me the thin line between good and evil, and how fortunate people are in our part of the world—something which is all too easily taken for granted.

———

Almost 100,000 people were killed in the earthquake which hit northern Pakistan and the disputed Kashmir region in October 2005. Millions more were left homeless. The earthquake measured 7.6 on the Richter scale. Kashmir was hardest hit, with most of the city of Muzaffarabad simply flattened. It was one of the most heartbreaking scenes I had witnessed in all my years reporting on natural disasters and, I suppose, it was even more poignant as it came less than a year after the awful death and destruction caused by the Asian tsunami.

All the hospitals in Muzaffarabad had been reduced to rubble, so a makeshift medical centre was set up in one of the few buildings remarkably left untouched by the earthquake. The medical staff who came to help had no real facilities. There was little water; the electricity was available only sporadically; while food was cooked outside. The place was dirty and the smell of sickness and death was totally over-powering. Hundreds of seriously injured people were treated in this makeshift centre; many of them had been brought down to Muzaffarabad from remote mountainous regions. We spoke to one man whose nine-year-old son had a broken leg but it was six days before the authorities had located their isolated village and taken the child and his seriously injured mother to the city for treatment. One of the local doctors, Dr Mukhtar Ahmed, had actually worked in a number of hospitals in Ireland. 'If you think things are bad in Ireland, think again,' he remarked. This man had lost 18 members of his extended family in the earthquake and, like most other people in the city, he was now living in a tent. Alongside his medical colleagues, he was working around the clock in the operating theatre as they attempted to treat the most seriously injured of the survivors.

The people were of all ages. Many were lying in beds in the makeshift wards. Their families were in and out of the building; there was constant movement and plenty of loud noise. It was far from the image of a modern hospital scene. The plight of these people had a huge impact on me. I could have told a hundred different stories in that hospital. There was so much suffering and so much loss. And, as we were being shown around, a young woman made eye contact with me. She was half-sitting up in the bed while an elderly doctor examined her lower body. He beckoned me over to the bedside. 'You see her eyes,' he said. 'They are her soul.'

The woman's name was Lubna. She was 35 years old and was the mother of eight children. One of her daughters had been killed in the earthquake. A wooden beam had crashed down on top of her own feet. She had been trapped for two days before rescuers had pulled her free from the rubble. The helicopter journey to Muzaffarabad was the first time she had ever left her remote mountain-village home. The medical team had saved her life but she had lost both of her feet. The stump of one of her legs was showing from under the grubby white sheet. I could see the stitches in her flesh. Yet, despite her loss—and being in a strange environment surrounded by pandemonium—Lubna still managed a smile. Her face was full of life. I couldn't get over her presence. It was a truly remarkable example of the goodness that exists in a human being.

'She needs help. With prosthetic legs, she could walk again,' the old doctor said. I decided to make Lubna's story the feature of that evening's television news report. In my piece-to-camera, which we filmed at Lubna's bedside, I repeated the doctor's appeal for prosthetic legs. It seemed wrong to move on without doing something to help this woman but we had other work to do. However, the story, when it was broadcast, touched many viewers. People started to phone with offers of help. By the time I got back to RTÉ, there was a significant pile of envelopes on my desk. As I opened the envelopes, I found myself taking out cheque after cheque, all sent to help Lubna get the medical treatment needed to help her to walk again. The generosity of people was amazing. The response to the two-minute television report on the main evening news generated over €50,000. The money was banked in an account looked after by the Red Cross. Some of the donations were spent on Lubna's medical treatment. Despite having lost her limbs in the earthquake, she would be able to walk again. Some of the money was spent building a new house for her family.

I first arrived in Pakistan two days after the earthquake hit in early October 2005. The earthquake zone was a five-hour car drive from Islamabad. It was a difficult journey, made all the more problematic by many diversions along the route. Landslides blocked part of the mountainous road. Even where it was relatively safe to drive, there were huge cracks in the tarmac. Along the roadside, trees were uprooted and buildings damaged. These were, however, only small signs of what lay ahead. The aid agencies and other emergency services were still desperately trying to get to the worst-affected places. Bad weather meant that helicopters were frequently grounded, and so the aid agencies and the authorities joined the long line of traffic that slowly drove upwards and higher into the mountains of Kashmir.

We had to take a chance driving through the rugged mountain pass at the entrance to Muzaffarabad. As we waited in the traffic for the single line of oncoming vehicles to clear, some boulders and rocks fell from a height onto the ground near the large opening to the tunnel passageway. The aftershocks of the earthquake were still being felt. It was a chaotic scene. A few cars turned back, their occupants obviously not prepared to take the risk of being trapped in the tunnel. However, having come this way, we decided to take our chances. Just like a few months previously in Sri Lanka, I was travelling with RTÉ cameraman Neilus Dennihy. We had met our driver, Abdul Samad, in Islamabad. A tall, skinny man, he was a member of the Pashtun tribe and came from a remote area in north-west Pakistan which bordered with Afghanistan. He hadn't a word of either English or Urdu, the language spoken by most people in Pakistan. Not long into the journey, we discovered that he didn't understand even pidgin English and would look blankly when we shouted words like 'left' and 'right'. Fortunately, we had a local aid worker accompanying us on the journey and the two men were able to communicate somewhat in a shared local dialect.

Most of the buildings in the mountainous region had collapsed during the earthquake on the morning of 8 October. Muzaffarabad had been badly hit. It was a city in ruins. Buildings had been flattened. Houses had been reduced to piles of rubble. The city's main market area was totally devastated. Only a handful of partially damaged buildings remained standing. The entire infrastructure in the city had also collapsed. There was no electricity and no phone communication, while water and food were in short supply. The aid agencies were scrambling to deal with a huge humanitarian disaster.

On the outskirts of the city, which was about the size of Limerick, we could see local people still searching for survivors. They were digging in the rubble of what had once been houses and apartments. Huge boulders and twisted steel gilders were piled high where, only a few days previously, there had been orderly neighbourhood streets. Thousands were dead. At that stage, there was talk of a figure of 30,000 dead. The numbers soon increased to 50,000, and then they were revised upwards to 75,000. With so many people living in the remote mountainous region unaccounted for, many international agencies eventually put the final region in excess of 100,000, making the Pakistani earthquake one of the worst natural disasters in centuries. Nobody was left untouched by the tragedy. We visited one local girls' school in Muzaffarabad where the classrooms had been full when the early-morning earthquake struck. About 700 children were dead and several hundred bodies had still not been recovered. Some survivors were located in the days after 8 October but those miracle stories were few and far between. In reality, the rescue teams were reduced to pulling dead bodies from the rubble. Everywhere we went in the city, local people pointed to rubble where bodies were still buried. In one place, a human arm was clearly visible. Bodies wrapped in plastic were laid out on the ground. There was an overpowering stench of death.

Few of the city's residents were untouched by the earthquake; most people had lost loved ones, homes and worldly possessions. These people now had to sleep outside at night. Some were fortunate to have small tents in which to shelter and store whatever small number of personal possessions they had managed to pull from the ruins of their former homes. Dotted around the city, these tent villages sprung up. We were no different—there was nothing left in the city—no hotels, no restaurants, nothing. During our first night, a small aftershock shook the ground. We slept out in the open, with a small blanket as the only shield against the night-time cold. A local sports stadium was also used to shelter many of those who were now homeless. These people were now dependent on the authorities and the aid agencies for food, water and shelter. Their plight was heartbreaking. We travelled with the local Concern staff to some of the remote areas in the mountains above Muzaffarabad, as vital supplies were delivered to these unfortunate people. One man told us how 500 houses on the side of the mountain had simply disappeared in the earthquake. The side of one mountain cliff had collapsed. It was startling to see this gaping hole in the mountain side. It was just too dangerous to try to recover the bodies of those who had died in the huge landslide.

The Pakistani earthquake was one of several big natural disasters to dominate 2005. The aftermath of the St Stephen's Day 2004 tsunami galvanised a huge international response, with governments and ordinary people digging deep into their pockets to send money for the relief effort. There was also support for the situation in Darfur, while few people were unmoved by the devastation caused in New Orleans by Hurricane Katrina. The earthquake in the mountains of Kashmir came at the end of a year of suffering and, maybe for that reason, there was donor fatigue. Whatever it was, the plight of those people—over 100,000 dead and upwards of three million homeless—seemed to matter less to the watching world. These people were the poorest of the poor. They had suffered a huge loss. Their situation made a huge mark on me personally, and Lubna's story came to symbolise their plight.

Maybe that explains why when the donations started to arrive in to RTÉ, I decided I could not move on as quickly from this story as from others. Few reporters are left unmoved by the stories of tragedy or trauma that they cover as part of their job as journalists. But the professional response is always to move on. There may be anger at the failure to resolve a conflict or to end a famine or respond quickly enough to a natural disaster, but, when the reporting job is finished, other stories have to be reported. That's just the way news reporting works. The anger doesn't disappear but there is simply not enough time to get deeply involved, and, in any event, that is not the role of a news reporter. Yet, somehow, for me, Pakistan was different—and the response to Lubna's story maintained the connection. However, I have to be honest and admit that when the time came to leave Muzaffarabad in early October 2005, I think both Neilus Dennihy and I were somewhat glad to be going home.

It had been a tough trip. I had spent five days in the same clothes and was badly in need of a wash as well as a good meal and a decent night's sleep. Abdul the driver had worked hard over the previous week although, in truth, he was a terrible driver and his four-wheel drive was a wreck of a truck. His lack of English had made it impossible to start even a limited conversation. The aid-agency worker whom we met in Islamabad had usually made an attempt at translating what we were saying. On the journey back to Islamabad, however, Neilus and I were alone with the driver. His lack of English was one thing but the fact that he couldn't speak even a few words of Pakistani was far more problematic. 'How is this guy going to read the road signs?' I asked.

I felt sorry for Abdul. There was a permanent air of misery about him. He was poorly dressed and had a light pair of shoes on his feet. I had said a few times over the previous few days that we would look after him when we got back to Islamabad. 'If we ever get back there, I'm going to give him my boots,' I joked with Neilus, pointing down to my heavy boots, recently purchased back in Dublin. 'I doubt if they'd fit him,' Neilus replied.

We had left some luggage and broadcasting equipment back at a hotel in Islamabad. The plan was to pick up this gear and switch accommodation to the local Marriott Hotel, which was nearer our editing facilities. We had no addresses for where we wanted to get to, and with a driver who was unable to ask directions, our plan was to get to the outskirts of Islamabad and then find a taxi driver who spoke English.

As we were leaving Muzaffarabad, our four-wheel-drive truck braked, and there was a huge thump. We had crashed into the car in front of us. There wasn't too much damage, although the front bumper had been knocked off our truck. Neilus and I hoisted the bumper up onto the back of the truck. We placed it on top of our luggage and recording equipment, securing it safely with some old rope. The truck with its unusual cargo was actually not out of place on the mountain road where jeeps and other vehicles with all sorts of luggage were a common feature. It was a tough journey down the muddy mountainous route as it bucketed down rain, with thunder and lightning for accompaniment. The wipers were constantly swooshing forwards and backwards. Visibility was poor. Abdul even stopped at one stage to check the tyres but fortunately we didn't have a puncture.

By the time we got to the outskirts of Islamabad, we were all tired and slightly irritable. I was having difficulty getting the driver to understand me—'Find a taxi rank and stop,' I said slowly on more than one occasion. I was too tired for this translation problem; all I wanted was a hot shower and some sleep. Neilus felt the same. We had worked very well together but now, as I struggled with the language barrier, he had had enough. He snapped, putting his hand over his ears. 'I don't want to hear. I don't want to listen to you any more,' he shouted. There hadn't been as much as a cross word between us over the previous days, or even a few months earlier as we had reported on the tsunami. But now patience was in short supply. As he sat there in the back of this wreck of a truck, with his hands over his ears, I could only laugh. It took a few moments but he also saw the funny side of our situation. We eventually came off the ring road outside the city and, through the rain, I caught sight of a taxi rank. One of the taxi drivers spoke some English.

'The Marriott Hotel,' I said. 'I need to get to the Marriott Hotel.'

'Yes,' the taxi driver said, nodding. 'Yes, yes.'

So, I sat into his little yellow Fiat taxi while Neilus and Abdul followed behind in the four-wheel-drive truck, with our luggage and front bumper securely stored overhead. After about 20 minutes, we pulled up outside a big international hotel—it was a Holiday Inn. By now, I had come to realise that this taxi driver's command of the English language was barely a step up from Abdul's.

So, we were on the way again. The yellow taxi leading as the four-wheel drive followed. After another 15 minutes or so, we finally arrived outside the Marriott Hotel. The rain took away somewhat from what I am sure was normally an impressive waterfall feature at the front entrance. The complex had a strong security presence along its perimeter gates. I left my colleague—and the truck and the taxi—at the main entrance, and walked into the marble reception area. I'm sure the manager was asking questions of his doormen as I approached the reservation desk.

'I'm looking for two rooms, please,' I said. The hotel manager was staring at me. Dishevelled is a polite way of describing my appearance. I was caked in dirt and probably didn't smell too good either. 'I'm afraid we're almost fully booked up, sir. I have only the bridal suite available,' the manager said, having checked his computer.

'Is he trying to get rid of me?' I thought. After a few questions and a little haggling, I managed to get a smaller suite with two single beds. 'Have you luggage, sir?' the manager asked politely. I almost laughed.

I returned to the main entrance and called in the little yellow taxi and Abdul's battered four-wheel drive. I doubt if the Marriott car park had ever seen the like before. The arrival of new guests spurred a host of hotel staff to the front door. However, before they could take our luggage—filthy bags and metal camera drums—the now-famous front bumper had to be removed from the roof of Abdul's truck. Several hotel porters in full uniform, with their peacock hats, looked on as Neilus and I struggled to untie the bumper. It was now time to bid farewell to the taxi driver and our travelling companion. We put a generous sum into an envelope for Abdul—what would probably have amounted to about half of a normal year's wages. Then I removed my boots at the main door of the exclusive Marriott Hotel in Islamabad and I handed them to Abdul. He embraced me like a long-lost cousin even though we had not been able to communicate over the previous week. He smiled and I knew he would have a good story to tell when he got home.

INDEX